Building Reading Comprehension Habits
in Grades 6–12
A Toolkit of Classroom Activities

JEFF ZWIERS
Menlo Park, California, USA

INTERNATIONAL
Reading Association
800 BARKSDALE ROAD, PO BOX 8139
NEWARK, DE 19714-8139, USA
www.reading.org

The International Reading Association attempts, through its publications, to provide a forum for a wide spectrum of opinions on reading. This policy permits divergent viewpoints without implying the endorsement of the Association.

Director of Publications   Joan M. Irwin
Editorial Director, Books and Special Projects   Matthew W. Baker
Managing Editor   Shannon Benner
Permissions Editor   Janet S. Parrack
Acquisitions and Communications Coordinator   Corinne M. Mooney
Associate Editor, Books and Special Projects   Sara J. Murphy
Assistant Editor   Charlene M. Nichols
Administrative Assistant   Michele Jester
Senior Editorial Assistant   Tyanna L. Collins
Production Department Manager   Iona Muscella
Supervisor, Electronic Publishing   Anette Schütz
Senior Electronic Publishing Specialist   Cheryl J. Strum
Electronic Publishing Specialist   R. Lynn Harrison
Proofreader   Elizabeth C. Hunt

Project Editor   Shannon Benner

Cover Design   Linda Steere; art by Digital Vision

Web addresses in this book were correct as of the publication date but may have become inactive or otherwise modified since that time. If you notice a deactivated or changed Web address, please e-mail books@reading.org with the words "Website Update" in the subject line. In your message, specify the Web link, the book title, and the page number on which the link appears.

Library of Congress Cataloging-in-Publication Data
Zwiers, Jeff.
 Building reading comprehension habits in grades 6–12 : a toolkit of classroom activities / Jeff Zwiers.
    p. cm.
Includes bibliographical references and index.
 ISBN 0-87207-539-7
 1. Reading (Secondary) 2. Reading comprehension. I. Title.
 LB1632.Z95 2004
 428.4'071'2--dc22
                                                                        2003026929

Third Printing, July 2006

CONTENTS

PREFACE

> How can I help my students develop *enduring* habits of comprehension?

> How can I meet the literacy needs of students with widely varied reading levels, cultures, and linguistic backgrounds?

> How can I integrate *helpful* and motivating assessments into my instruction?

> How can I develop reading activities that not only provide extra help for struggling readers but also benefit all my other students?

My guess is that you are reading this book because you are looking for answers to questions such as the ones above. These questions seem to surface every time I work with middle school and high school teachers in my role as a literacy coach, and they are (in my opinion) four of the most challenging questions that we face in secondary education—not because the questions don't have answers, but because the answers are as varied as the students in our classrooms and the contexts in which we teach. I'll be honest up front: This book does not have the answers—because there are no pat answers—but it does present practical ideas that have been working in a wide variety of middle school and high school classrooms. I have used the ideas, seen them used, and read about their effectiveness in books and articles.

The first step I take in my literacy coaching is to try to convince *all* teachers that they should be almost-experts in reading. I immediately hear, "Why not just leave reading to the English teachers?" The answer is, because teachers of other content areas, especially reading-heavy subjects such as social studies and science, are uniquely qualified to teach students how to actively think about the texts in their particular classes. For example, analyzing the causes and effects of historical processes differs from visualizing physical and chemical processes in science, which differs from interpreting character motives and figurative language in literature. It is eye-opening for teachers to realize how reading differs in the other content area classrooms around the school. I give teachers the analogy of mental workouts: Many students have not given their brains the types of vigorous thinking workouts—cross training, if you will—that teachers want them to have in different types of reading and learning. Once teachers see how different the comprehension process is in different subjects, I then bring up comprehension similarities from subject to subject.

Academic reading (reading for school purposes) requires the use of what most literature on comprehension calls *reading strategies* (e.g., Pressley et al., 1990). However, I prefer to use the term *habits* rather than *strategies* because I feel that *habits* more clearly describes the automatic and unconscious processes that are involved in constructing meaning from text. (The distinction of habits and strategies is explained in more detail in chapter 1.) This book, then, provides a crash course on reading comprehension habits. The upcoming chapters put the course material to work in the form of activities, or tools, for building comprehension habits in all classrooms. My goal with this book is to provide research-based, innovative, "for-tomorrow-morning-and-it's-midnight now" activities that are adaptable to multiple grade levels and subjects. I don't want teachers to spend a lot of precious planning time sifting through anecdotes and long stretches of text to find the tools they need.

You may have heard the old saying that if you give someone a fish, the person eats for a day, but if you teach someone to fish, the person eats for a lifetime. My ultimate desire here is for teachers to learn to fish—that is, to start with a solid theoretical base and then quickly be able to create *their own* tools to meet their specific student and subject area needs. When this happens, the four questions presented earlier begin to get answered, and students maximize their learning of content material while building lifelong literacy habits.

This book is intended for middle school and high school teachers of social studies, science, English, English language development (ELD; also known as English as a second language [ESL]), and any other subject with challenging texts and with readers who struggle to understand them. The activities in the following chapters are especially meant to help below-grade-level readers to access and organize the content of grade-level texts. The needs of English learners also were very apparent as I worked in classrooms to create this toolkit. I work with several school districts that have large numbers of English learners who have been in the United States for more than three years. Even though these students' needs are not identical to those of native-English-speaking mainstream students, many English learner comprehension issues can be addressed by the tools in this book. Of particular interest to teachers with struggling English learners will be the chapters on background knowledge (chapter 4) and understanding word meanings (chapter 7).

These activities are designed for struggling readers, yet teachers tell me that the activities have been effective and motivating for all students in their classrooms. This is probably due to the "multiple intelligences" nature of the tools, especially their applications in the visual and social intelligences. I chose to include as many extralinguistic (visual, kinesthetic, musical, etc.) activities as possible to reach students who have been "turned off" by traditional approaches to reading improvement. Whenever teachers can reinforce plain text with extralinguistic ways of learning, students' comprehension improves (Armbruster, Anderson, & Meyer, 1992). In other words, we need to *show* students—rather than just tell them—the habits that support comprehension. Following is a visual representation of the intended results of using this toolkit of activities.

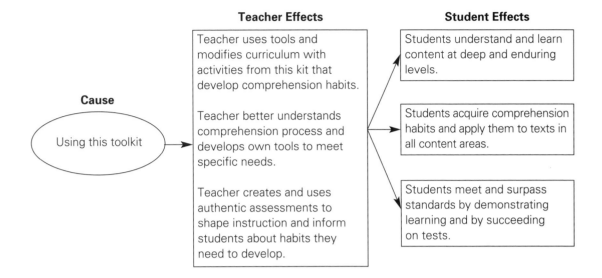

Teacher Effects

Teacher uses tools and modifies curriculum with activities from this kit that develop comprehension habits.

Teacher better understands comprehension process and develops own tools to meet specific needs.

Teacher creates and uses authentic assessments to shape instruction and inform students about habits they need to develop.

Cause

Using this toolkit

Student Effects

Students understand and learn content at deep and enduring levels.

Students acquire comprehension habits and apply them to texts in all content areas.

Students meet and surpass standards by demonstrating learning and by succeeding on tests.

Organization of the Book

Following this Preface, you will find a Master List of Activities that lists all the activities in the book, first in order of appearance and then in alphabetical order. You can use this list to locate a specific activity by name or to see what activities are offered in a particular chapter.

Part I discusses ideas for using comprehension habits as a foundation for developing literacy instruction. Chapter 1 provides a description of comprehension habits for upper grade teachers who desire a clear and concise foundation for building literacy in their students. The chapter also offers a practical explanation of the importance of student background, language, and thinking in developing literacy instruction. Chapter 2 reminds teachers of the key components of assessment and instruction as they relate to the development of comprehension habits.

Part II covers the comprehension habits themselves. Chapters 3–8 each cover a separate comprehension habit, with each chapter giving a description of the habit followed by recommended activities that help develop it. The six comprehension habits are as follows:

1. Organizing text information by sculpting the main idea and summarizing (chapter 3)

2. Connecting to background knowledge (chapter 4)

3. Making inferences and predictions (chapter 5)

4. Generating and answering questions (chapter 6)

5. Understanding and remembering word meanings (chapter 7)

6. Monitoring one's own comprehension (chapter 8)

In Part III, you will find reproducible forms and worksheets that are used in the activities. Feel free to photocopy these pages to hand out to students, or to make transparencies of them for use on an overhead projector during whole-class activities. You also can enlarge the pages to make posters to hang in your classroom. Sample reproducible forms and worksheets for this book also can be found at www.reading.org/focus/comprehension.html.

Finally, the book contains two appendixes with useful information to help you with some of the activities. Appendix A lists some multiple-meaning words and Appendix B lists affixes and roots (word parts). Both appendixes are particularly useful for building the habit of understanding words (chapter 7) while reading.

So, if you are up to the challenge of answering the four opening questions, becoming an almost-expert in reading, and fortifying your curriculum with effective and motivating literacy activities, then take a closer look at the rest of this toolkit. It will help you build your knowledge about reading comprehension so you can make the teaching of it more motivating for students. Then use the tools in this book as seeds for your own creative designs of instruction and assessment. Granted, it takes time and energy. Yet the rewards of seeing students become better readers of difficult texts—while they learn more content material—will be worth the effort.

Acknowledgments

I am deeply indebted to the following people for their ideas, flexibility, patience, and creativity: Carrie Holmberg, Kris Wallace, Mari Smith, Patricia Coccone, Maria Messina, Shannon Potts, Laura Dequine, Jan Wright, Wren Clark, and Marcela De Carvalho.

JZ

Feedback

Please send comments and suggestions about this book. Most teachers will modify the ideas in this toolkit to meet their needs, and I would like to hear about these modifications and any success stories you may have. Please also feel free to contact me with questions about specific situations that relate to older students' literacy. My e-mail is jazwiers@usfca.edu.

MASTER LIST OF ACTIVITIES

Activities in Order of Appearance

Activities in Alphabetical Order

PART I

Developing Instruction Using Comprehension Habits

A Crash Course in Reading Comprehension

* * *

Reading is like rocket science—
only more complicated.

The purpose of reading is to construct meaning. To the average literate person, reading appears to be quite simple. We look at the letters to make sounds to make words to make sentences, and then we understand. However, even a basic understanding of text depends on countless invisible thought processes that work together at lightning speed.

The first step in understanding the nature of reading comprehension is to appreciate the complexity of it. Most educators are fortunate to have had a large array of varied and rich literacy experiences, many of which were facilitated by easy access to books, literate parents/caregivers, good teachers, or all of these. The vital thought processes of reading became automatic for us, and this automaticity, ironically, hinders us from seeing how complex comprehension can be for struggling readers, particularly those in grades 6–12.

A good analogy for reading comprehension's hidden complexity is driving. Most adults consider driving a car to be second nature because of miles and years of practice. We hop in, drive, and arrive, often without thinking about the many explanations (and perhaps expletives) that our driving instructors offered to us when we were learning. We have long forgotten the nervousness we felt and the huge amounts of information we had to store in our minds when we were learning to drive, venturing out on the road the first few times. Reading is similar to driving in that the brain, from processing pages and pages of text, develops a variety of strategies and connections that facilitate efficient comprehension. These strategies and connections, especially the automatic ones, are the habits this book seeks to build.

The Comprehension Habits

The past two decades have offered numerous books and articles on reading comprehension strategies. Palincsar and Brown's (1984) reciprocal teaching concept is based on four key strategies: questioning, clarifying, predicting, and summarizing. A large number of successful programs and activities were then founded on these strategies. Keene and Zimmermann's *Mosaic of Thought: Teaching Comprehension in a Reader's Workshop* (1997) added strategies of background knowledge and schema, inference, synthesis, and metacognition to the list. Other researchers took ideas from the list and created studies that showed the benefits of teaching individual strategies to students in explicit ways (Beck, McKeown, Hamilton, & Kucan, 1997; Ciardiello, 1998; Friend, 2001). In creating this toolkit of activities, I analyzed hundreds of resources on comprehension strategies and synthesized them into the following six habits:

1. Organizing text information by sculpting the main idea and summarizing
2. Connecting to background knowledge
3. Making inferences and predictions
4. Generating and answering questions
5. Understanding and remembering word meanings
6. Monitoring one's own comprehension

As stated in the Preface, I feel that *habits* more clearly describes the automatic and unconscious processes that are involved in constructing meaning from text. These should not be considered the *only* six habits, though; they are simply the habits that I have found to be most effective and teachable in secondary contexts.

Comprehension habits are the split-second thoughts that kick in constantly to help a proficient reader actively construct meaning. They make up the majority of the thinking processes we use during reading, even though we seldom notice them (Taylor, Graves, & van den Broek, 2000). For example, a good reader seldom stops and thinks, "I need to relate this to my background knowledge," or "This would be a good time to predict," or "A quick summary right now will help me comprehend better," or "At this point I should visualize." Rather, a good reader does these things in the blink of an eye without, in a sense, even thinking. Because they happen so quickly, automatic habits keep the reader from losing the flow of the meaning and from letting any important thoughts seep out of the "attention tank." Figure 1 shows the complexity involved in keeping track of cognitive processes, connections, and information during reading.

The habits work together and overlap as they construct meaning (Villaume & Brabham, 2002). They are highly intertwined. For example, upon finishing a paragraph, I might quickly summarize the last three sentences, question a character's motives, infer possible causes for an event, tweak my main idea, wonder about a word, and predict what may happen in the next section—all while I am reading the first sentences of the next paragraph.

We must remember that *all* students are capable of developing these habits in order to become better readers.

How the Habits Work

One of the most important habits of comprehension is mentally organizing a text's information to match what the author had in mind. This is the ongoing process of seeing and inferring logical connections between chunks of text and using them to create a coherent main idea (Taylor et al., 2000). Organizing, in a sense, *is* comprehension. The other comprehension habits support this process by adding and subtracting key information to and from the evolving main idea.

Here's how it works. During reading, a reader constantly tries to make sense of the information stated in the current sentence by connecting it to two other sources of

Figure 1.   Attention in the Reading Process

Reading Progress

ATTENTION TANK
(Information Stored From
Comprehension Habits)

Purpose for reading
Main idea

Summaries 1 and 2

Connections to prior knowledge
and mental images

Prediction 1
Prediction 2

Inference 1
Inference 2

Question 1
Question 2

Unknown Word 1 guess
Unknown Word 2 guess

Overall monitoring of comprehension
(Am I getting this?)

Comprehension "Events"
(Comprehension Habits in Action)

Purpose being met? (Yes)
Main idea further sculpted from new
information, summaries, and
results of events below

Summary 3 generated

Mental image of main character
changed, using new text info and
own related experience

Prediction 1 confirmed
Prediction 2 disconfirmed and
changed to Prediction 3
Prediction 4 generated

Inference 1 confirmed
Inference 2 confirmed
Inference 3 generated
Inference 4 generated

Question 1 not yet answered
Question 2 answered
Question 3 generated

Word 1 guess confirmed by reading
on and using context
Word 2 meaning still unclear
Word 3 guess generated

Comprehension is adequate

ATTENTION TANK
(Modified)

Purpose
More defined main idea

Summaries 1, 2, and 3
Revised connections to prior
knowledge and mental images

Prediction 3
Prediction 4

Inference 3
Inference 4

Question 1
Question 3

Word 2 guess unconfirmed
Word 3 guess unconfirmed

Overall monitoring of comprehension
(Am I getting this?)

Comprehension "Events"

Purpose being met? (Yes)
Main idea slightly changed in light of
new information and events

Summary 4 generated

Similar situation visualized that
happened last year

Prediction 3 unconfirmed
Prediction 4 confirmed
Prediction 5 generated

Inference 3 not confirmed
Inference 4 confirmed
Inference 5 generated

Question 1 not yet answered
Question 3 not yet answered
Question 4 generated

Word 2 guess unconfirmed
Word 3 guess confirmed by using
word parts and reading on
Word 4 guess generated

Comprehension has broken down:
need to reread two paragraphs
because they don't seem to fit

information: (1) concepts found in preceding sentences and (2) the reader's own background knowledge (Alvermann & Phelps, 2001). Connections to previous concepts found in the text help a reader keep track of elements such as people, objects, ideas, and events while he or she reads. These connections, which are the comprehension habits discussed in chapters 3–8 of this book, help the reader to identify how the different facts and events depend on one another to form the author's message. The second type of connection, background knowledge, helps a reader to visualize the text's descriptions and fortify his or her understanding of implicit and explicit ideas in the text.

Good readers use comprehension habits to add "branches" of key information to the main idea as they read. Then, they seek to either strengthen the branches or prune them by judging how logically relevant they are to upcoming text (Fletcher & Bloom, 1998). Strengthening branches is the process of finding text information that agrees with or repeats the original summary, prediction, or inference that supports the main idea. Repeated ideas or references in a text usually strengthen the main idea. Pruning, on the other hand, is the process of discarding or modifying a "wrong" or unimportant branch, such as a prediction that did not come true, a summary of irrelevant information, or a hypothesis that was disproved later in the text. For example, I recently read an article on space travel in which the title and pictures led me to predict that traveling the speed of light might be possible in the near future. I soon had to prune this assumption away, however, due to the author's arguments and the details presented in the article.

In order to create, strengthen, and prune the needed branches for sculpting the main idea, the reader must store and manage multiple thoughts at the same time (Taylor et al., 2000). These thoughts include facts, predictions, summaries, inferences, questions, word meanings, and the ever-evolving, overarching main idea. For this reason, good comprehension depends on the reader's ability to effectively allocate attention to multiple thoughts and textual details all at the same time. In other words, good reading requires effective mental multitasking. (See the Mental Multitasking Practice activity in chapter 8.)

In Figure 1, notice the many thoughts being stored and processed in the brain's attention tank during reading. As we read, we retain and modify our collection of thoughts in a way that maximizes our ability to construct meaning. For example, yesterday I quickly used the title of an article to begin sculpting a main idea. Then, in the first paragraph I thought about a similar incident in my family, created a prediction about the rest of the article, and generated two questions that I hoped the article would answer. (This all happened as I was reading the second paragraph.) I retained all of these thoughts as I read. Whenever a new piece of information confirmed or contradicted a thought, I made the necessary adjustments. My rough main idea, predictions, and questions were a few of the connections that helped me construct a meaningful and organized mental framework for comprehending the text of the article. If I had lost track of these thoughts, my comprehension would have suffered.

For this reason, teachers must do more than merely teach the strategies; we must help struggling readers *automatically* and unconsciously use strategies, even to the point at which they cannot help but to use them. (A student once said to me, "I am trying not to predict and infer so much, but I can't help it.") Strategies will then become habits that allow the brain to do other things during reading, such as organize the details, concepts, and abstract ideas that are presented. The mental capacity to effectively remember, manage, and prioritize thoughts comes from years of reading millions of pages of a variety of narrative and expository texts—and from good teaching. The good teaching part is where we come in. Many classroom activities, when effectively modeled, scaffolded, and practiced, can help struggling students make up lost time and pages.

Comprehension Habits for Expository Texts

Struggling readers tend to have trouble with the content vocabulary, background knowledge, abstract thinking, and habits necessary for organizing the large amounts of information found in middle school and high school texts. For this reason, high-quality literacy instruction in all content areas is vital for meeting the demands of increasingly complex expository materials in secondary curricula—not to mention the demands of high-stakes exams, college courses, and the real world of work. In my experience working in secondary schools, I have noticed that struggling readers benefit greatly from extra modeling, practice, and explicit literacy support, particularly with nonfiction texts. Why? Because in addition to the lack of emphasis in earlier grades on nonfiction comprehension, secondary classes often are taught by teachers who got into the exciting business of education in order to teach the ideas and concepts of their content areas—not to teach reading. These teachers earnestly want their students to read better but are overwhelmed by the different reading levels among their students, the lack of appropriate materials, the pressure to cover a year and a half of content standards in one year, and the lack of time available for literacy training.

Students who struggle the most with reading and language tend to benefit significantly from teachers who are dedicated to building comprehension habits (Ryder & Graves, 2002). Many content area teachers (including teachers of English and ELD courses) do not realize that they can—and should—teach comprehension while at the same time teaching their content. *In fact, teaching rich content is one of the best ways to build comprehension habits—and vice versa.* In other words, when a topic is interesting or is taught in an engaging manner, students are more likely to put effort into actively thinking about the text (Guthrie & Wigfield, 2000). Active thinking is a catalyst for developing automatic comprehension habits. Worksheets, grammar activities, and "answer 10 questions" exercises have become insipid and ineffective long before many of our struggling readers and long-term English learners reach us. Students in the upper grades are ready for more respect as adolescent thinkers, and they are ready to be challenged to think in more complex ways than what many curricula currently offer. It is up to us to give our students the tools for such thinking and to model how they are used.

"Academicizing" the Comprehension Habits That Students Already Use

We must continue to help struggling readers make connections to background knowledge and thinking processes *that they already use* for making sense of their world outside of school. Some teachers have asked me, "How can I teach inference to students who don't know how to infer?" I remind them that every student already uses *daily* all the comprehension habits mentioned in this book. The comprehension habits are the integral thought processes we all use for making our way through each day of life—for reading the world, as Freire and Macedo (1987) say. For example, many students already interpret metaphors in songs, infer feelings from pictures, guess word meanings from a billboard, ask questions about a movie, visualize a story that is read to them, predict the end of a television show, or summarize what they did last weekend. Our students simply need to transfer and extend the comprehension habits they already use outside of school to the comprehension of academic texts inside of school (i.e., they need to "academicize" their existing habits). It is our job as teachers to create, model, and support experiences in which students can successfully do this.

The Comprehension Challenges of Linguistically and Culturally Diverse Students

A large number of struggling readers did not spend their childhood years in U.S. "mainstream" homes and schools (U.S. Bureau of Census, 1993). Some of these linguistically and/or culturally diverse students are immigrants, often called English learners. Some grew up in U.S. homes where a non-English language was spoken, and some grew up in households where a nonschool version of English was spoken. Most diverse students have not been privy to the large amounts of cultural and academic "capital" that the majority of mainstream students bring with them to school (Delpit, 1995). This capital, as you might guess, plays a large role in comprehension. In addition to this capital, language has been and will continue to be a major factor in the development of comprehension for these students.

Most of the ideas in this book were created with diverse students in mind. We must constantly remember that these students often have different ways of viewing the world—views that can clash with the texts and teaching styles that we may currently use in the classroom (Peregoy & Boyle, 2000). When this clashing occurs, comprehension suffers. Many teachers have U.S. mainstream backgrounds and, therefore, find it difficult to empathize with the many academic and nonacademic issues of diverse students. Such students can lack the specific background knowledge, academic language, and culturally bound perspectives needed to make the connections and inferences that many mainstream English-using authors assume that their readers will make.

Diverse students also come to us with varying degrees of literacy in their native languages. It is much easier to teach students to read in English if they already know how to read in Spanish, Arabic, Russian, or Mandarin. Literate students already have built up many of the automatic habits of comprehension and have trained their brains to process written text (Urquhart & Weir, 1998). They have developed abilities in mental multitasking and hierarchically organizing written information. Reading in their first language has challenged them to think in complex ways and to process text quickly. Other English learners, however, come to us with limited literacy experience in any language, and these are the ones who struggle the most to catch up to those students who have had the opportunity to practice with words and written ideas since infancy.

Many English learners in the classrooms I observe can fluently read aloud words in English but do not sufficiently understand the text. They say the words, and they may speak in

English to their peers, but they cannot put it all together to understand it in the way the author and teacher intend. These students may even know the meaning of each individual word in the text, but they may lack the ability to put those words together the way the author intends. An English learner also may misinterpret dialogue, metaphors, slang expressions, and word variants, such as verbs or adjectives that have been turned into abstract nouns.

Unfortunately, many teachers and authors are not sensitive to thinking patterns that differ from their own, and they have had little experience thinking outside their cultural-linguistic boxes. The majority of U.S. teachers have not had their thinking shaped by the many factors that have shaped the thinking patterns, habits, and attitudes of their diverse students. These factors may include war, culture shock, loss of family members, poverty, hunger, hard labor, leaving home forever, racism, linguistic prejudice, illness, differing religions, differing adult–child interactions, family illiteracy, caring for siblings, frequent moves, gang involvement, divorce, drugs, and pregnancy—just to name a few. Moreover, these factors may be compounded by radically different educational experiences that students may have had in the schools of their home countries.

As teachers, we must strive to see classroom learning through the eyes of our diverse students and then provide texts and teaching that relate to their diverse backgrounds and interests. Even our teaching of expository text comprehension can be improved significantly by a better understanding of how linguistically diverse readers may relate to a topic (Gillet & Temple, 1999). Many of the ideas in this book equip the teacher to build text "scaffolds" with diverse readers in mind. These scaffolds are organizational frameworks onto which a student can build concepts and organize text information for the purposes of increased understanding of complex language, retention of the information, and development of comprehension habits to use for future similar texts.

One helpful way to engage diverse students is to show as you read by using visuals, drawings, or graphic organizers. The use of visuals to show the connections and structures in varying texts is especially helpful to those learners who are still familiarizing themselves with the complexities (and inconsistencies) of English (Peregoy & Boyle, 2000). English learners, for example, encounter frustration much sooner if spoken or written words are the only medium used in a lesson or text. Visual aids extend students' mental endurance and better communicate what the words truly mean in order to improve overall comprehension. This toolkit of activities contains many visual ways to organize information and build the habits that diverse and mainstream students alike can use to improve comprehension.

For students who lack academic English and/or reading experience, learning by immersion and osmosis isn't enough. They need extra and explicit support in order to reach grade-level comprehension (Irwin, 1991). It is our job to provide this support in the form of extra modeling, practice, feedback, and scaffolding. These are a few of the essential elements of instruction described in the next chapter. Why include them in this book? Because we all can do with a quick reminder of best practices and effective teacher behaviors. A set of tools is one thing; knowing when, where, and how to use them is another. Therefore, peruse the suggestions in chapter 2 and reflect on how to incorporate them into your teaching on a daily basis.

CHAPTER

Assessment and Instruction That Build Comprehension Habits

* * *

Teaching is the ultimate synthesis
of science and art, of organization
and improvisation.

The primary purpose of this book is to help teachers fortify instruction with activities that develop automatic reading comprehension habits in students. In a sense, we want to "soup up" current instruction with the best tools available in order to provide our students with ample modeling and practice in active text processing. We want students to be engaged, challenged, and saturated with academic thinking—without being overwhelmed. Unfortunately for many of our struggling readers, there often has been too little engagement and too much overwhelming. The first step in the process of enhancing our instruction is to find out what our students do as they comprehend and learn. This is what I call *useful assessment*, also referred to as *authentic assessment* or *assessment that informs instruction and learning*.

We must monitor student progress *while* students are comprehending, not just after. This helps us see students' strengths and weaknesses in using their habits to construct meaning. Many elementary teachers already do this informally in their minds. They usually know which students are struggling and in which areas. For example, a teacher knows that Ana doesn't use context very well to figure out new words, Robert doesn't connect to background knowledge very well, and Celia excels at making logical predictions. Yet in middle school and high school, with larger numbers of students and a focus on content, teachers are much more challenged to observe student comprehension and keep track of their observations. With some teachers having as many as 170 students to keep track of, this is understandable, but it also is rectifiable. The trick is to modify instructional activities so that they also serve as assessments. This book includes suggestions for doing this.

Assessing Reading Comprehension

Comprehension is a highly individual process, and assessing it is far more complex than many decision makers lead us to believe. To climb inside a reader's mind and accurately "measure" the quality, speed, and durability of the countless connections and processes that occur during his or her interaction with text is impossible. How can we see and measure the lightning-fast inferences that zip through readers' minds as they read? How can we measure the nature and quality of thinking itself? How can we see what the student is visualizing and how he or she is modifying that scene based on the text? Each student brings a different set of tools and materials (skills and background knowledge) to each text. All we can do is learn as much as we can from what we observe. To do this, we must sharpen our observation abilities and instruments.

What do we want to know about a student's comprehension? Table 1 breaks down the six habits a bit further to help you create checklists or rubrics for observing students. You can then use this book's activities as lenses to see how well your students are comprehending and in which areas their comprehension processes are breaking down.

We must provide clear feedback to students with regard to their progress (Marzano, Pickering, & Pollock, 2001). Students want to know their academic strengths and weaknesses. A score of 84 on an essay or multiple-choice test provides little feedback, but the chances of learning improve when the assessments are interesting and meaningful. Assessments that allow more choice, creativity of expression, and validation of original thought tend to be more successful (Wiggins, 1998). For these reasons, I encourage teachers to create nontraditional and less "assess-y" assessment strategies such as graphic organizers, charts, checklists, matrices, and anecdotal records. These types of assessments are usually more engaging and useful than many question-based forms of reading assessment. In fact, some of the best assessments I have used are ones that students don't consider to be assessments.

Every teaching activity can be a window into comprehension. Consider using the following steps to help you use the activities in this book as assessments:

1. Know what aspects of the comprehension habit(s) you want to assess. Refer to Table 1 for ideas.

2. Decide what type of evidence a student can provide to show the quality of the aspects in step 1. The evidence may be the information in a graphic organizer, drawing, discussion, written text, and so on.

3. Most teachers do not have time for step 4, so if you do not, you should pick one or two key aspects of comprehension that will show up in the activity and focus on them while discussing work with students and/or grading student work. For example, in the Prediction Chart activity (chapter 5), I might focus on the quality of evidence for predictions, how well the prediction relates to the main idea of a text, or both. Then, I focus the discussion or my written comments on these aspects.

4. If you have a few minutes, create a checklist (or rubric) that lists what is to be learned and how it is evidenced by the activity. These checklists also are very helpful for informing students about what they are expected to know, do, say, and think. You can

Table 1.　What We Would Like to Know About the Comprehension Habits

Comprehension Habit	We Want to Know How Well a Reader...
1. Organizing text information by sculpting the main idea and summarizing	• Recalls important details that relate to the author's purpose and main idea (i.e., the big picture) • Recalls sequence • Organizes the information hierarchically during and after reading • Uses textual aids and visual cues • Considers purposes—author's, teacher's, reader's
2. Connecting to background knowledge	• Connects to related background knowledge (cultural, experiential, cognitive) • Modifies background knowledge, using the text's descriptions in order to create new patterns of information • Combines previous experience with text descriptions to create useful pictures in the mind
3. Making inferences and predictions	• Stores inferences and predictions in short-term memory for later use during reading • Uses all aspects of text (e.g., visuals, headings) to create inferences • Reflects on previous texts or experiences to make a connection or assumption • Relates text to current events and classroom themes • Uses cause and effect and fact and opinion to infer and predict • Interprets figurative language • Generates relevant predictions with logical evidence that relates to main idea and/or author's purpose • Revises predictions based on new evidence in text
4. Generating and answering questions	• Generates relevant implicit and explicit questions to interact with the text • Generates questions that the author wants the reader to ask • Uses questions before, during, and after reading • Actively seeks to answer questions during reading
5. Understanding and remembering word meanings	• Uses sentence structure and semantic clues to predict word meaning • Uses context to figure out the meanings of multiple-meaning words • Uses knowledge of key vocabulary, prefixes, suffixes, and roots
6. Monitoring one's own comprehension	• Uses fix-up strategies when comprehension breaks down • Adapts reading and thinking to fit the type of text (narrative/poetry, functional, expository/social science, science, math)

even include a section in which to take notes on the specific evidence of the habit or skill. See the following example:

Prediction		Evidence Notes
Uses evidence from background knowledge to make prediction	1 2 3 4	
Prediction logically and helpfully relates to the main idea of the article	1 2 3 4	
Revises predictions according to new information in text	1 2 3 4	

5. Share your observations and assessments with students as a whole class and then individually. (Hand out the checklist or rubric before teaching the activity so students know what is expected of them.)

Even though high-stakes tests are an ever-present influence on what we do in school, all teachers are likely interested in taking their students much further down the road of reading comprehension than what is measured by such tests. Fortunately, improved test scores are a positive side effect of building comprehension habits (Marzano et al., 2001). Yet the main benefit is students' improved abilities to reason, infer, judge, organize, interpret, apply, communicate, and comprehend the world—abilities that are shallowly tested by the multiple-choice test experience but deeply tested by higher education and life.

Instructional Habits

We should begin with clear content and comprehension goals in mind in order to create an environment in which all students progress toward these goals as efficiently as possible. To create and maintain a complex environment that is optimally conducive for all students' learning, a teacher must have a well-developed set of lesson elements and teacher behaviors (I call them *instructional habits*) that automatically kick in before, during, and after each lesson. The rest of this chapter briefly outlines several instructional habits and key components of instruction that should become a natural part of teaching, especially the teaching of comprehension habits that will form a foundation for students' lifelong learning.

Connecting the New to the Existing
We must provide teaching that helps students relate new concepts, skills, and strategies to what they already know (Gillet & Temple, 2000). (Many teachers are tired of hearing this, but we all could always do a better job at it, particularly with struggling readers and English learners.) Chapter 1 mentioned the importance of helping students build academic habits on the existing foundation of their knowledge and skills. If we don't help students connect, they

quickly lose interest and become overwhelmed with too much disjointed information. To combat this, we can do several things: (1) relate current learning to previous lessons, other courses, current events, school issues, or life outside of school; (2) incorporate familiar texts such as movies, songs, images, television shows, commercials, community issues, and controversial topics; (3) show students the similarities between thinking inside school and outside school by using a Venn diagram or T-chart; (4) fill in the necessary background knowledge before the lesson or reading, using pictures, stories, gestures, drama, and so on; and (5) try the activities in chapter 4 of this book.

When students feel that they are not starting from scratch and that they already know something about a topic, they will be much more likely to be interested in learning a little more about it—especially if they feel that it relates to their lives in some way (Delpit, 1995).

Modeling Comprehension

Modeling, according to Vygotsky (1934/1978), is a key component in learning. Yet I have noticed a serious lack of modeling of reading in upper grades. Many teachers of grades 6–12 do not know how to model reading comprehension, and, therefore, they do not do it. They assume that students already know how to read and just need extra time to figure out the meaning of texts on their own. When the many invisible thinking processes (habits) that facilitate comprehension of school texts do not occur to students, it is mainly because they have rarely seen or heard them applied to school texts by another person. They have not had the chance to be an apprentice, so to speak. Even though teachers tend to assume that secondary students are past needing it, our students *still* need to observe another person modeling an academic task more than just once (Wilhelm, 2001). Teachers are the best-qualified people to show students how good readers think. For example, we should model our thinking when reading challenging content texts and performing tasks such as filling in graphic organizers, drawing mental images from a text, and creating written responses.

One form of modeling is reading aloud. Reading aloud is vital for building fluency and language (Robb, 2003). Many struggling readers did not have this type of modeling when they were young, but it is still vital even in middle and high school, and even in social studies and science classes. Moreover, students tend to enjoy it because they think that the teacher is doing the hard work.

Think-alouds (Farr, 2001) also are very effective ways to show students how proficient readers think while reading. By verbalizing our thoughts, we can make visible the many complex habits that help us comprehend, and we can show how much mental work it is to read for meaning. We can show how we also get stuck, figure out words, ask silly questions, make predictions, infer, and so on. Plenty of think-aloud suggestions are found in the following chapters of this book.

Scaffolding Students' Comprehension

Students need to be given opportunities to do what the teacher has modeled, but with teacher assistance that gradually diminishes as students master the skill. "Just enough help to get them to the next level of learning" is one way to remember the term *scaffolding*, which is often seen as the gradual release of responsibility from the teacher doing the task to the student doing it independently (Alvermann & Phelps, 2001).

As an illustration of scaffolding, imagine a master artist with several apprentices. The master artist does not simply let her apprentices gather in the corner and create products on their own all day. She works with them, models various steps, voices her thought processes while she works, asks for comments, and provides clear feedback. On the other hand, she does not give a long lecture as the apprentices listen and take notes, with the goal of passing the multiple-choice test on sculpture the following Friday. The latter scenario would be similar to the teacher-centered formats sometimes used in modern schools, which tend to be too rigid and incomprehensible for struggling readers, not to mention boring and irrelevant to students' lives.

In scaffolding, the teacher does most of the task in the beginning and then uses scaffolding activities to build student abilities and independence at the task. For example, a teacher may start a lesson on figurative language with a popular song and then show students how to fill in a chart that helps them to analyze the relation between literal and figurative meanings (see LitFigs activity in chapter 7). Gradually, the teacher allows students to fill in the chart, with less and less assistance, until eventually the chart is taken away and students can discuss figurative interpretations without extra support.

We need to keep in mind that we are striving to do far more than build student proficiency at specific tasks such as answering questions about a text or filling in charts. Rather, we intend for the thinking abilities required for success on such tasks to develop into mental habits that kick in automatically when students read any type of text in the future: SAT tests, DVD machine instructions, newspaper articles, project reports, business letters, and, eventually, *War and Peace* by the fire at age 75. The years between 6th and 12th grade are delicate and crucial years for strengthening, refining, and expanding the habits that facilitate comprehension (Robb, 2003). With sufficient scaffolding, we can help our students to move on, prepared for any comprehension challenge that might arise.

Giving Minilessons

An important component of comprehension instruction are minilessons—short and targeted lessons that teach a particular aspect of reading when the need arises (Lyons & Pinnell, 2001). For instance, a teacher may notice three or four students who struggle when asked to summarize. During an appropriate time, the teacher takes the students aside to provide a minilesson on summarizing. Steps for teaching the lesson include the following:

1. Introduction—Let students know what they are about to learn. Connect the new material to students' prior knowledge and the text currently being studied.

2. Teacher modeling—Show students how to use the strategy. Teacher think-aloud techniques are effective for this.

3. Student modeling and guided practice—Have students gradually take charge of the strategy and begin to require less support from you.

Table 2.	Minilesson Topics
Reading	Writing
• Understanding unknown words in context • Classifying and categorizing information • Using the glossary or index • Making inferences and drawing conclusions • Identifying story elements (setting, plot, etc.) • Interpreting symbolism • Seeing Spanish-English connections • Using text structure to comprehend • Generating under-the-surface questions • Discerning fact from opinion • Identifying cause and effect • Taking multicultural perspectives • Interpreting idiomatic expressions • Using word parts	• Writing hooks and grabbers • Going from graphic organizers to written compositions • Taking different points of view • Considering audience and purpose • Using similes and metaphors • Writing business letters • Using appropriate words • Creating topic sentences • Using paragraphs • Using quotation marks • Using capital letters • Addressing counterarguments • Using appropriate words

4. Independent practice—Give the students opportunities to try the strategy in new situations and then to reflect on how it has been useful.

Table 2 shows some ideas for using minilessons with your class.

Building Academic Language to Facilitate Comprehension

For students to understand the concepts and content in their texts, they need to understand the academic language that authors use in these texts. Teachers must make this challenging language more understandable for struggling students, many of whom struggle because of diverse language backgrounds. Some important ways to make academic language more comprehensible include the following:

- Clarify content and language objectives before, during, and after instruction.
- Take observation notes on students' language use in small groups and in pairs. Share academic language phrases that you hear from students by writing them on an overhead transparency or on the board. For example, you might write such phrases as "He is different from her because...," "I disagree because...," "This argument outweighs theirs because...," and "We should consider...."
- Provide wait time (five seconds or so) after you ask questions, in silence with no hands raised. This gives time for students with slower language processing to formulate answers. Also, allow students to provide answers nonverbally at times (e.g., thumbs up/thumbs down, shake or nod of the head, gestures).
- Ask questions that prompt critical thinking and allow for open-ended responses.
- Require students to support their answers, opinions, predictions, and inferences with evidence and examples from the text or real life.

- Model the use of academic language and show students how the language is used to describe comprehension. Use posters with academic language on them.
- Use gestures for academic terms. For example, move your hands in a certain direction and then turn around in the opposite direction for the terms *however*, *but*, and *on the other hand*.

Table 3 shows some ideas for promoting academic language among your students and for specific language to associate with each comprehension habit. Use the table to create posters from which students can borrow terms when they are developing the habit. You can also refer to the posters while teaching.

Table 3. Examples of Academic Language Starters	
Comprehension Habit	Academic Language That Expresses the Comprehension Habit
Organizing text information by sculpting the main idea and summarizing	The part where...is important because.... The gist of it is.... The main idea is.... The key details that support the main idea are.... The purpose of this text is.... The author wanted to tell us.... It's about a...that....
Connecting to background knowledge	This relates to what I learned in my other class about.... I remember when I had a similar experience. Before I form an opinion, I need to learn more about.... In my family, we....
Making inferences and predictions	I think we could infer that...because.... I hypothesize/predict that.... Based on...I guess that.... The picture (or other graphic) means.... Given that...I bet that....
Generating and answering questions	Why...? How...? Would...? Should...? Could...? I wonder.... I found the information in (resource).... One answer might be.... What do you think about...? What is your opinion of...?
Understanding and remembering word meanings	The meaning that works best in this sentence is.... Because the prefix means...I think the word is.... I can remember this word by picturing a....
Monitoring one's own comprehension	I forgot who he was so I went back and re-read.... This doesn't seem to fit with the main idea. I think the author intended to teach.... My predictions and questions helped me understand....

Using Graphic Organizers and Other Visuals

All learners have varying degrees of what is often called *visual intelligence* (Gardner, 1999). Visual intelligence is the mental skill a learner uses to organize and process information by seeing and creating images. Most authors of narrative and expository texts expect readers to visualize many concrete and abstract ideas while reading. Teachers must, therefore, be adept at developing visual lesson components that help students cultivate their visual abilities as they learn.

Visuals are summaries of the text's information that show, rather than just tell, what the words mean. For English learners, visuals help make language stand still long enough to sink in and be understood (Urquhart & Weir, 1998). Visuals are helpful in all of the three stages of reading: before, during, and after (Alvermann & Phelps, 2002). The most common visuals are pictures, videos, maps, and graphic organizers such as diagrams, charts, and tables.

Pictures, videos, and maps show physical descriptions of a text's information and images. Graphic organizers, on the other hand, are drawings that use geometric shapes or tables to show connections between pieces of information (Hyerle, 1996). For many learners, seeing the connections in a visual and organized way helps them to better comprehend and remember information. Graphic organizers also can make invisible and complex comprehension strategies more explicit, visible, and tangible to students (Merkley & Jeffries, 2001). When teachers and students see and understand their own thinking processes while reading, they internalize the comprehension habits found in chapters 3–8 of this book.

One of the most important features of graphic organizers is their ability to help a reader create a mental picture of the text's information (Hyerle, 1996). This allows the reader to clarify and keep track of the relations, sequences, and important concepts in the reading. Ideally, the process of using (i.e., designing, filling in, studying) visual representations of text will eventually develop into an automatic habit that no longer necessitates the use of the actual graphic organizer. For example, I have used Venn diagrams so often that now, when I am reading a text that compares two concepts, I picture the two intersecting circles in my mind, which helps me retain the information. This process is now a constructive mental habit for me.

As you develop your own expertise and insights as a builder of graphic organizers, you should pass on these tips to students. Provide a hefty supply of varying models and explain why they are made the way they are. Ask students for other ways of graphically showing different types of information beyond the Venn diagram or semantic web.

Students who learn to make their own graphic organizers are far better at remembering and understanding the information in texts than those students who just fill out a graphic organizer made up by the teacher (Peregoy & Boyle, 2000). When students use and construct graphic organizers during learning, they must mentally manipulate the information in what they are reading. For example, most graphic organizers give much-needed practice in identifying key elements of text and reducing (i.e., summarizing) them to fit in the spaces provided for writing.

For students, the process of designing the graphic organizer reinforces their understanding of the material by requiring them to reconstruct the information in their own words and to create connections that you or other students may not have noticed. This creative design process gives them more ownership of their learning and of their interpretations of the text. This ownership translates into better comprehension and retention (Hyerle, 1996). And the more students enjoy a task and find it relevant, the less they mind the extra thinking.

I have seen many teachers put up a wonderful visual and then only use it once. Remind yourself to use each visual to its maximum potential in all stages of the lesson. Refer back to it often. Add to it. Have students add to it and teach others from it. Use it as an anchor for the concepts in the lesson. Finally, use it to review key concepts before giving summative assessments.

Assessing With Graphic Organizers. As discussed in the beginning of the chapter, graphic organizers can give you the chance to informally assess the ways in which students are understanding text information. Students' ways of thinking, interpreting, and organizing text information into graphic organizers often prove to be very innovative and insightful. You can make simple rubrics or checklists that go with the graphics to be used. For example, for a Venn diagram, you could use the following checklist:

☐ Correctly identifies four shared features

☐ Correctly identifies three contrasting features on each side

☐ Uses examples and evidence from text to support statements

☐ Makes valid inferences and hypotheses

☐ Summarizes using own words

☐ Effectively explains to partner how to use the graphic organizer

---

Putting More MoMaMu Into Lessons

MoMaMu is a mnemonic that stands for movement, kinesthetics, gestures, and hand motions (Mo); manipulatives, real objects, and hands-on projects (Ma); and music, chants, rhymes, songs, and rhythm (Mu). MoMaMus are extraverbal, nontraditional methods that reinforce content learning and make language comprehensible. These techniques can be especially helpful when teaching new vocabulary and concepts (Marzano et al., 2001). Unfortunately, I have noticed that the quantity and quality of MoMaMu techniques seem to decrease each year from grades 1–12. By high school, many classes are seriously lacking in these extraverbal techniques, a situation that consequently deprives many struggling students of optimal learning conditions. MoMaMu methods are helpful for teaching all students, but they are especially helpful (even vital) for reaching those students who struggle with reading comprehension and the processing of academic language (see McLaughlin & Vogt, 2000).

Some activities, such as hands-on science experiments, already have several MoMaMu techniques. But, we might ask, will every student adequately learn the standards for a given lesson? And if not, could additional MoMaMu techniques (e.g., chants, objects, or role-playing) be used to improve learning? The answer is almost always *yes*. This is because many students need to learn the same concept in more than one way. Often it is the nonverbal way that clarifies the verbal learning and makes it stick in the brain. For this reason, the more

Table 4.	Questions and Examples for Integrating MoMaMu Techniques	
Technique	Reflection Questions	Examples
Mo (Movement)	• How can some kind of movement, either with hands or the whole body, show this concept? • Can students come up with their own motions?	• Hand motions for comprehension habits and thinking skills • Moving to sides of the room depending on which side of controversial issue the student takes • Mime, skits, drama, role-play
Ma (Manipulatives)	• How can I bring in or create objects or simulated objects that show concepts? • How can students manipulate things to show learning and remember concepts?	• Clothes, sticks, clay, cardboard, index cards, sentence strips, posters, models, dice, instruments, tools
Mu (Music)	• How can I, the students, or both create a song that embodies the learning that needs to happen? • Is there a song already out there that can serve our purposes? • What vocabulary should be in the song? • What instruments might be fun to use with the song?	• Chants, songs, raps, poems

standards there are, the more MoMaMu techniques we should use. I strongly encourage middle school and high school teachers to use these techniques more than they already do. Unfortunately, many teachers consider techniques such as chants and hand motions to be a waste of time or too juvenile for their students and, therefore, do not even attempt them. Yet I have had numerous teachers come to me and say something like, "I thought my students would boo and hiss as if I were treating them like babies, but they loved it! And they still know the content after three months!"

Perhaps the biggest gap that MoMaMu fills is the need for spicing up boring teaching. The next six chapters have a number of MoMaMu techniques that can be used to jazz up content and comprehension learning in the pre-, during-, and postreading stages. Gradually, we must make them a natural part of our teaching; Table 4 shows some ideas for how to do this.

I even have a MoMaMu chant for teachers to remind them to fortify the different stages of each lesson with these techniques:

First we engage so they won't mentally check out,
With photos, show-and-tell, role-plays, and read-alouds.
And we focus and connect to what they already know,
With Quickwrites, brainstorms, and K-W-Ls.

We always make what we say as clear as we can,
With charts, doodles, drama, and moving our hands.
For some good oral practice and vocabulary fun,
We use chants, raps, tunes, and popular songs.

Before students read, they must warm their brains up,
With anticipation guides, THIEVES, or think-aloud stuff.
Then as they read, they think and organize,
With semantic webs, sticky notes, grids, and timelines.

Before they write, again they think and organize,
With Venn diagrams, story maps, and outlines.
They can debate an issue or do a poster presentation.
They can even write a letter to the United Nations.

For fun, you can circle and label each technique shown here with one or more of the elements of Mo, Ma, or Mu. You also will notice visual and cooperative elements. (Try turning the chant into a rap.)

Facilitating Meaningful Academic Communication

The act of communicating a concept to another person helps us learn it better (Lyons & Pinnell, 2001). When we communicate, we are forced to organize and clarify our thoughts into coherent sentences before we speak. This process makes an imprint on the brain, creating ownership of the information and, subsequently, facilitating more enduring learning. The process of discussing ideas with other people also forces us to challenge our own preconceptions, negotiate meaning, and sharpen our thinking. Several types of activities are helpful for promoting interaction in classrooms:

- **Students teaching other students**—Students learn a lot when they can effectively teach the target concepts to other students. This is especially true when the other students being taught do not already know the information. Jigsaw Summaries are good examples of this type of learning (see chapter 3).

- **Pair activities**—Pair activities are effective because they can be constructed quickly (e.g., "Turn to a partner..."), and anxiety is low because only one other person is listening. See Think-Pair-Share and variations (chapter 4).

- **Group projects and discussions**—Groups of three to five students can provide powerful learning experiences when handled correctly. Students need to have their roles clearly defined. Initially, teachers should model what to say and how to say it by using minilessons and a lot of guidance during the process. Reciprocal Teaching (see activity in chapter 8) is a popular example of cooperative group work. Following are a few of the possible group roles:

Clarifier	Graphic designer	Presenter
Comparer	Inferrer	Problem solver
Discussion director	Notetaker	Questioner
Encourager	Predictor	Summarizer

Promoting "Minds-On" Reading in All Stages of Reading

Active reading means struggling, connecting, reflecting, organizing, notetaking, and *thinking hard* in order to create an accurate representation of the text. "Minds-on" reading means comprehending a text before, during, and after reading. Using these pre-, during-, and postreading stages, which also boast an array of fancier names (into, through, beyond; initiating, constructing, extending), is, in a sense, a separate habit. If we can get students to build the habit of actively processing text in all three stages, comprehension will improve. Refer to the reproducible Comprehension Bookmark (see page 185) to see possibilities for each stage. Copy it and give it to your students for ongoing reading. You can even laminate it and have students use it as a checklist over and over.

These three stages are important because struggling readers often view reading as just a "during" process (or worse, just a decoding process). Comprehension increases drastically when students learn to use the strategies within the pre- and postreading stages, which are teachable and worth the time spent on teaching them. Using these stages is particularly effective with expository readings, which tend to be the texts that give students the most trouble (Brown & Stephens, 1999). So we must provide plenty of support during all three stages, especially in the prereading stage. Students should rarely "go in cold" to a reading assignment without some kind of brain warm-up or content preview (Alvermann & Phelps, 2001).

Why should we spend time on pre-, during-, and postreading activities? Prereading activities do the following:

- Introduce focal lesson concepts and important words and terms
- Build foundational background knowledge
- Provide motivational "hooks" for reading
- Make connections to prior lesson content, activities, and readings

During-reading activities do the following:

- Coach students through various stages of reading a text
- Model and build reading strategies so they become habits
- Help students to organize and retain the information
- Help build ongoing assessments of strategy use and comprehension
- Allow for student-centered and collaborative learning

Postreading activities do the following:

- Model different ways of summarizing and synthesizing information
- Help to organize and retain information
- Allow students to apply the text to their lives
- Help students to reflect on the readings and bring closure to the prereading and postreading activities

Table 5 is a list of selected activities from this book that particularly lend themselves to one or more of the three reading stages. They are listed under pre-, during-, and postreading categories, but most are very effective in more than one stage of reading. You can cross-reference this list to find activities that meet your needs. In each of chapters 3–8, there is a similar chart that helps you see which activities are especially helpful for different content areas. In Table 5, the chapter numbers indicate where each tool is found in this book. The symbols tell which comprehension habits are emphasized; see the key at the end of the table for an explanation of the letter symbols. You also can refer to similar tables in each chapter that show when and in which content areas the tools are best used.

Using Best Practices Weekly

We don't have enough time for good teaching practices. We need the *best* teaching practices that we can design. We must fill our lessons with activities that maximize learning and the building of good academic habits. Best practices can be used all year long with a variety of subjects and texts. I often tell teachers who are reluctant to change teaching practices to start with one or two activities and to keep doing them throughout the year, while adding one more each month. By the end of the year, the best practices will replace most of the mediocre practices. (And you'll enjoy teaching even more.) Try creating a literacy binder for quick reference while lesson planning. One teacher created the following chart in order to catalog the best practices that she used consistently each week:

Prereading	During Reading	Postreading
Anticipation Guides (+ Why)	LitFigs	Quickwrites
Brainstorm and Sort	RATA (Read-Aloud Think-Aloud)	Think-Pair-Share
K-W-L Plus	Reciprocal Teaching	Language Experience Approach Plus
Quickwrites	Semantic Webbing	Semantic Webbing
Think-Pair-Share		
Word Bank		

Getting the Most Standards and Habits Out of Each Minute

Given our limited time and resources, we should strive to develop as many habits, skills, and content standards as we can with the same activity. So take a critical look at the teaching activities you use and notice which ones seem to address more content and thinking in less time. For example, a diorama or a map-coloring activity may take up more precious time than they are worth in terms of standards achievement and thinking practice. On the other hand, a group activity that generates a matrix with information from a social studies text might address multiple objectives at once (e.g., organizing information, categorizing, summarizing, learning content, discussing, figuring out vocabulary).

Table 5. Activities Listed by Reading Stage

Prereading Activities	Comprehension Habits Emphasized	Chapter
Anticipation Guides (+ Why)	B, I, P	4
Brain Warmers	B, M, P, Q	4
Brainstorm and Sort	B, M, S	4
CATAPULT Into Literature	B, M, P, Q, W	4
Closed Eyes Visualize	B, I, P, S	4
Concept Poster Chat	B, M, P, S	4
Do the BK	B, I, S	4
Give One–Get One	B, M, Q	4
Guess and Adjust	I, M, P, W	7
Inference Advertisements	I, M, P, Q, S	5
K-W-L	B, P, Q, S	4
Main Idea Café	I, M, P, S	3
Question Tree and Sea	I, Q, S	6
Quickwrites	B, I, P, S, W	4
Show and Not Tell	I, P, S	5
Summarizing Training Camp	M, S	3
Text Structure Organizing	B, M, P	4
THIEVES	B, M, P, Q, W	4
Think-Pair-Share	B, I, P, S, W	4

During-Reading Activities	Comprehension Habits Emphasized	Chapter
Background Knowledge Backpack	B	4
Cause and Effect Timeline	I, P, S	5
Evolving Main Idea Three-Column Notes	C, M, S	3
External-Internal Story Line	C, I, M, S	5
Keyword Construction	M, S, W	3
LitFigs	I, W	7
Main Idea Formula	C, M, P, S	3
Main Idea Memory Storage	C, M, Q, S	3
Mental Multitasking Practice	C, M, S	8
New Words in Context Chart	I, Q, W	7
Outline-ish Thoughts	I, M, S	3
Path to Purpose	C, M, S	4
Prediction Basketball	I, P	5
Prediction Chart	I, P, Q	5
Prediction Signals	I, P, W	5
Question the Author	I, P, Q	6
Question Tree and Sea	Q, S	6
Quickwrites	B, I, M, P, S, W	4
RATA (Read-Aloud Think-Aloud)	B, C, I, P, S, W	8
Reciprocal Teaching	B, C, I, P, Q, S, W,	8
SCUBA Diving Into Word Meaning	I, W	7
Semantic Webbing	M, S, W	3
Sorry, I Lost My Headings	M, Q, S,	3
Sticky Note Snapshots	B, C, I, P, Q, S	4
T+B=I Inference Machines	I, P, S, W	5
Think-Aloud Note Grids	C, I, M, P, Q, S	8
Vee Map	Q, S	6

(continued)

Table 5. Activities Listed by Reading Stage (continued)		
Postreading Activities	Comprehension Habits Emphasized	Chapter
Central Question Diagram	B, C, M, Q, S	6
Character Report Card	I, S	5
Connect the Words	M, S, W	7
Dialogue Comic Strip	I, M, S	5
Hot Seat	I, M, Q, S	6
Jigsaw Summaries	M, S	3
Language Experience Approach Plus	I, M, S	3
LitFigs	I, Q, W	7
Matrices	M, Q, S	3
Multiple Meanings Table	W	7
Quickwrites	C, I, M, Q, S	4
Semantic Webbing	M, S	3
Socratic Sessions	C, I, M, Q, S	6
Story Map	I, M, P, S	3
Vocabulary Bank Notes	W	7
Webpage Creation	B, I, M, Q, S	3
Word Bank	W	7

B = Background Knowledge Usage; C = Comprehension Monitoring; I = Inferring; M = Main Idea Sculpting; P = Predicting; Q = Questioning; S = Summarizing; V = Visualizing; W = Word Meaning Interpretation

Building Textbook Reading Habits

Many students in upper grades do poorly in school because they cannot read their thick, imposing books. However, this can be prevented by taking the time to show students how to read the textbooks that carry the bulk of the content to be learned (Alvermann & Phelps, 2001). Most content area teachers have not devoted much time or energy to their own skills in teaching reading. In the upper grades, many social studies, math, and science teachers expect English teachers to teach reading. English teachers, however, expect the teachers of previous grades to already have taught reading.

Content area teachers (especially in science and social studies) should commit to extensive teaching of expository reading, especially because English classes do not have time for it. Content teachers are experts at the thinking needed to comprehend their content material. They can effectively model the ways in which historians, mathematicians, and scientists actually think as they read a text. Ultimately, content teachers usually discover that building comprehension habits is well worth the extra time when students, as they improve their reading, excel at learning and retaining more content. To aid this process, many of the activities in the following chapters are geared toward nonfiction and textbook reading.

Developing Literacy Teacher Habits

To teach the "rocket science" of reading comprehension, simply pulling ideas from books and workshops and then stuffing them into the curriculum is not enough. There is too much going on in the thick of each lesson to plan everything beforehand. For this reason, we need to develop automatic literacy-related instructional habits that engage every time we make instructional decisions. The following list shows just a few of the important habits of a literacy-minded teacher, some of which are borrowed from the points previously discussed:

- Teach to different learning styles (MoMaMu).
- Model your thoughts, questions, confusion, and problem-solving steps.
- Clarify objectives (know, do, say, think).
- Relate learning to real life.
- Maximize student interaction and use of academic language.
- Provide useful feedback that directly relates to higher success on assessments.
- Take notes on behavior and individual student progress during learning activities.
- Creatively tap into learning from previous lessons and from students' lives.
- Draw, doodle, and act to make language and concepts comprehensible.
- Strategically move around the classroom to observe and support learning.

The suggestions in this chapter for building comprehension habits are just starters; they are meant to be adapted by you to fit your needs. I am convinced that the thorough development of comprehension habits is one of the most important gifts we can give to our students for the future. The next six chapters provide a variety of tools for building these good habits in any class where students read.

PART II

Six Comprehension Habits

CHAPTER

Organizing Text Information by Sculpting the Main Idea and Summarizing

* * *

Knowing where you have been
and where you are is of great benefit
to knowing where you are going.

Finding the main idea has never been fun for most struggling readers. They have been asked to find it countless times and have produced inadequate answers. After repeated failures, many students just give up on the search altogether. They figure out how to work the system instead, most often by searching for answers to questions or by copying. Unfortunately, getting the main idea is the most vital type of thinking we can do to comprehend a text. We cannot sidestep it. Nor can we avoid the related habit of summarizing that supports the main idea. For these reasons, this chapter provides a variety of ways to help students develop better organizing abilities in subtler and less painful ways.

Have you ever started reading a book that was just too stuffed with information to absorb it for more than five minutes? You either take a lot of breaks or choose not to read it. Our students do not have these choices. We ask them to read and learn it all, but the texts are overloaded with information. What does a good reader do? A good reader reduces text to just the essentials. The good reader then proceeds to organize the essentials by using a process I call *sculpting the main idea*—the process in which a reader looks at emerging clues and develops the text's core information *before and during* reading, not just after.

The good reader uses this evolving main idea to decide what to store in the summaries. Summarizing is the process of reducing a just-read portion of text into a manageable chunk of important information. This chunk, in turn, helps guide the reader in sculpting the overall main idea. As one can see, this becomes a codependent cycle: As the main idea becomes more defined, the reader can more effectively decide which information goes into the summaries that support the main idea. As the summaries increase in number, they help the reader sculpt a better-defined main idea.

This chapter offers ideas for helping all students to develop these symbiotic organizing habits:

- Identifying, generating, developing, and sculpting the main idea of the passage
- Summarizing portions of text to strengthen, change, and challenge the evolving main idea

Sculpting the Main Idea

"What's the main idea?" might be the most popular question asked by teachers and tests. Yet many students have never been directly taught how to figure out the main idea of a text. This is because secondary teachers tend to assume that the students learned such a basic skill in previous years of schooling. However, getting the main idea is a complex and challenging habit to develop, and it gets more challenging as texts get more complex in middle school and high school. Therefore, getting the main idea is a habit that we cannot afford to stop developing in our students (Baumann, 1986). Of course, teachers reading this chapter are probably already quite convinced of this need.

Main Idea Components

For the purposes of this book, I will define sculpting the main idea as the process of creating a compact chunk of information that includes the topic, what is said about the topic, and, usually, the text's purpose. These items can be shortened to the What? What about it? and Why? components to help students remember the process. Starting with the text's title and other initial visual clues, we begin to formulate the main idea. Some titles are misleading, however, and we must test our hypotheses about the main idea and look for evidence as we read. If evidence comes along that contradicts our existing main idea, we must "trim" away pieces and "attach" new ones that align with the text.

Topic (What?). The topic is a word or phrase that describes what the text is about. It usually is a main subject, process, or event. Sample topics include "a quest to destroy a ring," "ionic and covalent bonding," and "unsung heroes of the American Revolution." Students should be trained to generate a possible topic every time they see a title and then to combine it with other prereading clues such as visuals, charts, boldface words, and so on. Fortunately, in most expository texts the topic can be found in the title of the passage. But if it is not so obvious, we need to train students to generate it. This can be done in two ways: (1) Show students how to focus on repeated references, that is, ideas that are central and repeated throughout the text (Friend, 2001); and (2) "Be the text's author at a party," an activity in which the student thinks like the author in order to come up with answers to cocktail party questions such as, What's your writing about? (see the Hot Seat activity in chapter 6). For example, if asked the above question about my book, I might answer, "reading strategies." The next question partygoers might ask is, What does your text say about that? This second question is the What About It? component discussed next.

Description (What About It?). We must train students to dig a little deeper into what *this* specific text says about the topic. Think about the many times we have asked students the question, What does the text say about it (the topic)? What important ideas did this text offer to further describe the topic? This step is key because it helps (forces) the student to find that just-right area between too broad a topic and a description that is too detailed. Following are some examples of What About It? responses:

- The main characters sought to destroy the ring because if it fell into the wrong hands the world would be overcome with evil.

- These types of bonds between atoms are different in that covalent bonds share an electron and ionic bonds are created by attraction between positively and negatively charged atoms.

- Many people, even though they didn't become famous, helped to produce food and weapons in order to make the American Revolution a success.

Text Purpose(s) (Why?). The text has a reason for which it was written—and for which it is read. The better a reader figures out these reasons, the better he or she will comprehend the text. Knowing the first two components just discussed can help a reader figure out the text's purposes. Then again, knowing the purpose(s) can significantly help a reader generate the first two components. For example, knowing that the teacher is trying to teach me about the influence of Confucius on Chinese thinking, I will approach the text by focusing my summaries and main idea on this "influencing." Following are three types of purposes that help shape the main idea and summaries.

Author's Purpose. Knowing why the author wrote the text gives us immediate clues to help us organize and gather information from it. For instance, if we quickly guess that an author of an editorial about deforestation is trying to convince us to take her side, we can better organize the article's contents in our minds. If we figure out that a history textbook author wants to inform us about the hardships of the Great Depression, we have a good start on the main idea. Good readers automatically ask themselves questions such as, Why did the author write this? or What does the author want me to get from this?

Struggling readers who improve at asking and answering these questions become better readers. We need to train students to ask such questions as they look at the initial text clues. Remind students to reserve a small portion of their brain to keep track of the author's purpose while they are reading because it may change, particularly in works of fiction. We should teach students that most authors write with one or more of the following purposes: to inform, to explain, to promote thinking, to persuade, to entertain.

Teacher's Purpose. For most of the reading done outside of school, the reader gets to choose the text, and he or she chooses it for a purpose already in mind. For instance, an engineer reads a manual to learn a new computer language, a counselor reads the recent psychology journal article that relates to a current case, a college student reads the requirements for a scholarship application, and so on. School tends to turn this practicality around and assign texts because the state, the school, and/or the teacher have purposes for reading that they impose on students. Students who understand these purposes usually exhibit better comprehension and perform better on assessments (Readence, Bean, & Baldwin, 2001).

Teach students that one great way to learn these purposes is to ask, because most teachers are happy to respond.

Reader's Purpose. We might be surprised—even shocked—to find out how many of our students don't have a reason for reading. The most common reason that arises, which is not a good one, is that the teacher requires it as a way to answer questions or respond to a writing prompt. Yet, even faced with this external pressure, good readers will ask, What will I get out of this? and then generate a working answer as they begin to read. The readers who use the author's and teacher's purposes to help form their own purposes tend to exhibit improved comprehension. Teachers can model this habit with think-alouds (see chapter 8) to show how expert readers establish purpose. For example, you can say, "Looking at the title and pictures, the author probably wants me to learn…," or "If I look at the objectives for the lesson that the teacher put on the board, this text will help me…."

Consider putting up a copy of the Steps for Purpose poster (see page 156). Model the steps for students and then have them do the steps in pairs or groups. After reading, have them check to see if the purposes were fulfilled. Also try the Path to Purpose activity in chapter 4.

The Role of Flexibility

The reader must be flexible when forming and refining the main idea. The main idea generated in the beginning of a reading may be very different from the main idea at the end of a reading. Perhaps the beginning of a text is so difficult or unfamiliar that the reader can only form a very generalized main idea. For example, I may start off thinking that *Moby Dick* is going to be about a great whale hunt. Then, as I look at the style of writing and the emphasis on character actions and thoughts, I realize that it is much more about the human psyche. We must, therefore, be willing to adjust my expectations during reading in order to effectively use each new section of text. In other words, readers must be open to sculpting major changes in the main idea along the way, particularly when the text contains new concepts and unfamiliar vocabulary.

The Role of Memory

A good reader monitors the quantity and quality of information that goes into his or her memory (Taylor et al., 2000). In the beginning of a reading, there is more room in the memory, and, therefore, more extraneous information can fit. Gradually, the less important details are discarded to make room for the more important ones. A reader must decide if each piece of current information is important enough to store; the reader does this by deciding how well it supports (or changes) the evolving main idea. The reader also continues to monitor how well the key information is supported throughout the text. Gradually, as the important details that need to be stored accumulate, the brain consolidates them into summaries. Refer back to Figure 1 (page 4) to see the many pieces of information that need to be stored in memory as we read. Also see the Mental Multitasking Practice activity in chapter 8 for a way to help students improve their memory of the thoughts they have during reading.

Components in Summarizing

The "clay pieces" of information that we gradually add to sculpt the main idea as we read are the summaries. Summarizing happens when we employ a portion of our thinking cells to condense a portion of text into a manageable chunk. You will probably summarize this paragraph when you reach the end of it. Why do we summarize? The main reason is brain capacity. Let's say, for example, that we can only hold seven separate pieces of information in our brains at one time. (I chose the number seven because it is the quantity of digits of many phone numbers. It could be any number over two.) Many texts have a lot more than seven pieces of information. So what do we do when we hit the limit of seven (or whatever the number may be)? We group several related pieces together into one category and give it a name, which is actually a summary (Baumann, 1986). This makes room for other important pieces that may come up. This process is similar to putting files into folders on a computer, which then fit into other folders, and so on. Imagine a computer with every single file sitting individually on the desktop. They would not all fit and, therefore, must be organized.

Teaching summarizing can help students improve their grasp of the main idea and, subsequently, their comprehension of the text (Friend, 2001). Now it's time to dig a little deeper into the thinking that goes into summarizing: The two components of summarizing are categorization and classification.

Categorization

Categorizing is the process that occurs when a reader has a category name, such as title, main idea, or summary, and then finds information to fit underneath it. This type of organization is common in textbook chapters, but it does not help if students do not look at or think about the category name and how it connects to the text that follows. The mental process of categorizing may look similar to the steps shown in Figure 2.

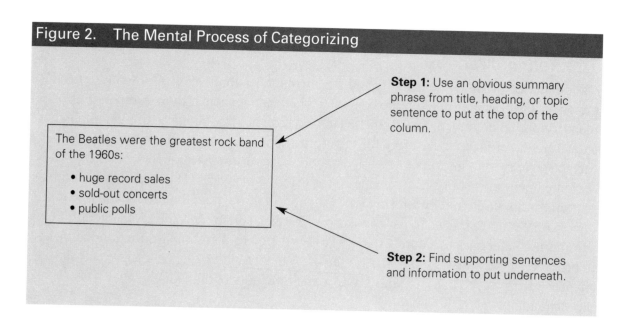

Figure 2.   The Mental Process of Categorizing

The Beatles were the greatest rock band of the 1960s:

- huge record sales
- sold-out concerts
- public polls

Step 1: Use an obvious summary phrase from title, heading, or topic sentence to put at the top of the column.

Step 2: Find supporting sentences and information to put underneath.

Classification

Classifying is even more useful for summarizing. Of the two components of summarizing, classifying is the more inductive and, hence, the more challenging habit for struggling readers to develop. As Jaworski and Coupland (1999) say,

> Academic study, but in fact all aspects of experience, are based on acts of classification, and the building of knowledge and interpretations is very largely a process of defining boundaries between conceptual classes, and of labeling those classes and the relationships between them. (p. 4)

To classify while reading, the reader analyzes the details, such as words, sentences, or paragraphs, and then looks for what they have in common. The reader then groups them by their possible commonalities. Often the reader will need to generate a rough category name for this group that describes why they are together (e.g., "These sentences all describe how atoms attract to make molecules."). This category name is the summary phrase under which the reader will continue to classify future sentences. The mental process of classifying is shown in Figure 3.

A big help for summarizing is being able to recognize topic sentences in a paragraph. The topic sentence tells the reader what the whole paragraph is trying to say, and, therefore, indicates the main idea or the summary category under which we can organize the paragraph's details. However, we should avoid teaching students that the main idea is usually found in the first sentence of a paragraph. Baumann (1986) found that only about 15% of paragraphs in adult expository material have the topic sentence in the initial position. He also found that only 30% of the paragraphs have the main idea explicitly stated anywhere in the paragraph. These findings strongly suggest that we must teach students to overcome the lack of an explicitly stated main idea and learn to generate their own summaries and main ideas. The rest of this chapter contains activities for building main idea and summarizing habits in all content area classes.

Remember, we are not teaching a *new* habit here. We are developing in our students the existing habit of organizing information into summaries, and we are teaching them to do it in academic ways. In each activity found in this chapter, start with the ways in which students already use this organizing habit in nonacademic contexts. Start with the concrete and familiar;

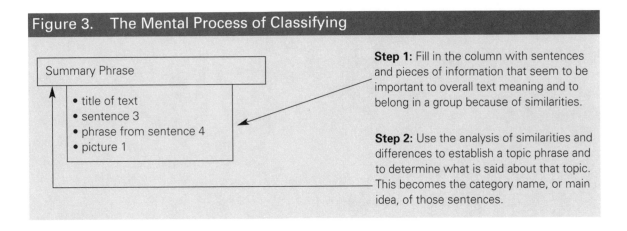

Figure 3.   The Mental Process of Classifying

Summary Phrase
- title of text
- sentence 3
- phrase from sentence 4
- picture 1

Step 1: Fill in the column with sentences and pieces of information that seem to be important to overall text meaning and to belong in a group because of similarities.

Step 2: Use the analysis of similarities and differences to establish a topic phrase and to determine what is said about that topic. This becomes the category name, or main idea, of those sentences.

then move to the more abstract and academic. For example, in Main Idea Formula, you can start with common texts such as movies, television shows, posters, songs, and so on. Point out to students how easily they can generate main ideas and summaries from this material. Then, transition this activity into the topic or text of the upcoming lesson.

Tools Chart for Organizing Text Information

Table 6 shows the appropriateness of this chapter's activities for various content areas. On the left side of the table, a ✓ in a column indicates that the activity is useful in that stage of reading. On the right side of the table, a ✓ in a column indicates that the activity is helpful for comprehension of common texts used in that content area. A ✓✓ on the right side of the table means the activity is especially helpful for that type of text and that you should try it as soon as possible. Take the time, however, to look at all the activities and spend a few moments thinking about how you might use them in your teaching. I have been pleasantly surprised at the variety of creative ways that teachers have adapted most of these activities and organizers.

Don't forget to apply the general teaching suggestions from chapter 2 to the activities in this chapter. When you find an interesting activity, refer to chapter 2 and ask how you can best integrate its instructional suggestions into the activity to meet your specific needs.

Table 6.	When and Where to Use the Activities in Chapter 3						
Before Reading	During Reading	After Reading	Activity	Social Studies	Science	English/ EL
	✓	✓	Evolving Main Idea Three-Column Notes	✓✓	✓✓	✓
	✓		Interpretive Drawings	✓		✓✓
	✓	✓	Jigsaw Summaries	✓✓	✓✓	✓✓
	✓	✓	Keyword Construction	✓✓	✓✓	✓
✓		✓	Language Experience Approach Plus	✓✓	✓✓	✓✓
✓		✓	Main Idea Café	✓	✓	✓✓
	✓	✓	Main Idea Formula	✓✓	✓✓	✓
	✓		Main Idea Memory Storage	✓✓	✓✓	✓
	✓	✓	Matrices	✓✓	✓✓	✓✓
✓	✓	✓	Outline-ish Thoughts	✓✓	✓✓	✓
✓	✓	✓	Semantic Webbing	✓✓	✓✓	✓
	✓		Sorry, I Lost My Headings	✓✓	✓✓	✓
✓	✓	✓	Story Map	✓		✓✓
✓		✓	Summarizing Training Camp	✓✓	✓✓	✓
	✓		Think-Aloud Summaries	✓✓	✓✓	✓✓
	✓	✓	Webpage Creation	✓✓	✓✓	✓

Activities for Organizing Text Information

EVOLVING MAIN IDEA THREE-COLUMN NOTES

This activity helps students to sculpt the main idea and create summaries while reading. The summaries are based on the detail notes that are placed in the far right column of the page. This is an adaptation of two-column notes, also called Cornell notes, a note-taking technique found in many resources (e.g., Brown & Stephens, 1999).

Procedure

1. Create three columns on the board. (When students do this activity by themselves, they will do it on a sheet of paper.) The left column is labeled "Main Idea," the middle column "Summaries," and the right column "Details."

2. Based on the title of the text to be read, generate a possible main idea with the students and write it in the Main Idea column. This main idea can and may change throughout this process.

3. Read the first paragraph aloud, and take notes in the "Details" column. Details include key words, phrases, and examples.

4. Use these detail notes to create a one-sentence summary to go in the middle column. Create several one-sentence summaries of different sections or paragraphs of a text.

5. Connect, mentally and/or with arrows, the summaries to the main idea.

6. Show students how the process went from column 1 to column 3, then to column 2 and back to column 1.

7. Refine and rewrite the main idea in the left column as it evolves.

INTERPRETIVE DRAWINGS

In this activity, students pick an important part of the text (or just use the main idea) and create a drawing or visual representation of it. With expository texts, these can be in the forms of graphic organizers with connecting arrows. Emphasize that the drawing is to help oneself understand and remember the text better. Students also can think of it as a way to teach others about the text without writing an essay.

For narratives, this activity can be very effective at getting students to think at deeper levels than just the literal meaning (Hibbing & Rankin-Erickson, 2003). Analogies, symbols, and metaphors can be portrayed interestingly in drawings. This activity also is effective for building habits of generating inferences and visualizing.

Procedure

1. Offer plenty of visual examples: previous drawings, modern artwork, textbook pictures, cartoons, and so on. Some examples can be very simple or basic, to show students that they do not have to draw well to do this activity.

2. Think aloud what you would do to create a drawing that summarized a text. Pick different texts and show how you would draw something to fit each one's information and remember it. For example, you might draw a raft on a river for a story about Huck Finn. You could draw a map with symbols on it to show different groups involved in or events of the Spanish conquest of Mexico. You could sketch a cell for a text on cell division.

3. Give students an easy text from which to create their own interpretive drawings. Remind them that there are no wrong "answers" and that they do not have to be artists. Remind them that some very expensive abstract art does not necessarily fit what they would think of as an attractive look. Tell them to be artists who try to capture the moment, mood, meaning, symbolism, importance, or purpose of the text.

4. Optional: You could call this activity "Picture Cheating" and tell students to pretend they are artists who need to create a picture that gives away the meaning of the text to unmotivated students who do not want to read it.

5. Optional: Have students write their explanation of the drawing's meaning on the backs of their papers. This is a subtle way to get them to verbalize a summary or main idea.

6. Put students into pairs or groups and have them respond to one another's drawings. Point out that responding entails guessing the meaning, praising the work, and asking questions; remind students not to be critical.

7. Have students share their own drawings with the class and explain them.

JIGSAW SUMMARIES

Jigsaw groups (adapted from Aronson, 1978) provide students a way to build summarizing habits while also pushing them to communicate meaningful messages with other students. Students in one group become experts on a portion of the text and the experts then teach that text to a different group.

Procedure

1. Divide the chosen text into three to five sections. Plan to have the same number of students in each group as there are text sections.

2. Prepare an Expert Sheet or study guide that will help students become experts as they summarize a section of text. The sheet may have questions (open-ended or under-the-surface), a task, and/or a graphic to fill in, and so on.

3. Use a pocket chart, random numbers, or some other method to create home groups. Then assign each student a letter that corresponds to his or her expert group and the text that the group will study. (See Figure 4.)

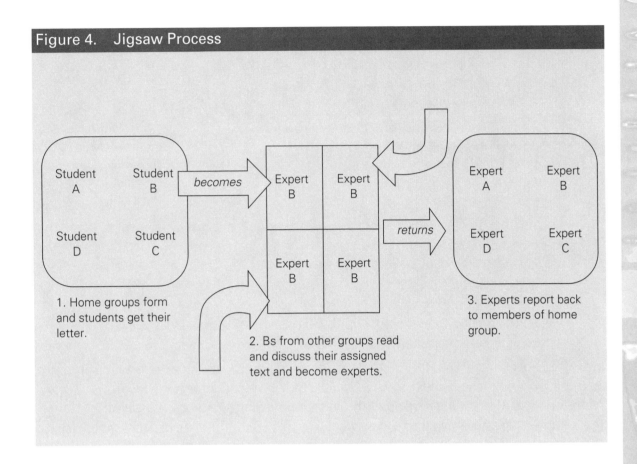

Figure 4. Jigsaw Process

Student A / Student B / Student D / Student C

becomes

Expert B / Expert B / Expert B / Expert B

returns

Expert A / Expert B / Expert D / Expert C

1. Home groups form and students get their letter.

2. Bs from other groups read and discuss their assigned text and become experts.

3. Experts report back to members of home group.

4. Have students with the same letters get together in expert groups and read (silently) their assigned section. Then, have them discuss their conclusions, summaries, opinions, answers, task, or graphic organizer and how they will teach it to their colleagues in the home groups.

5. Have the experts report back to their home groups to summarize and teach the important parts of their text sections.

6. Hold a class discussion about the text, perhaps with graphic aids that you have created to organize the information.

Variation

4 × 4 Jigsaw Circle: Have eight students each read a different section of text. Then, put four of the students in an inner circle and four in an outer circle. Each student in the inner circle exchanges information about what he or she has read with a partner in the outer circle, and then one circle rotates. The students repeat the process with a different partner, then rotate again. This process repeats until all four pairs have shared their reading with each other. (See Figure 5 for a visual representation of the process.) You may want to give the students a time limit—say, five minutes—for each partner session. You also can have students fill in a table or chart that you create, or have them answer teacher-generated questions about their sections of text.

Figure 5. 4 × 4 Jigsaw Circle

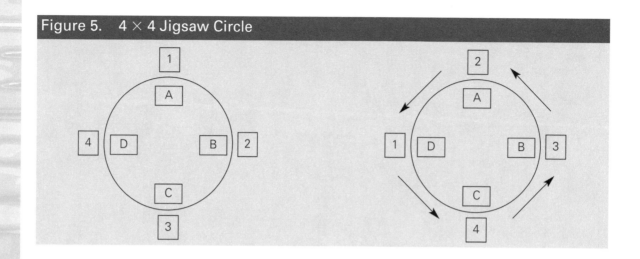

KEYWORD CONSTRUCTION

In this activity, adapted from Bleich (1975), students reduce the text to a single word, phrase, or quotation, and then rebuild from that. The thinking processes of tearing down, synthesizing, and rebuilding develop the brain's summarizing muscles, so to speak.

Students take notes and then choose what they think is the most important word or concept of the entire text. The word does not have to be in the text, but the activity often is more manageable (and just as successful) if students are asked to take the word or phrase from the text. Character names and other proper nouns are usually not effective keywords, and their use should be discouraged. Use of creative and unconventional words should be encouraged, just as long as the students can defend their choices with valid evidence and reasoning.

Procedure

1. First, model this activity for students. Choose a text and use sticky notes to write down important information, doodles, and summaries from the text. Place the sticky notes on the boxes in the top half of the Keyword Construction sheet (see page 154).

2. Verbalize how you choose your own keyword for the text. Have students discuss your decision, if desired. Refer to specific evidence in the text that supports your choice. Let students hear how you chose your word over other options. Use the Keyword Construction form as a scaffold.

3. Now, begin to scaffold the activity. Choose a new text and repeat the process, this time inviting the class to participate. Have students discuss and choose several keywords as a class. You can keep them from using certain "obvious" words that might limit their thinking by making a "no-use" list.

4. Now, let students in pairs or small groups read a new text and choose a keyword. Have them write their keyword in the key-shaped area at the center of the page. In the bottom section, they can write their reasons for the word's importance—reasons that come from the text and their ideas of the purpose of the text.

5. Have students use the keyword and build a summary of the text from it. The summary should include several reasons why the keyword is important. The sentences should connect the keyword with the purpose of the section and the current content being learned.

6. You can use the Keyword Construction activity as a platform for written assignments, persuasive essays, and even drama or music projects.

LANGUAGE EXPERIENCE APPROACH PLUS

The Language Experience Approach (Van Allen & Allen, 1976) requires students to generate language that describes a shared learning experience. You can modify the traditional Language Experience Approach, however, in order to scaffold the language that goes into the written product. That is, build on students' existing language structures and vocabulary and help them to create a product that is a little more advanced than what they could have produced without your help. It becomes a shared, modeled, and scaffolded writing experience that helps students see how to organize thoughts into a summary of any type of learning.

This activity helps students to do the following:

- Organize and remember content material
- Identify important information to summarize
- Use complete sentences and correct punctuation
- Build academic language and thinking
- Maximize clarity by choosing the best words
- Learn minilesson concepts that they see written in their own words

Procedure

1. Students need a topic for the writing assignment. They can take notes individually or cooperatively on a text or other learning experience: a science procedure, mathematical problem-solving process, story, historical event, art procedure, game rules, class opinions, video, slide show, and so on. If students are working in groups, have them discuss the most important pieces of information that each group will share as the class creates a whole-class paragraph.

2. Have the students (as a whole class) orally share with you, sentence by sentence, a summary that you then write on the board or on poster paper. (Using the board allows for erasing, and the finished summary can later be transferred to a poster. A large poster is helpful because it can be displayed for several days without taking up board space.)

3. Allow students to modify words and phrases and to argue whether a sentence is important enough to include. Have students support their sentences with reasons for their importance. Encourage them to relate these reasons to the author's purpose, the content objectives for the lesson, or both. You can give a limit for the number of sentences students can contribute because it is a summary.

4. As students share, gently help them to refine their words and sentences by suggesting there may be better choices or by offering alternatives. Refer to any academic language you have used in class. For example,

> Student: We find the opposite of the fraction.
>
> Teacher: Is there a better word than *opposite* that we have used in this class?
>
> Student: *Reciprocal.*
>
> Teacher: Do others agree? OK, let's put, "First, we find the reciprocal of the fraction."
>
> Teacher: Instead of using *but* again, can we use the word *however*?
>
> Teacher: Should we put, "We feel that since..." or "We know that because..." to begin this sentence?

5. Similar to a think-aloud, verbalize why you might choose certain words over others and why or why not to include certain information. Avoid changing the students' language too much. Offer or elicit certain keywords and key academic language that students may not produce at first. This is a great way to scaffold academic language and thinking.

6. Read aloud the finished summary, and have students make any last-minute corrections. Students can copy the paragraph in their notebooks if there is time.

7. Continue to use the Language Experience Approach Plus paragraph as a text for teaching minilessons about such topics as academic language, main ideas, topic sentences, adjectives, adverbs, punctuation, pronunciation, persuasive writing, voice, word choice, and so on. Remember that learning from a text is a lot more engaging if it is one's own text.

MAIN IDEA CAFÉ

This activity emulates a café setting where intellectuals share thoughts and opinions about the nature of life, literature, and the world.

Procedure

1. Select important headings, quotations, or visuals (clues) from the text that students will read. Put them on separate strips of paper or on notecards.

2. Tell students the title of the text to be read.

3. Hand out one clue to each student and allow each student time to read and think about his or her particular clue in order to predict how it might fit into the overall meaning of the text.

4. Have students circulate around the classroom to get other opinions by reading their clues to other students. (You can limit circulation to groups of four to six.)

5. In pairs, have students guess the meaning of the clues as they relate to the predicted main idea and/or purpose of the overall text.

6. Tell students to notice how their predictions about the main idea and/or purpose improve as they hear more and more clues and predictions from other students.

7. Optional: Ask students to guess the sequence of their pieces in the text. They can line up in physical order according to their clues, for example.

8. Lead a brief discussion on what the students predict the text is about.

9. Have students read the text. Stop them at times and have them check to see if their predictions about the main idea are correct.

MAIN IDEA FORMULA

We need to train students' brains to sculpt main ideas and create good summaries. By using a math-esque formula, I have seen many students perk up because they like math and want to know how the two subjects connect. The formula is a visual way to show how readers think when they generate main ideas.

Procedure

1. Bring in, and have your students bring in, "texts" such as videos, taped television shows, photos, songs on tape or CD, and so on. Ask the question, What was it mainly about? for these and other well-known texts. Then, discuss the purposes for reading various texts. Many narratives, for example, have a plot that carries the author's message or purpose.

2. Ask students why we teachers think the main idea is so important. Ask, Why should we train our brains to know the main idea? Highlight student answers that emphasize that the main idea gives the direction, foundation, or purpose.

3. Explain the parts of the formula and have students generate answers.

Topic + What is said about the topic + Purpose = Main Idea

Topic +	The discovery of North America by the Chinese
What is said about the topic +	Historical Chinese maps and documents show the arrival of the Chinese people on the west coast of North America 70 years before Columbus's first voyage.
Purpose =	To challenge people to consider evidence of early Chinese contact with Native Americans and to show how history is up for continual debate
Main Idea	Based on evidence from accurate Chinese maps and documents, the Chinese may actually have landed on North American soil before Columbus did. This should cause us to rethink our traditional accounts of history and even question how history is written.

Other examples of the formula equation include the following:

- The movie's main idea = A high school student + he goes back in time, messes up his young parents' lives, almost preventing his own birth, and then fixes it + purpose of entertaining people with a story about time travel and courage.
- The article's main idea = space travel + not worth the cost to taxpayers + attempts to persuade readers to stop paying taxes and to vote for a certain person.
- The picture's main idea = a child dying + the horrors of war and the innocent victims + showing viewers the smaller stories of war the television does not highlight.

4. Now show how the main idea can change during reading. The second and third parts (variables) of the equation often change as one reads. Think aloud (i.e., verbally model for the students) how to identify or generate a main idea with a variety of texts. Use interesting material to make the process engaging. Also, throw in some texts that challenge *you* (e.g., song lyrics or articles provided by students) to offer a more genuine sense of how a teacher also might struggle with text and think about how to understand it. Model the following processes for students:

a. Think about the title. What does the author think the text is about? Why might the author have written it?

b. Skim the text. Notice the text structure. Is it a narrative, description, list, sequence of events, comparison/contrast, opinion, or other type of text?

c. Read the first paragraph or two. Ask yourself, Why did the teacher assign this text? What can I, or should I, get out of reading this?

d. Use steps (a) through (c) to create a rough draft (mental or written) of the topic of the text plus what is written about that topic and a possible author's purpose. This draft must be short.

e. Read the rest of the text:

- Look for the most important information from each paragraph or section of text, and relate it to the rough draft main idea. For example, while reading a paragraph, always be thinking, "This is about..." or "This strengthens or changes the overall main idea because...." (Use a sticky note to jot down the idea.)
- Notice highlighted and repeated words, subheadings, diagrams, and other clues that signal importance; these might be words such as *important, relevant, in conclusion, that is, ultimately, main problem, for example*, and so on.

f. During reading, makes notes of key points in the margins or on a separate piece of paper.

g. Sculpt the main idea to accommodate new pieces of important information.

h. Go back and skim or reread the text, and use your notes to finalize the main idea.

5. Have students practice the previous steps with you as a guide. Provide feedback as you gather glimpses of student thought processes. In longer passages, you can lead the students through a passage, pausing to give the students a chance to summarize each manageable section. Ask the students if the summary still supports the overall main idea of the passage. If not, then ask students to resculpt the main idea.

6. Allow students more independence in their practice as you give them increasingly challenging texts. Have them compare their main ideas with others, working in pairs and groups.

MAIN IDEA MEMORY STORAGE

This activity is a visual and kinesthetic simplification of the active thinking we use to comprehend. It is based on research related to semantic organizers and their positive effect on comprehension and retention (Marzano et al., 2001). Main Idea Memory Storage gives students practice in keeping one "mental hand" on the main idea and the other "mental hand" on the summary chunks of information that relate to the main idea. This can be done alone or in pairs, and silently or as a think-aloud. As always, you should model the activity sufficiently before the students take over.

Procedure

1. Choose a narrative or expository text that is challenging to the students.

2. Think aloud about the process of using initial clues to form a rough main idea. Write the main idea on a sticky note (use clear ones if you are working on an overhead projector) and place it in the top box of the Main Idea Memory Storage form (see page 155). Then explain to students that you will modify the main idea while you read. You can even assign the left hand only to the main idea and say that the summaries can be touched only by the right hand.

3. Read aloud from the text and stop at an appropriate point to summarize. Create a summary note (use a different color of sticky note than the main idea note, ideally) and place it on one of the six boxes under the main idea note. Discuss with students whether the summary requires you to change your main idea note or not. If so, write a new main idea note and replace the old one. The old one can go down on the lower right stack. Repeat this step six times.

4. When your six summary boxes are full, explain aloud to students as you shuffle them around based on importance, the upper three being more important than the lower three, and explain how you can consolidate two or more notes into one (e.g., by classifying and categorizing). As you run out of spaces in the six boxes, you can move old or less-important information to the four boxes on the lower left of the diagram.

5. As you read the text, continue to use sticky notes to modify the main idea and move around the important information found in the text.

6. When a revised main idea forms, move the former main idea to the bottom right space on the diagram.

7. Notes that hold important supporting information can be shuffled around to fill the six spots along with the most important supporting summaries.

8. When students understand what to do, have them go through the process in pairs as you assist them. They can then share their diagrams with others and defend their choices.

Variations

- Students can use a 5" × 7" card instead of the head diagram for the main idea, writing the main idea in the center of the card and then attaching the sticky notes all around the sides of the card.

- If you don't like the head drawing or the use of sticky notes, you can fold an 8½" × 11" sheet of paper horizontally and, using a pencil, write the main idea above the fold and the smaller summaries below. Then, simply erase as you need to change the information.

MATRICES

A matrix (i.e., grid or table) allows a student to organize various categories of information according to different variables that are placed in columns and rows. Using matrices for organizing information is an adaptation of a well-known vocabulary strategy called *semantic feature analysis* (Johnson & Pearson, 1984). It is an effective way to get students to analyze ideas, reduce information to the minimum, and then rebuild it in their own words.

For many expository descriptive texts, particularly in science and social studies, a matrix is an effective way to organize important information. Matrices help students to compare characters, solutions to problems, symbols, wars, policies, time periods, and so on. More than just a "data entry" tool, matrices can be used as springboards to discussion, inference, and further research.

Procedure

1. Examine the chosen text and find the categories to put in the left-hand column of the matrix. Then decide which variables (often these are adjectives) to put across the top row, such as in the following example:

War	Cause	Effect	Cost
WWI			
WWII			
Vietnam			
Gulf			

2. Model the process of filling in some of the cells as you read and think aloud. Show students how to self-question in order to fill in answers: What were the effects of the Gulf War?

3. Find evidence from the text(s) to support your entries.

4. Have students finish the matrix in pairs or individually.

5. Have students give evidence for some of their answers. Have them refer to the text.

6. When finished, have them analyze the grid for patterns and relations. With these patterns and relations, students can generate hypotheses for discussion or research.

7. Have students write a conclusion based on the information on the matrix. (You can model this the first few times.)

OUTLINE-ISH THOUGHTS

They may not seem exciting, and they aren't, but outlines are some of the most prevalent and powerful types of texts around. Sooner or later, their time must come. Cute graphics and semantic maps will not serve our students forever. Students will see information organized in outline form their entire lives (e.g., in articles, tables of contents, directions, textbook chapters, study guides, and more). Most authors think in some kind of outline-ish way. If readers think "outline-ishly" too, then comprehension improves. Hence, teaching outlining skills can be very helpful for developing the lifelong habits of organizing, summarizing, and prioritizing information (Readence et al., 2001).

Procedure

1. Show students a wide variety of outlines.

2. Dissect the outline and discuss why headings and subheadings are named the way they are. Does every detail fit underneath the correct subheading? Ask students why a detail fits under a heading. Ask how the same level of details is related and see if they refer to the heading.

3. As a class, generate outlines of everyday and relevant things: school, sports, food, friendship, music, weather, war, art, parents, cars, movies, television shows, and so on.

4. Have students work together to create an outline of a recent topic discussed in class. Share all the ideas generated and create a whole-class outline on an overhead transparency or on the board.

5. Model how to take ideas from a text and create an outline. Use titles and subheadings.

6. Provide a partially filled outline or semantic web of a longer passage that contains supporting details and paragraphs but no paragraph summaries or main idea for the text. (Many study guides for textbook chapters are in the form of partially filled outlines.)

7. Have students fill in the blanks and discuss their results with other students.

Variation

Show students how to create outlines from semantic webs (see the following Semantic Webbing activity) and vice versa. A possible resource is Inspiration software; however, make sure that students understand the process of converting webs to outlines and can do it by themselves without relying on software.

SEMANTIC WEBBING

Semantic webs and organizers have long been used effectively for hierarchically organizing information. They actually are outlines presented in visual form. Many semantic organizers have a central concept, surrounded by key supporting concepts that increase in level of detail as you move away from the central concept. For the purposes of reading comprehension, the central concept usually is a main idea or the author's purpose. As one moves outward from the main idea, the next spaces shape headings and key supporting concepts, then subheadings, and finally, key details. Semantic target and semantic web organizers, which are easily drawn as follows, can both be used for this activity:

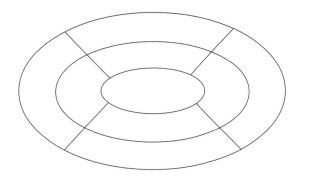

Semantic Target

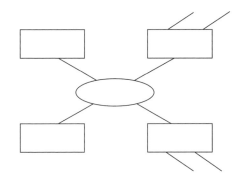

Semantic Web

Procedure

1. Choose a text that lends itself well to webbing. (Most knowledge is organized hierarchically with categories, under which fit discrete pieces of information depending on their characteristics. Therefore, texts that compare, persuade, analyze, describe, classify, and interpret all lend themselves well to semantic organizers.)

2. For prereading, write on the board a topic or a preview question that relates to the text's key ideas, and write some key vocabulary terms. Draw a simple semantic organizer on the board or on a separate poster sheet. Ask students to guess which terms might be grouped together and which terms might go in the organizer's boxes (or other shapes). To model this process, fill in the boxes' headings during class discussion. (Eventually, students will fill in the boxes without your help.)

3. After filling in the main headings (categories), students will have a general idea about the text and can summarize what they expect the text to cover (perhaps in a Quickwrites or Think-Pair-Share activity [see chapter 4]).

4. During reading, have students read silently as they fill out their own organizer. For some groups, you can read the first part of the text and even model the building of the organizer on the board. Emphasize the use of key words and phrases that are in the words of the reader, rather than sentences copied from the text. Students also can draw symbols or images in the boxes to better remember the information.

5. Using the semantic organizer as an aid, have the students retell (to a partner or small group) the important points of the text. Then, the listeners can remind the teller of any important information not included. Putting the pieces of the text back together in their own words helps students take ownership of the information, which solidifies it in their minds. The semantic organizer helps the brain build visually based connections.

6. The semantic organizer also provides an excellent framework for writing that is based on the text. The boxes can help a student get ideas for appropriate paragraph separations. Give students a list of transition and connector words to choose from, depending on the style of the writing they are doing. Have students help you create a paragraph on the overhead to model how to transfer the semantic web into written text. Students can write along with you.

Variations

- **Details-First Webbing:** This type of semantic webbing starts with the details of a text and organizes them into categories, which then helps students discover the main idea or central theme. The best way to generate the details list is to pick out keywords from the unit you are teaching (Figure 6 provides a sample details-first web for an exploration unit). Note this activity is similar to Brainstorm and Sort (see chapter 4).

- **Main-Idea-First Webbing:** This variation is effective when students have a good grasp of the main idea and the categories that form it—when the ovals and boxes of the semantic web organizer are mostly filled in. Main-Idea-First Webbing helps to generate and organize

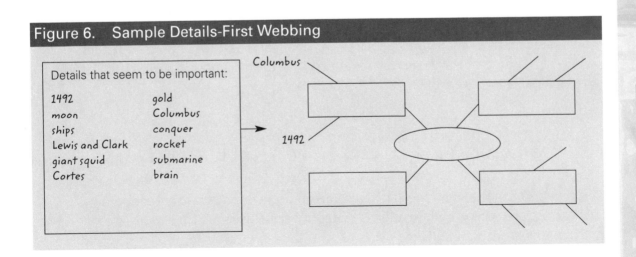

Figure 6.   Sample Details-First Webbing

Details that seem to be important:

1492	gold
moon	Columbus
ships	conquer
Lewis and Clark	rocket
giant squid	submarine
Cortes	brain

Columbus

1492

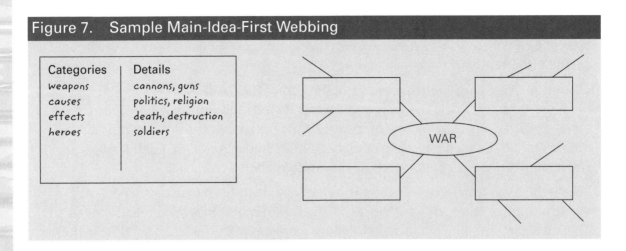

Figure 7. Sample Main-Idea-First Webbing

Categories	Details
weapons	cannons, guns
causes	politics, religion
effects	death, destruction
heroes	soldiers

WAR

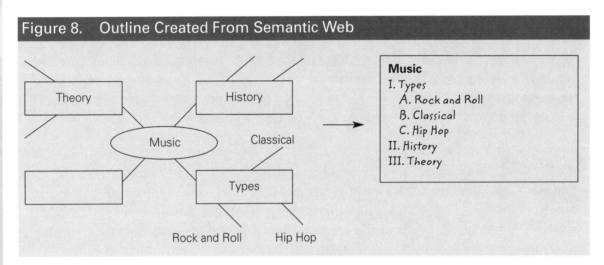

Figure 8. Outline Created From Semantic Web

Theory

History

Music

Classical

Types

Rock and Roll   Hip Hop

Music
I. Types
   A. Rock and Roll
   B. Classical
   C. Hip Hop
II. History
III. Theory

the details, along with any further categories that might arise. Figure 7 shows a sample main-idea-first web for the topic *war*. In this example, the class started with the topic in the center. Students worked in pairs or groups to generate possible main categories, then generated details for the other column. There was ongoing discussion about the web elements and how to organize them.

• Show students how to go from a semantic web to an outline. (See Figure 8.) The central concept is the main idea; the next boxes out become the headings numbered I, II, III, and so on; and the branches are the A, B, and C, and so on.

SORRY, I LOST MY HEADINGS

This activity forces students to read text sections and generate a tentative heading or subheading for a section's information (see Figure 9 for an example). It also gives good practice for text-marking and note-taking.

Figure 9. Sample Headings Generated From Text

Scientific Achievements of the Maya

Almost 2,000 years ago, the Maya civilization began to develop. In the field of mathematics, they were the first to invent the concept of zero. They studied the stars and made precise calculations for their calendars.

Mayan Cities as Centers of Worship

The Maya also built great cities like Chichén Itzá and Uxmal on the Yucatan Peninsula. The pyramids in the centers of these cities were constructed to honor the various gods that the Maya worshipped.

Procedure

1. Take a chapter or article and photocopy it with the headings blocked out with tape or correction fluid. Put a line or a box where each student-generated heading will be.

2. Model for students how you notice and mark (by underlining and note-taking) the important information in a section of text, and then think aloud for them how you create your own headings.

3. Discuss with students whether each of your headings is too general or too specific. This can be a very useful and powerful step. It helps students to refine their thoughts to be clear and focused, and to see ideas at the right "distance." It will help students in writing as well.

4. Have students work in pairs or individually to fill in the rest of the headings and discuss them with others before sharing all the headings as a class.

STORY MAP

The story map is a tried-and-true way to show the important elements of narrative text (Buehl, 2001; Johns & Berglund, 2001). It also can be used with history texts as an outline of an important event, with supporting events leading up to the climax (perhaps for a war). Different versions of this graphic abound, so feel free to adapt this one to suit your needs. Science teachers have even used it successfully. (Also see the related Inner-Outer Prediction Chart in chapter 5, page 89.)

Procedure

1. Model on the overhead or board how to fill in the story map (see the following steps 2–8) for various texts such as short stories, songs, fables, television shows, movies, and any novels that you already have read in class. (A full-size Story Map to photocopy for this activity is provided on page 157.)

2. First, fill in the character names around the oval in the bottom right corner. You can add doodles or notes, such as *protagonist* and *antagonist* labels, next to the names.

3. Fill in place and time. Discuss why the author might have chosen this setting.

4. Put the main problem or conflict in the large diagonal box. If you are filling in the map during reading, emphasize the use of pencil, because the conflict may change.

5. On the left-hand lines, put the important events that lead up to the final climax or resolution of the problem. This is great practice for summarizing because the lines do not allow much space.

6. Summarize the climax or resolution in the banner box at the top.

7. Put the final events on the "ending events" and "changes" lines at the right. These are the important events and changes in the characters or situations that resulted after the resolution.

8. Discuss the message or lesson that the author might have intended when writing the text. Consider historical, moral, social, political, and entertainment purposes. Write the theme, message, or lesson in the box on the right.

9. Have students use the map with additional texts on their own.

Variation

Modify this graphic organizer according to the particular story you are using. For example, some stories have an early resolution and a large number of ending events, so you could add more lines in that section.

SUMMARIZING TRAINING CAMP

Good readers do not go back over a text several times in order to produce the needed summary. Good readers summarize in a split second and move on. This training camp helps readers to quickly see what's important, reduce it to a memorable chunk, and relate it to the main idea.

Procedure

1. Pull a paragraph or passage from an article, textbook chapter, or use other types of text such as a webpage or painting, drawn cartoons, etc. Let students know the title of the text from which the selection was taken.

2. Put the selection on the overhead projector or the board. Remind the students that the author included this paragraph or passage for a reason, and point out that it is important to find out what that reason is.

3. Read aloud the selection to the students. (Try to use paragraphs without obvious topic sentences.) Model how to be on the lookout for topic or summary statements to save time in summarizing.

4. Underline details, phrases, and words that are important to the topic as you read.

5. At the end of the selection, quickly write a summary of why it is there. You can ask the following questions:

- Is the author describing a thing, person, process, story, or event?
- Is the author describing something by using literary devices such as metaphor, analogy, hyperbole, and so on?
- Is the author explaining a cause and effect, or a problem and solution?
- Is the author comparing or contrasting two or more things?

6. Practice makes mostly perfect. If we model the process and then give students a variety of interesting texts to break down, students can build summarizing skills without even realizing it. On a regular basis, give students a short paragraph, article, picture, video clip, poem, song, or other type of text for which they can generate a possible summary. Ideally, the text will be interesting, motivating, and standards-based. Some teacher resources contain ready-made passages and even include summaries to compare with student responses.

Here are some tips for good summaries:

- Use your own wording, but don't include your ideas or opinions.
- Don't repeat ideas or distort the author's meaning.
- Use summarizing lingo: *The author says that, states that, explains that, points out that, mentions that, emphasizes that, argues that, maintains that, highlights the fact that,* or *concludes that....*

THINK-ALOUD SUMMARIES

Thinking aloud is one of the most powerful ways to build the habit of summarizing. Why? Many struggling readers have never seen what constitutes good, active thinking during reading. Think-alouds (Davey, 1983; Farr, 2001; Robb, 2003), which are found in most reading strategies books, make the invisible more visible. If you use think-alouds on a regular basis, students can gradually acquire any comprehension habit.

Procedure

1. Model how to use prereading strategies (title, visuals, etc.) to generate an initial prediction of what the main idea and purpose for reading might be.

2. Read the text aloud and stop from time to time to give a brief summary, for example, "So far, this is about...."

3. Further on in the text, before you give your next think-aloud summary, give students some time to summarize inside their minds or on paper. Then, verbalize your think-aloud and have students agree or disagree. You can let them do this by holding up cards marked "yes" or "no," giving a thumbs-up or thumbs-down, or by using some other method. Discuss differences and why information should have been included or left out.

4. At the end of the text, give an overall summary of the main idea and describe how your original purpose was met or not met. For example, I recently read an article to sixth graders about the platypus. I then wrote down some thoughts I had:

> "This first section talked about how difficult it is to study platypuses (is it platypi?) because they spend so much time in the water and underground."
>
> "The second section covered how they were dying because of litter and debris from nearby cities."
>
> "This part talked about the interesting feeding habits—using electric responses in its bill to find food in murky water."
>
> "This described the strange trait of laying eggs despite being a mammal, and the fact that it has a venomous spur on each ankle."
>
> "This photo showed the amazing adaptations of the platypus that have allowed it to survive since the time of the dinosaurs."

WEBPAGE CREATION

This activity provides an effective way to see and develop the nonlinear and hierarchical connections that are so vital in the comprehension of difficult material. Using simple (and free) webpage creation programs, such as Geocities, Microsoft Word, or Netscape Composer, students can summarize a text or content area concept. Even creating a paper copy of the webpage can be effective and motivating for students.

Webpage creation is a way to build habits of summarizing, main idea sculpting, categorizing, identifying the author's purpose, and classifying.

Procedure

1. Show students at least six exemplary webpages with varying content. Explain the parts and possible variations. Print the examples onto color overhead transparencies, if possible. Work with students as a class to create a rubric for this activity (see chapter 2). Have students use the sample webpages and the rubric to guide them during the process of creating a webpage. They can then ask you what score they would receive on the rubric during the creation process in order to make corrections as indicated by the criteria in the rubric.

2. Optional: Translate one webpage's contents into a semantic web and/or outline to show how the hierarchical relations can be represented.

3. Discuss with students how creating a webpage helps to build habits such as organizing information and summarizing. Use a Think-Pair-Share activity (see chapter 4) if there is time.

4. Use a short reading sample and show students how you takes notes on the following comprehension processes: summaries, questions (answered and not), visualizations, (realized and not), connections to prior knowledge, etc. Take notes in a two- or three-column format or use a semantic web.

5. On the overhead or a computer screen, quickly design a webpage with a column on the left and a bar across the top. Show how you take the summaries and turn them into one- or two-word headings for the category buttons in the left column. For example, the Webpage Template (see page 158) has buttons with causes, effects, people, places, and purpose from my notes on the history chapter that they will read. In the center space, create a brief overview in your own words that describes the text's main idea. Finally, model how to create the subpages, the pages to which the buttons on the main page will point. You can color code these pages.

6. Students create a similar layout because they will read the text and fill in the details for the button headings on separate pages.

7. Eventually, you can have students create category names that will become the buttons for the webpages. Students can put these on the paper draft and also can draft the pages (on a different color of paper) that will connect to the buttons. These "branch" pages will contain the details.

8. Optional: Extend the webpage beyond summarizing to include other habits and content area concepts. Suggest the following buttons or images that will connect to other pages:

- Suggestions to help readers read this text
- Prior knowledge that helped me
- Things I visualized while reading
- Questions answered and not
- Predictions realized and not

- Elaborations on the text, alternate endings, or subplots
- Purposes of the author, teacher, and me
- New words from the text
- Information from prereading
- How the webpage could have been better
- Inferences

9. Use a word-processing program to enter the textual information that will be contained in the webpage. (This does not have to be complete before students begin the webpage creation.)

10. Publish the webpage on a school or public website.

Connecting to Background Knowledge

* * *

I am a collage of all that I have
heard, seen, wondered,
and dreamed.

Background knowledge is like a backbone for comprehension. (For this reason, I sometimes call it *backbone knowledge*.) We can't do without it. Why? Because as we read, we must connect the text's information to related knowledge and experience in our brains that we, in a sense, use as raw material to construct meaning as the text dictates. We compare this evolving meaning with each successive piece of text and we modify or discard any inconsistencies (i.e., we "prune away" the less useful information).

Authors expect readers to possess and use certain pieces of background knowledge. This fund of background knowledge often consists of facts, concepts, experiences, and ideas about culture (Alvermann & Phelps, 2001). An author will use idioms, analogies, technical words, and descriptions that the intended readers of the text are supposed to understand already; the author does not take the extra time to elaborate on what he or she considers to be common experience or knowledge shared by most of the prospective readers. For example, an author might omit common details about a typical ocean beach. When the text deviates from this common fund of background knowledge, however, then the author must take the time to describe how it differs from readers' common expectations (e.g., an ocean beach with mounds of red seaweed and pink sand). The problem for many struggling readers and English learners is that their funds of background knowledge and vocabulary are not what the authors of middle school and high school texts expect them to be.

A useful analogy for using background knowledge in reading is that of constructing a house. (Of course, it helps for you to have background knowledge of house building in order to read and understand this analogy.) The builder must bring a variety of materials to the building site. The builder looks at the plans (the text, in our case) and then searches for the materials that the plans require. If the materials are not handy, the builder goes to the store to obtain them (a reader refers to other resources). Perhaps a substitute material can be used (related background knowledge) that is modified to fit the needs of the plan. Sometimes the builder brings prefabricated sections to the job (background knowledge patterns or schema). These save time by avoiding the need to put many separate pieces together. For example, if a

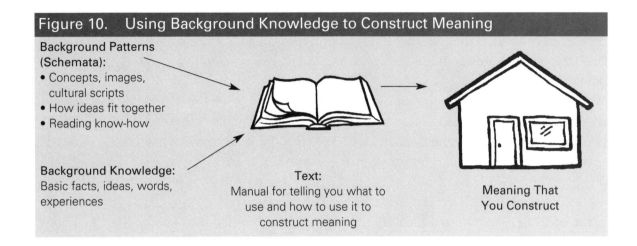

Figure 10.   Using Background Knowledge to Construct Meaning

Background Patterns (Schemata):
• Concepts, images, cultural scripts
• How ideas fit together
• Reading know-how

Background Knowledge:
Basic facts, ideas, words, experiences

Text:
Manual for telling you what to use and how to use it to construct meaning

Meaning That You Construct

reader already knows what a typical U.S. wedding ceremony entails, the author does not need to spend pages on common details that the reader can fill in with cultural background knowledge. But when that background knowledge is not there (e.g., for a recent immigrant from Laos), the knowledge needs to be built up in some way or comprehension will suffer. Refer to Figure 10 for a visual representation of how this process works.

Using and Developing Background Knowledge Patterns

Background knowledge patterns, also called *schemata*, are the larger chunks of information that a person uses to make sense of text. Background knowledge patterns tend to be complex concepts of culture, beliefs, expectations, values, and past experiences that we use to comprehend the nature of things and events. For example, if you read, "I found coal in my stocking, knocked over the tree and started a fire, and smiled at my grandfather who was wearing a red suit," readers with the cultural schema of Christmas morning in the United States would quickly *get the drift of it*. Others might *scratch their heads* in wonder, even though they *grasped* the meaning of each individual word in the sentence. Additional examples of background knowledge patterns include common ideas about restaurant settings, greetings, sports, hobbies, politics, rural and city scenes, human behavior and emotions in response to certain situations, and idiomatic expressions such as the italicized phrases in this paragraph.

Here is another example of a text that may stump some readers who do not have the matching background knowledge pattern already in mind as they read:

> The process is actually quite simple. First, you separate them into several piles according to shape and color. Then you separate them again according to their age. The oldest ones need the most care and cleaning. After they are clean, you carefully look for the spot where each one belongs. Then you write down which ones are still missing so you can search the many places where they might be found. You look in drawers, under furniture, and inside the pockets of old clothes. You keep hoping that you will find one more little prize.

Some reading teachers probably saw the first line of the text above and immediately skipped the whole passage, thinking it was the same vignette (about laundry) that they have seen in many literacy trainings. Others read on and realized that this was a different text and proceeded to connect the clues to fit background knowledge. Some eventually figured out that the text was about coin collecting by using text clues and background knowledge. (If you didn't, now you know.)

We have countless background knowledge patterns that we use to organize how we think and live. These include patterns for hygiene, eating, romance, religion, communication, work, relaxation, and how people behave or learn in a given context. We need these patterns to make quick sense of a current situation. For example, if I read that a young girl is heading off to her first day of school, my background knowledge kicks in and I picture her walking into a sunny classroom, with students seated in perfect rows as a teacher smiles and introduces her to the class. The text may drastically change this image, but at least I have a starting point. Remember that diverse learners who did not have mainstream upbringings in the United States may have background knowledge that is much different than what mainstream American authors envisioned when they were writing their texts (Peregoy & Boyle, 2000). In such cases, it is even more important to predict what kinds of background information diverse students will need in order to comprehend successfully.

Background knowledge significantly contributes to other comprehension habits such as inferences, predictions, questions, and visualizations. In making inferences and predictions, we mix our knowledge of what we know has happened or what normally happens with what is said in the text in order to create meaning that is not directly stated (Keene & Zimmermann, 1997). In creating questions, we have certain areas of knowledge with holes in them and the text piques our interest to fill those holes with a question. We then use the text to construct an answer. In visualizing, we use previous images stored in our brain in the form of basic shapes, colors, and movement in order to form new mental pictures.

Visualizing

When we use background knowledge to create mental images and associations that aid us in comprehension, we are visualizing. Proficient readers routinely create a variety of mental pictures during reading. We use the text's information to bring up prior mental images that we obtained from life, pictures, movies, television, or other sources. We adapt the images as we read in order to fit what the text says. The more vivid the mental pictures we can create, the more comprehensible and memorable the text tends to be (Hyerle, 1992).

Why is visualizing so important? When we visualize, we use mental energy to create meanings and connections in the form of images. It is this mental organizing that helps the images and their information stick in our brains. With reading, as with most learning situations, we are more likely to learn something if we take control of the learning process and are active constructors of meaning rather than passive receivers. Research has shown that when students are taught to visualize text images, they experience better recall and are better able to make helpful inferences and predictions (Gambrell & Bales, 1986). In the case of narrative text, we make a "mental movie" of what is happening in the story. Think about scenes from books you have read and how they are still in your mind even after many years.

Sometimes the images stick so well that we think we saw them in a movie or even that we actually experienced them.

For expository materials, such as those in science or economics, we can make mini-mental-movies (e.g., of the water cycle or cell division) or concept posters (e.g., of a supply-demand chart or a Venn diagram) in our minds that show connections. In science, I might visualize a scene of two atoms sharing an electron or a graph of cell division rates. The quality of these images, of course, depends on my prior experience with texts and images containing atoms and graphs. In social studies, I might visualize ships setting sail for Africa or a Mayan woman grinding maize for the next meal. For math, I might picture the vehicles described in a word problem before I begin working the problem.

We often begin to create mental pictures from the very start of a reading session. We use the title or first sentences of the text, create rough mental images, and continually revise them according to each new sentence. Table 7 shows how this process works. Read the passages in the left column of the table, and notice how the reader's mental pictures on the right change with each sentence.

A reader who makes similar visualizations while reading the sentences in Table 7 will better remember the main idea that being an astronaut is very demanding. In my observations of many struggling readers, I have noticed very positive results from (a) using images to provide background knowledge, (b) training students to actively process images already in the text (they sometimes skip them without this training), and (c) training students to create their own mental images as they read. Activities in this chapter that are particularly helpful for visualization include Background Knowledge Backpack, Closed Eyes Visualize, Concept Poster Chat, Path to Purpose, Sticky Note Snapshots, and Text Structure Organizing.

Drawing while reading also helps students to actively and visually comprehend, provided that the drawing is accurate enough and does not use too much time. If we train

Table 7. Visualization	
Science Paragraph Sample	Images Visualized by Me
Astronauts do much more than just float around in space and smile for cameras.	A smiling astronaut in a spacesuit, with the Earth in the background
They learn how to eat, sleep, and exercise while being weightless.	Several astronauts in gray shirts, inside a cramped ship, one using a rowing machine
For example, you can't just set your sandwich down and expect it to stay on the table!	Bread, cheese, meat, and tomatoes floating around inside a space shuttle
Astronauts also perform a large number of work tasks, such as spacecraft maintenance, testing, and experimentation.	An astronaut outside with a big wrench; other astronauts inside looking at computers
They even study the effects of life in space on the human body, in order to see how we might do on trips to other planets.	Someone taking a blood sample from an astronaut to see any changes
So if you sign up to be an astronaut, remember that it is more work than any job you may ever have on Earth.	Me in a spacesuit taking in the view of the Earth, and the boss astronaut yelling, "Get back to work!"

students to create symbols or doodles while reading, they will tend to better remember the information they read. This should not surprise us because the process of visualizing and then drawing what we see requires active thinking. We must, of course, extensively model for students how to make quick and accurate drawings and doodles. One suggestion is to use a piece of paper with four television screens drawn on it (see the Visualization Stations form on page 166). Students can be given a short amount of time to make sketches on the four screens to depict what is happening in the text while they read or listen to someone read aloud (Hibbing & Rankin-Erickson, 2003). Activities such as this also can give you a quick view into what is happening in a student's brain while he or she is reading. If the student is way off the mark, you can intervene.

Movement, or kinesthetics, also can help students develop their background knowledge and visualization habits. When students see you act out an idea (character, scene, or process) or, even better, when students also do the movements, these actions become imprinted in the brain as background knowledge. Then, the ideas are easier to visualize and recall when a text refers to them. Do the BK is an effective kinesthetic background knowledge activity.

How Students Use Background Knowledge

Every student has stores of background knowledge and experience just waiting to be tapped in order to improve his or her comprehension of school texts. Every day, students connect experiences to their background knowledge in order to communicate, learn, and carry out life tasks. Our task is to build on the ways in which students already connect to and use their background knowledge in nonacademic settings (and in other classes) in order to meet the academic comprehension needs in classroom settings. For example, a student may draw from his or her experience working on a farm when describing hard work to a friend, but may not yet connect to this experience when the topic of feudal systems is introduced in social studies or when learning about animal adaptations in science. It is our job to see that this "extra" connecting happens—and then becomes a habit.

We are not teaching a new habit here. We are developing in our students the existing habit of using background knowledge in more academic ways. In each activity found in this chapter, I recommend starting with the ways in which students use the habit in nonacademic contexts. Start with the concrete and familiar, then move to the more abstract and academic. For example, in the Brainstorm and Sort activity, you can start with common topics such as soccer, school, music, friendship, food, cities, or cars. Point out to students how easily they categorize and classify the pieces of their background knowledge. Then, transition this activity into the topic of the upcoming text or lesson.

Tools Chart for Background Knowledge

Table 8 will help you figure out when to use this chapter's activities in which content areas. On the left side of the table, a ✓ in a column indicates that the activity is useful in that stage of reading. On the right side of the table, a ✓ in a column indicates that the activity is helpful for comprehension of common texts used in that content area. A ✓✓ on the right side of the table

			Table 8. When and Where to Use the Activities in Chapter 4			
Before Reading	During Reading	After Reading	Activity Name	Social Studies	Science	English/ EL
✓		✓	Anticipation Guides (+ Why)	✓✓	✓✓	✓
✓		✓	Background Knowledge Backpack	✓	✓	✓✓
✓			Brain Warmers	✓✓	✓✓	✓✓
✓		✓	Brainstorm and Sort	✓✓	✓✓	✓
✓			CATAPULT Into Literature			✓✓
✓	✓		Closed Eyes Visualize	✓✓	✓✓	✓✓
✓			Concept Poster Chat	✓✓	✓✓	✓
✓			Do the BK	✓✓	✓✓	✓✓
✓		✓	Give One–Get One	✓	✓✓	✓
✓	✓	✓	K-W-L	✓✓	✓✓	✓
✓	✓	✓	K-W-L Plus	✓✓	✓✓	✓
✓	✓	✓	Path to Purpose	✓✓	✓	✓
✓	✓	✓	Quickwrites	✓✓	✓✓	✓✓
	✓		Sticky Note Snapshots	✓✓	✓✓	✓✓
✓	✓	✓	Text Structure Organizing	✓✓	✓✓	✓
✓			THIEVES	✓✓	✓✓	
✓	✓	✓	Think-Pair-Share	✓✓	✓✓	✓✓

means the activity is especially helpful for that type of text and that you should try it as soon as possible. Take the time, however, to look at all the activities and spend a few moments thinking about how you might use them in your teaching. I have been pleasantly surprised at the variety of creative ways in which teachers have adapted most of these activities and organizers to work in all content areas in all stages of reading.

Don't forget to apply the general teaching suggestions from chapter 2 to the activities in this chapter. When you find an interesting activity, refer to chapter 2 and ask how you can best integrate its instructional suggestions into the activity to meet your specific needs.

Activities for Background Knowledge

ANTICIPATION GUIDES (+ WHY)

Anticipation guides (Tierney & Readance, 1999), also known as prediction guides, activate a student's prior knowledge and set a purpose or framework for the reading. They are most useful when the text contains controversial issues, problems, or opinions that do not have one easy answer. The guides serve as springboards for modifying beliefs and opinions about a topic (Duffelmeyer, Baum, & Merkley, 1987). They can be used to bring up and examine commonly held assumptions such as "The Earth is round" (not precisely) or "an animal is a bird if it has a bill" (not the platypus). Figure 11 shows a sample anticipation guide for a text on computers.

Procedure

1. Identify major concepts in the reading or lesson.

2. Create statements that question certain notions, beliefs, or opinions or that may challenge what students already know. You can use the reproducible Anticipation Guide on page 159

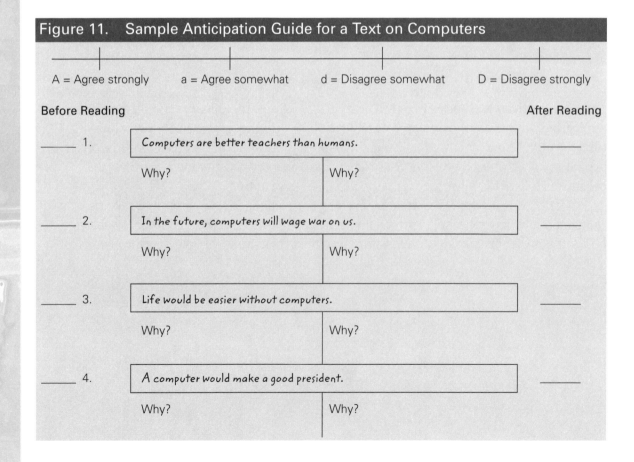

Figure 11.   Sample Anticipation Guide for a Text on Computers

A = Agree strongly   a = Agree somewhat   d = Disagree somewhat   D = Disagree strongly

Before Reading   After Reading

_____ 1.   Computers are better teachers than humans.   _____

        Why?   Why?

_____ 2.   In the future, computers will wage war on us.   _____

        Why?   Why?

_____ 3.   Life would be easier without computers.   _____

        Why?   Why?

_____ 4.   A computer would make a good president.   _____

        Why?   Why?

to save time; write your questions or statements in the numbered boxes and then make a copy for each student.

3. Hand out the guide and briefly explain the statements. Have students mark their responses of agreement or disagreement in the "Before Reading" column.

4. Have students give reasons for their opinions by answering the "Why?" question on the left under each statement.

5. Have students read the text. During reading, the students can refer to the guide and take notes.

6. After reading or other follow-up activities, have students mark the "After Reading" column and fill in the "Why?" section on the right under each statement.

7. Conduct a discussion comparing the before and after results. Your discussion should refer to evidence in the text and should cover students' reasons for changes in their before and after answers.

Variation

Anticipation Questions: You also can have students answer several questions before the reading or lesson. Then, they read the text and answer the questions again after reading. For generating good questions for this activity, see chapter 6.

BACKGROUND KNOWLEDGE BACKPACK

The Background Knowledge Backpack is a simple way to help students build the habit of accessing different types of background knowledge for comprehension.

Procedure

1. Use the reproducible Background Knowledge Backpack form on page 160. Read aloud a text to the students and stop several times to fill in the "pockets" in the Backpack. Model this activity many times so students can see the different types of useful background knowledge that can be used. Figure 12 shows a sample of the completed form.

2. Have students read the text from where you left off and pause at times to fill in the pockets. (They can do this in pairs as well.) Let students know that there is no set order and that all three types of background knowledge listed on the sheet can be used for the "My BK" pockets.

3. Have students (either in pairs or in groups) explain their "Text" pocket responses and how their background knowledge helped them to understand the material.

4. Have students share with the entire class as you write a similar diagram on the board or overhead.

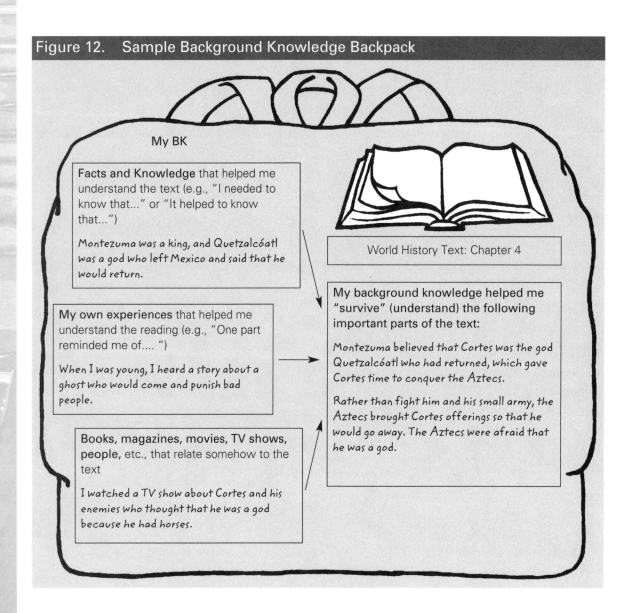

Figure 12. Sample Background Knowledge Backpack

My BK

Facts and Knowledge that helped me understand the text (e.g., "I needed to know that..." or "It helped to know that...")

Montezuma was a king, and Quetzalcóatl was a god who left Mexico and said that he would return.

My own experiences that helped me understand the reading (e.g., "One part reminded me of.... ")

When I was young, I heard a story about a ghost who would come and punish bad people.

Books, magazines, movies, TV shows, people, etc., that relate somehow to the text

I watched a TV show about Cortes and his enemies who thought that he was a god because he had horses.

World History Text: Chapter 4

My background knowledge helped me "survive" (understand) the following important parts of the text:

Montezuma believed that Cortes was the god Quetzalcóatl who had returned, which gave Cortes time to conquer the Aztecs.

Rather than fight him and his small army, the Aztecs brought Cortes offerings so that he would go away. The Aztecs were afraid that he was a god.

5. As a slight variation, students can create a similar diagram that has "What I didn't understand" on the right and "What I needed to know" on the left side.

BRAIN WARMERS

These activities serve as excellent prereading "hooks," attention grabbers, motivators, and background knowledge builders. Readers, especially those who struggle with grade-level material, should seldom dive into a text without some kind of preparation. Here are a few quick ideas that you can use to prepare students to read.

Backward Predictions: Read the ending of a text or story and have students predict the beginning; then read the entire story to see if the students were correct.

Debate: Debate an issue that students will encounter in a text. For example, present the issue on the board, then take the less likely position (devil's advocate) to spark some argument that will arise in the reading.

Guess and Adjust: This vocabulary activity, found in chapter 7, is also an effective way to get students to generate some central concepts that will arise in the text.

Read-Alouds: Read aloud the title and first part of the text and then have students visualize and predict what the rest of the text will be about. See RATA (Read-Aloud Think-Aloud) Word Clues in chapter 7.

Reading Reason Vote: Have students generate reasons to read the specific text after they have done some prereading (e.g., with the CATAPULT or THIEVES activity from this chapter). Write down the reasons, add any of your own, and then hold a class vote for the top three reasons to read the text.

Role-Plays: Have your students role-play an event or idea related to a story. Pick a scene or event from the text and have students create or participate with you in a simple role-play. Some examples are as follows:

- Balancing equations in algebra
- Revolutionary War protests
- A few poignant lines from a play
- The water cycle

Show and Tell Pictures and Objects: Use real items or pictures to prompt discussion or provide good material for a Quickwrites activity.

Video Clip: Show a relevant five-minute video clip that provides some background and gets students a little more motivated to read the upcoming text. Show other videos later on, if they fit. Combine this with Quickwrites and think-aloud activities.

BRAINSTORM AND SORT

Brainstorming is a commonly used prereading activity in which you elicit from students a barrage of ideas related to the text's topic. Brainstorming exposes students to the wide range of collective background knowledge that tends to connect to a text's topic. You can use the information gathered to introduce the text, build interest, and even build vocabulary and background knowledge that will aid comprehension. This adaptation is an excellent activity for building classifying and categorizing skills. It is similar to a procedure called List-Group-Label (Taba, 1967).

Procedure

1. Prompt the students to brainstorm ideas related to a topic of your choosing: "What do we know about...?"

Table 9.	Sort Chart From a Brainstorm Session on Friendship		
What Friends Do	What Friends Say	Qualities	Examples
Lend money	Encouragements	Faithful	Huck Finn story
Listen	Jokes	Caring	When Trish gave me
Spend time with you	Advice	Patient	her coat
			Robots in *Star Wars*

2. Accept all ideas, but it is important to have students explain how some of the more off-the-wall ideas may connect to the topic. Write the ideas on the board. Students can write them on a sheet of notebook paper, or you can give them copies of the Brainstorm and Sort form (see page 161) to use.

3. Ask students to begin to group ideas together into three to five columns or clusters.

4. Have the students, with your help, create categories under which the ideas will fit logically. You can make a sort chart with columns or create a semantic map for this. The category names go at the top of the columns in a chart or in the ovals of a semantic map. Table 9 shows a sample sort chart.

5. Model the thinking process involved in classifying and categorizing ideas (also an important skill for summarizing). Think aloud while sorting items. For example, "Is 'listen' a quality? It is an action so I think it would fall under the 'What friends do' category."

6. If you sort the information with a semantic map, you can use it to give a minilesson on going from maps to outlines, which can be useful later if the students are asked to outline the text.

7. Once the web is created, students can use the form as a note-taking sheet while reading.

Variation

Have students first come up with categories for the brainstormed information and then take time to discuss the placement of items in pairs or groups. Next, have them read a text on the topic. While they read, have students cross out the items that do not fit and circle the items that are reinforced by the text. Then, have students add to the semantic map or brainstormed list while they read. When they are more experienced with brainstorming and categorizing, students do this in groups on their own, particularly if different groups are reading different texts.

CATAPULT INTO LITERATURE

A prereading activity, CATAPULT (covers, author, title, audience, page 1, underlying message or purpose, visuals, and time) Into Literature is useful for getting students to survey and launch into works of literature. This activity and THIEVES give struggling readers some tricks of the book reading trade. If we can get students to set up as much content and theme as they can

Table 10. CATAPULT Process Steps

Covers (front and back)	What does the front cover show us about what we might visualize in the story? What does the back cover tell us about the story (the words, pictures, or both)?
Author	What is the author's background? Has he or she written any other stories that might be like this? What were they about? Are the same characters in this story as in the others?
Title	What does the title lead us to predict about the story? Let's hear some possible predictions.
Audience	For whom was this story written? Old; young; male; female; city-dwelling; country-dwelling; past, present, or future readers?
Page 1	Read page 1 and think about what the story might be about.
Underlying message or purpose	With what we have thought about so far, what message or purpose might the author have for the readers?
Look at visuals, maps, or sketches in the text	As we look through the story, what do the pictures, sketches, diagrams, or maps tell us? How will they add to our ability to visualize events and characters?
Time, place, characters	From clues so far, what can we say about when the story takes place, where it takes place, and the characters? What can we guess might happen to the characters?

before they read a text, they will have a much better framework on which to attach the details and ideas of the text. And students will be less likely to get lost in what they are reading.

Procedure

1. Model and scaffold the use of the steps shown in Table 10. Tell students to take notes during this discussion.
2. Create a half-sheet worksheet to remind students of the CATAPULT steps as they read (a reproducible CATAPULT Into Literature Practice form is provided on page 162).
3. If there is time, have students share either in pairs or with the whole class their CATAPULT notes.

Variation

CATAPULT Prereading Web: This is a modification of the CATAPULT acronym-based activity, done in the form of a semantic web in order to give more visual emphasis to prereading. In the boxes around the text's title, put whatever prereading elements from CATAPULT that you want to emphasize, as shown on the next page.

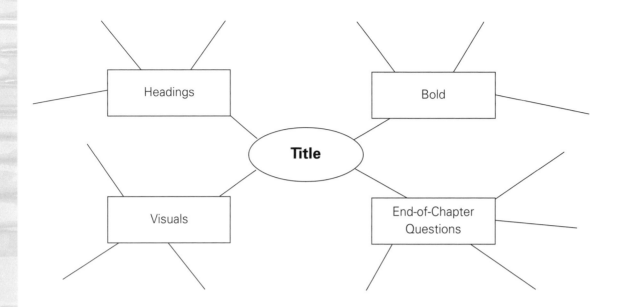

Have students use the web to fill in information that connects to each box. Students can then compare notes and/or you can have a whole-class share time to discuss the results. (Note that this modification is also effective for the THIEVES activity.)

CLOSED EYES VISUALIZE

Visualizing is vital for comprehension. It is similar to making a movie happen in your mind. Readers need to use mental pictures from television, books, movies, and their own experiences to create the pictures that the author expects a reader to create while reading (Hibbing & Rankin-Erickson, 2003). For example, the book I am reading may be about a desert in Texas, and although I have never been to Texas or even to a desert, I have seen deserts on television and I have a rough mental image of dry sand, cacti, and lizards. So, as I read, I modify this mental image into what the author intends for me to picture and to know.

Procedure

1. Explain to students that picturing text in their minds is vital for understanding it.

2. Show students a series of three or four pictures (or show short video clips).

3. After each picture, have students close their eyes and visualize what was in the picture. They also can write down words to describe the images if they want.

4. Tell students to visualize a variation of each picture. For example, if you showed them a picture of mountains, have them modify this mental image to have several mountain climbers on the cliffs in a snowstorm.

5. Tell the students that this is what happens during reading: We start with a rough image and the text makes us modify it with other details.

6. Have students visualize and imagine that they are in situations similar to those that will be encountered in the text they are about to study. (You can have them put their heads down if they do not like closing their eyes.)

7. Next, transition to written text. Read aloud a text and stop after the initial clues are given. Allow students to form an initial picture. Then read on and stop at appropriate times to allow students to modify their mental images. You also should model your thinking processes while reading aloud.

8. Play sound effects or music if either fits.

9. Finally, have students visualize while they read their own texts. During and after reading, they can keep a "visualizing log" by writing on notebook paper how the text caused them to modify their initial images and scenes. The following sample should give you the idea.

Initial Visualization	Modified Visualization After Further Reading
A small town with old cars and poor people	A village with no cars, dirt streets, brightly colored houses, and no people
An army with tanks, green uniforms, and missile trucks	An army with cannons and soldiers in red uniforms, all mounted on horses

Variation

Have students read a text section silently, or even aloud, and then give them time to visualize what happened or what was described in the text. They should close their eyes to do this. Next, have students draw the scenes they visualize. Then, they modify these scenes as they read the text. This process will show on paper how they modify scenes in their minds, which strengthens the mental flexibility needed for learning new concepts.

CONCEPT POSTER CHAT

Based on research that has shown positive effects from using advance organizers before reading (Stone, 1983), a Concept Poster Chat is a teacher presentation that uses a large poster that you create with markers while you explain the concepts to be learned from the text. It is a powerful way to build background knowledge and vocabulary, and it can be an excellent form of comprehensible input for English learners as well.

Procedure

1. Decide the key points that you want your students to get from the text. Think about how you can draw these points on one or two large posters. Examples include an illustrated timeline, a diagram, a story map, a character description, a Venn diagram, a cause and effect chart, a map, and a drawing of a scene.

2. Lightly sketch in pencil the main lines, symbols, and words you will cover when you fill in the poster for the class. A little bit of forethought can make a huge difference in learning with this activity.

3. Mount the poster on the wall. In class, draw over the pencil lines with a thick marker as you preview key concepts in the text and draw symbols to illustrate key vocabulary. You can even use props, drama, and physical objects if they fit the discussion. Students can take notes, if needed.

4. The teacher talk time during the Chat activity should not be more than 10 minutes. Have students do one or two Think-Pair-Shares (about 3–5 minutes each) during that time in order to process the information. The whole activity, including the Think-Pair-Shares, should not last longer than 20 minutes.

5. Keep the poster on the wall for reference during the lesson or unit. Refer back to it often.

DO THE BK

Do the BK (BK stands for *background knowledge*) is a kinesthetic way to build background knowledge for a text. The activity is based on multiple intelligences research (Armstrong, 2003; Gardner, 1999) that shows that many learners connect to experiences that they have seen or done themselves. This is effective because the teacher models the activity, which allows students to see it live multiple times. Then the students get to do the activity multiple times. When students later read the text that relates to the actions, they connect immediately and their comprehension improves.

Procedure

1. Choose a challenging idea (a concept, set of vocabulary words, process, or section) from the text that will be assigned.

2. Generate ways to act out the idea. This can include miming or gesturing. For example, you might decide to act out the water cycle by being a cloud (arms making a circle), then moving your arms downward like falling rain, then running as if you are a stream traveling to the ocean, and finally rising up and becoming a cloud again. For social studies, you might decide to act out the initial events that sparked the Mexican-American War or create gestures for the Eightfold Path of Buddhism.

3. To teach key vocabulary words, refer to the Go Beyond the Verbal activity in chapter 7. Key vocabulary words in all subject areas are almost always better learned through motions.

4. Do the motions as you explain the idea you are trying to convey. As a variation, you could act it out silently and have students guess what you are doing.

5. Have students act out the idea in unison as you lead them.

6. If there are multiple parts to the idea (such as the water cycle), shout out parts and have students react with the appropriate action.

7. Have students read the text that contains the idea from this activity.

Variation

Have students generate ways to act out certain parts of the text. For example, choose four challenging concepts, and have eight groups come up with ways to act them out. The groups can present their "motion pictures" of the concepts to the class.

GIVE ONE–GET ONE

Give One–Get One (Kagan, 1997) is a social way for students to tap into and build background knowledge for a text. It is similar to a brainstorm session but has a more communicative twist.

Procedure

1. Generate a topic idea from the text and put it on the board. Some examples are as follows:

- What I know about whales
- Examples of friendship
- Keywords for studying space
- Reasons to exercise
- Favorite idioms, metaphors, sayings
- What we learned last month about electricity
- What will the text teach us about gravity?

2. Have students fold a piece of paper in half horizontally and number 1–4 above the fold and 5–8 below, as shown:

3. Have students write down ideas related to the topic you gave.

4. Have students circulate throughout the room and exchange their ideas for at least three different ideas from other students, which go on lines 5–8. They need to get the student's name for each corresponding idea and write it in the "From" column.

```
Ideas I will give:
1._____
2._____
3._____
4._____

Ideas I got:              From
5. _____         ____
6. _____         ____
7. _____         ____
8. _____         ____
```

5. After several minutes, have students regroup and share with the class the ideas they heard from other students.

6. Have the students use academic language such as "Julie had a similar thought," "Manuel predicts that...," or "Katia differs in opinion because she...."

7. Discuss all the responses and then introduce the text.

K-W-L

K-W-L (Ogle, 1986) has a long and effective history in the scaffolding of expository texts. Basic K-W-L uses three columns in which to write down information that we Know (background knowledge), Want to know (establishing purpose and asking questions), and have Learned (main idea). In addition to teaching students to connect to background knowledge, this activity also can develop habits of summarizing, questioning, predicting, inferring, and figuring out word meanings.

Procedure

1. Create three columns on the board and head them with "What we know," "What we want to know," and "What we learned."

2. Ask students what they know about the subject or text you are about to study. Prompt the students with pictures, titles, or subjects to fill in the first column (some teachers put "What we *think* we know" in the first column to avoid confusing students with potentially incorrect information).

3. Ask students what they want to know, and fill in the second column with their questions.

4. Have students read the text or do research on the topic.

5. In the third column, have students answer their questions from the second column and add any extra key information that they learned.

Variations

Many teachers have successfully adapted K-W-L to expand its effectiveness for teaching comprehension. Following are some ideas.

- **Extended K-W-L:** Sampson (2002) creates more than a simple K-W-L accountability for obtaining information in the K-W-L process. Six columns are used in this variation: the three traditional K-W-L columns, a column for checking off whether the text(s) confirmed the information in the "What we think we know" column, and two other columns for noting the sources of the information (see the example).

What We Think We KNOW	Confirmed?	Source	What We WANT to Know	What We LEARNED	Source

When using this activity, remember that not all the items in the first or second columns will be confirmed or answered.

- **K-N-L:** This variation uses content standards in the second column (what students *need* to learn) rather than items students are curious about (see example). You will need to help students with the second column, writing in content standards and taking time to explain them.

What We KNOW and Can Do	What We NEED to Learn	What We LEARNED (and/or What We Can Do)

- **K-W-H-L-S:** In this version, you add two extra columns (see example), one for how students will learn the information and one for how they will show what they learned.

What We Think We KNOW	What We WANT to Learn	HOW We Will Learn It	What We LEARNED	How We Will SHOW That We Learned

- **K-W-L-U-M:** For this version, you can add either or both of the last two columns shown in the example.

What We Think We KNOW	What We WANT (Need) to Learn	What We LEARNED	How We Will USE (Apply) What We Learned	What MORE We Want/ Need to Learn

- **W-W-W-W:** You might want to include other columns in K-W-L such as What the Teacher Wants Us to Learn, Why We Should Learn It, Who Needs to Know This in Life, and What Other Points of View There Are.

K-W-L PLUS

K-W-L Plus (Carr & Ogle, 1987) uses graphic organizers (within the context of a K-W-L chart) to help students further organize information into additional categories before, during, and after reading.

Procedure

1. Give students an initial topic or some clues, such as a text title or pictures, and ask students to think about what they might know that might relate to the topic. Have students brainstorm in order to fill in the step 1 area of the graphic organizer (see Figure 13 for a sample).

Figure 13.   Sample K-W-L Plus Activity

What we think we KNOW	What we WANT (need) to learn	What we LEARNED
Step 1 Voting, ballots, communism, freedom, choice, Magna Carta	**Step 3** What is communism? Why don't more people vote? What is the Magna Carta? Why was it important?	**Step 5** Democracy rule by all people. We can decide who leads us. Many have died for our freedom to vote.
Step 2	**Step 4**	**Step 6**

Step 2 diagram:
- Magna Carta → Foundations
- Not Communism → Democracy
- Democracy → Elections, Freedom
- Elections → Voting, ballots
- Freedom → Choice

Step 4 diagram:
- What was the Magna Carta? / Why was it important? → Foundations
- What is communism? / What is democracy? → Democracy
- Democracy → Elections, Freedom
- Elections → Why should we vote? Should all be allowed to vote?
- Freedom → Are there degrees of freedom?

Step 6 diagram:
- The Magna Carta limited power of king → Foundations
- Democracy rule by all people → Democracy
- Democracy → Elections, Freedom
- Elections → We can decide who leads us.
- Freedom → Many have died for our freedom to vote.

2. Have students generate several categories under which each of their responses can fit. Put these categories into the boxes of a semantic map that they will draw in the step 2 area. The first several times you use this activity with your class, you should think aloud when modeling and scaffolding the process of generating categories, sorting, and creating the graphic organizer.

3. Have students generate questions, with some guidance from you, for the step 3 area in the second column. They can relate their questions to information in the first column; you can even draw arrows across the columns to show how their questions in step 3 relate to their ideas in step 1.

4. Have students create questions that correspond to the boxed categories in step 2. Have them create a new semantic map in the step 4 area that has these questions around it.

5. Now have the students study the text. As they read, have students take notes on what they learn and write them in the step 5 column or on sticky notes. Students also can draw arrows from the answers they found to the questions in steps 3 and 4.

6. Have students use the original semantic map from step 2 as a template that they now change to fit what they learned. Have them write that information in the semantic map in the step 6 area, including any answers to the questions in step 4. They also can generate new categories here, if any should arise.

7. Students can compare their final graphic organizers with other students in pairs or groups to share information and to discuss any differences in categories and the importance of the information included.

PATH TO PURPOSE

This activity helps students build the vital habit of focusing on initial text clues in order to establish a working main idea (and purpose) for reading. In this activity, which is very similar to a semantic web, a reader taps into background knowledge to create a possible "map" for progressing through a text and gathering important information along the way.

Procedure

1. Remind students that the author wrote the text for a purpose. Model for students how to look at the title and other initial clues to guess the purpose. Ask them, Why did the author write this?

2. Write the author's purpose in the oval at the top of the reproducible Path to Purpose form on page 163. (You can do yours on an overhead transparency and students can be given blank photocopies for their own future work.) Use pencil so that you can make changes during reading. Remind students that the purpose can change. Around the oval, you can put the reasons (evidence) for the purpose you generated.

3. In the signs along the road on the form, put major clues, headings, and ideas that help you make your way to the destination (purpose). Around the signs, you can put supporting details and paraphrases that describe the importance of the sign's heading. The signs can be filled in at any reading stage: before, during, or after.

4. Revise the purpose while reading if the text changes your initial guesses for it.

Variation

Another use for the Path to Purpose form is as a chart that compares two sides of an issue. The issue or problem to be solved would go in the oval and the signs would contain key points on opposite sides of the road. (Some teachers have used this variation as a scaffold for persuasive essay writing.)

QUICKWRITES

Quickwrites require each student to reach inside his or her mind and pull out something related to a prompt in order to put it on paper. They are informal and low-stress ways to jump-start the brain of each student, particularly those who may not share in a whole-class brainstorming session. They are a way for students to connect to what they already know or just learned and to organize their thoughts enough to write them down.

Procedure

1. Give the students a question or prompt related to the text about to be read, and have students write down whatever comes to their minds without organizing it too much or worrying about grammar. The topic should relate to the text being studied in some way: connection to background knowledge ("Describe a time when..."); a controversial topic or question that relates to student life; explanation of content concepts or vocabulary; or predictions, summaries, inferences, hypotheses, and so on. All students should be able to write something.

2. You may need to offer some students extra support, particularly those with limited experience or knowledge about the topic. There often will be students who say, for example, "I don't have problems with friends," "I don't want to go anywhere," or "I've never seen a...." Be ready to modify the prompt to get all students to participate.

3. Quickwrites can become a part of a student's journal and be used for assessment, especially if the student so chooses. They also can be used during Think-Pair-Share activities or even as a Ticket Out the Door, in which each student writes a summary of what he or she learned and hands it to you on the way out of class.

Following are some sample Quickwrites:

History: I think wars start because people want to take over people's lands and control them. I'm not sure why people want to take over lands or control people—maybe because of selfishness or greed, maybe because they want to make people convert to their religion. The war in my country hurt many people who were innocent and just wanted to have a normal life.

Math: First, you have to get the similar terms together, but they have to have the exact same variables and exponents. Then you get the variable you want to solve on one side and the numbers on the other. You need to make sure to do the same thing to one side that you do to the other, like two sides of a seesaw. Then I get the variable all by itself by multiplying or dividing and that is the answer.

Science: The Punnett square helps you figure out the chances of a plant being tall or not if two parent plants have a dominant and recessive gene mix. It is a 75% chance that the plant will be tall because it shows in 3 out of 4 boxes. It will be short 25% of the time because the tt is only in one box. I think this works for humans but not sure because we have much more complicated DNAs and genes to mix.

Variation

Pen Go–Pen Stop: In this variation, students are given a prompt and a minute to think, and then they write as much as they can when you say "Pen go." A few minutes later, you say "Pen stop" and the students must stop writing. This variation helps students to challenge themselves to write as much as possible—while also making sense.

STICKY NOTE SNAPSHOTS

This is a visualizing activity for both fiction and nonfiction texts that uses 3" x 3" sticky notes. It is effective because it allows students to move the images while at the same time creating them to meet the specific needs of the text. Other habits that are developed with this activity include inferring, predicting, and summarizing.

Procedure

1. Tell students that they are to draw either pictures or diagrams that are created in their minds as they read a section of text. For example, you can assign one sticky note snapshot per page of text. You should use this activity to build the habit of choosing the most important information to visualize. Tell students to draw the most important concept that the author tried to teach on each page (or in each section). They should not copy any visuals that are already in the text. (Students who do not like drawing can describe what they see in their minds with written words.) Figure 14 shows a sample sticky note snapshot with a corresponding section of text.

2. Students can include a brief written explanation on the front or back of each sticky note snapshot.

3. When they finish reading, have students place their snapshots in a photo album (or on a poster) dedicated to that text, with captions written below or above the snapshots.

4. Use the snapshots to scaffold writing responses.

Figure 14.   Sample of a Sticky Note Snapshot With a Science Text

Escape Velocity

Suppose you walk outside your space station on Mars. You throw a baseball straight up into the air. If you are not superhuman, the ball will rise for a while and then fall because of the planet's gravity. If your arm were strong enough, however, you could make the ball escape beyond the pull of gravity and it would continue out into space indefinitely.

The speed needed to throw a ball so that it can escape a planet's gravity pull is called "escape velocity." This velocity is related to the mass of the planet. If the planet is very massive, then its escape velocity is high because the gravity is strong. A less massive planet wouldn't require as much force to defeat gravity's pull. For example, you don't need to have a strong arm to throw a ball out into space from an asteroid.

The escape velocity of the Earth is around 25,000 m.p.h., whereas that of the moon is only 5,300 m.p.h. You would need a strong arm on both the Earth and the moon to launch a ball into space. Another factor influencing escape velocity is how far you are from the planet's (or moon's) center. The further away you are from the core, the lower the escape velocity.

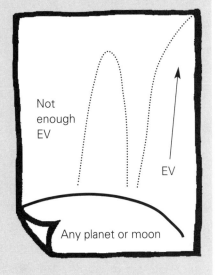

TEXT STRUCTURE ORGANIZING

This activity trains students to recognize the common forms of text structure. Good readers automatically consider how the text is structured in order to improve comprehension (Alvermann & Phelps, 2001). Even a quick glance at the title and headings of a text often can tell a reader how the author constructed the text. Yet many texts do not give obvious clues, and the reader has to take a closer look at embedded clues to help figure out the structure.

Remind students that a text may contain more than one (or even all) of the types of text structures that follow. The author for instance could describe a problem and then its causes with a cause-and-effect paragraph, then compare and contrast possible solutions, and then persuade the reader to lean toward one solution.

Procedure

1. Show students grade-level reading samples that have the text structure you wish to teach.

2. Circle the signal words and phrases that indicate the type of text structure.

3. Model how to fill in the graphic organizer for the text. (See Table 11 for samples and ideas.)

4. Have students help you fill in the boxes and outer details of the chosen graphic organizer. Discuss the hierarchical nature of most texts: overall purpose or main idea, then supporting main points, and finally details to support the main points.

5. Give students another text to read and another organizer that they can fill in while working in groups or pairs.

6. Optional: Have students use the graphic organizers to write their own texts based on the structures. The more familiar students are with the structures in their own writing, the better they can use them for reading (and the better they get at writing, too).

7. Give students a choice as to how they want to organize and visualize their thoughts. It might be one of the graphic organizers in Table 11, a sketch, or even an outline.

THIEVES

Many teachers employ the services of rather intimidating textbooks to provide instructional support in the classroom. These books are difficult for many students to read. This and the CATAPULT Into Literature and Text Structure Organizing activities give struggling readers some tricks of the textbook reading trade. Eventually, these activities can build prereading habits that will last students for as long as they read textbooks.

THIEVES (adapted from Manz, 2002) is an acronym that helps students go through all the necessary prereading steps before diving into a textbook chapter: title, headings, introduction, everything they know, visuals, end-of-chapter materials, and "so what?" It is a

Table 11. Organizing Text Structure

Text Structure	Purpose	Features	Key Terms	Graphic Organizer
Description	To explain an idea, person, place, or thing	Focus on one thing and its components	• is, are • consists of • also • this, that • in fact • for instance • most important	
Sequence	To describe the order of events or how to do or make something	The specific order of events or steps	• first, second • then, before, now • not long after • while • finally	
Cause and Effect	To explain why something happens or exists	Reasons and results	• so • so that • because of • as a result of • since • in order to	
Persuasion	To get the reader to act or to agree with one side of an issue or argument	Both sides presented; one side is favored; counterarguments addressed	• granted, despite • you must admit • then again • we should • it is important • therefore, even though	
Compare and Contrast	To show how subjects are alike and different	Two or more items with similarities and differences	• differs from • similar to • by contrast • unlike • similarly • yet, although, but, however, on the other hand • either...or, not only... but also	
Problem and Solution	Presents a problem situation and possible solutions	A problem, along with pluses and minuses of all solutions	• the main difficulty • one possible solution is • one challenge • therefore, this led to, so that • if...then, thus	

way to get students to build extensive knowledge of the text even before they read the first "normal" words of a chapter.

Procedure

1. Tell students something such as, "We now get to become information thieves. Let's see how much information we can steal from the chapter before we actually read it."

2. Model how to go through each of the items in Table 12 as you look at the chapter. Use an overhead to write down the information. You can use the reproducible THIEVES Practice form (see page 165) with boxes for each letter, and can give students a THIEVES Bookmark (page 164) to fill in as they read.

3. After going through steps 1 and 2, have students use the THIEVES Practice form in pairs with another section of text.

Table 12. THIEVES Sample Session	
Component	What the Teacher Says and Does to Model
Title	What does the title tell us? Let's think of all the possibilities.
Headings	What do the headings tell us? They are the minititles of each section. What questions can we make from them that we think the section will answer? Let's also look at the table of contents, ask some questions, and make some predictions.
Introduction	Read the chapter introduction if there is one and think about it. Read the first paragraph of normal chapter text as well. Why do we think the author wrote the text?
Everything I know	Jot down all the facts and ideas about the topic that you think will be helpful for understanding. Create some questions about your own knowledge that you think the text might answer. Use the back of your paper, if needed.
Visuals	Let's look at all the diagrams, charts, and pictures. Let's read the captions. Why did the author include them? Can we think of any questions about them?
End-of-chapter material	Let's look at the end of the chapter to read any summaries (Don't ever forget to read the summary! It will save a lot of time.) and to see which questions the author thought were important. This can help us focus on what the author's purpose is. Let's try to guess the answers to a few questions using the information we have gathered so far. Write down a couple questions that look important. Also, we should notice every boldface or italicized word, especially if it is a new word or has a new meaning in this subject area. Look at any other text clue that might strengthen your initial idea (i.e., make you a richer thief).
So what?	Now, let's ask why we are reading this text. Why might I be interested in it? How might it connect to my life? Why does the teacher or our state want me to know this? Why did the author take the time to write this? For money? To teach us about the topic? For artistic expression? To improve my life somehow? For future classes?

THINK-PAIR-SHARE

A Think-Pair-Share (TPS) is a quick (2–5 minutes) verbal interaction between two or three students that allows them to quickly process the academic language and content being learned. TPS is not just a background knowledge activity, so also keep it in mind for building other habits and for the during- and postreading stages. TPS can be very effective during teacher presentations for creating "breaks" that push students to organize thoughts well enough to communicate them. TPS also allows a student to hear how another person is processing the learning, which further builds background knowledge.

You can use TPS in many different areas of instruction, such as vocabulary, content concepts, opinions, compare-and-contrast activities, sharing parts of homework, summaries of text or visuals, connecting to background knowledge or other classes, making predictions or inferences, and solving problems.

Procedure

1. Create a question or prompt that will get students to use their background knowledge and experience to answer it. Figure 15 offers tips for generating Think-Pair-Share questions or prompts.

Figure 15. Tips for Generating Think-Pair-Share Questions or Prompts

1. Create questions or prompts that zoom in on key content concepts in the text and relate to previous learning:
   - What was the Magna Carta and why was it important?
   - Why do authors use metaphors to enhance a story? Give examples from our last book.
   - Draw and explain how the circulatory system interacts with the respiratory system.
   - Explain how a certain quotation from the story proves that the character fits your description.
   - Explain how to divide fractions.

2. Create open-ended questions or prompts that connect to students' lives and allow for personalized, divergent responses:
   - If you were a colonist, would you have...? Why?
   - How does our community deal with waste and pollution?
   - Describe how acids and bases are used at your house.
   - If you found a wallet with no ID, what would you do? Why?

3. Create questions or prompts for academic skills and other habits that you want to emphasize while reading and throughout the presentation, lesson, unit, or year. These skills might include generating questions, summarizing, predicting, inferring, classifying, persuading, evaluating, analyzing, comparing, and so on:
   - How might this war be similar to the Civil War?
   - What were the causes and effects of the first Gulf War?
   - Generate two below-the-surface questions about molecular bonds.
   - Summarize how to solve equations by using the substitution method.
   - What can you infer about the character's feelings from her actions?

4. Focus and Connect (FoCo): Create questions or prompts that focus students back on the author's purpose and connect the text to the essential standards for which you are using it:
   - What does this have to do with our goal of learning the many ways in which different people helped in the war?
   - How does this connect to our objective of learning how to persuade others?

2. Have students think in silence for 30–60 seconds to mentally prepare what they will say. They can write down thoughts, too.

3. Put students into pairs. During the pair work, students should do the following:

- Face their partner, show interest, and listen actively. They can even take notes.
- Take turns talking.
- Stay on the topic.
- Remember what their partner says in order to share it with the class later.
- Give reasons for any opinions, such as evidence from the book, class discussions, or one's own life.
- Use the vocabulary and academic language that you have modeled.
- Ask their partner questions that call for clarification and evidence: Do you mean that...? Why do you think that? Where does it say that? (Caution students to be polite and respectful in their questioning of one another.)

4. After pair time, ask students to share with the class what their partners said. This forces them to listen and also publicly validates what each partner has said.

Variations

- **Double Prompt Pair-Share:** Create two different questions for the TPS, one for each student, so they cannot simply say things such as "ditto" or "I agree" or "you said my answer."

- **Think-Pair-Square:** After pairs are done sharing with one another, have them turn to another pair to share. This gives students a chance to share with three people instead of the entire class.

- Insert various reading and writing components. For example, you could have TWPS (Think-Write [Quickwrite]-Pair-Share), TPWS (Think-Pair-Write-Share), RPS (Read-Pair-Share), RWPS (Read-Write-Pair-Share), and so on.

Making Inferences and Predictions

* * *

The more you infer and predict,
the more chances you
have of being right.

Humans are wired to infer and predict. We watch people around us and look at their facial expressions to see how they feel. We make inferences about motives when we listen to politicians. We predict a book's enjoyableness by the picture on the cover. We infer that a restaurant is expensive because it has valet parking.

Making an inference in reading is the process of combining the current text information with one's own experience in order to create meaning that is not directly stated in the text (Dole, Duffy, Roehler, & Pearson, 1991). It means creating connections and making educated guesses that go beyond the author's exact words or images. I sometimes describe inference as taking little "thinking steps" off the safe path of the literal and seeing if they lead to where the author intends. If the inference is correct, then we have learned something new and will have that learning better anchored in our brains. If it is wrong, then we *still* learn something new—to make a different inference in a similar situation in future texts.

An inference about future information in a text is a prediction. We use the text clues and our background knowledge to predict what will happen next in a story or what we will learn later in a text. We then go through the text to confirm, discard, change, or make new predictions, depending on new evidence. Prediction provides us with motivation and purpose for reading. It also helps the mind prepare itself to understand the upcoming ideas in the text. As we predict, we need to reflect on the main idea in order to make a logical prediction. This necessitates a certain amount of focus on text details and an ongoing handle on the main idea.

We must teach students to effectively and automatically mix the text and their background knowledge to make good inferences and predictions. If students rely too heavily on the text, they will miss a large amount of deeper meaning; if they rely too heavily on background knowledge, they will lose the direction of the text.

Types of Inferences

Text-to-Text Inferences

These inferences allow us to connect one part of a text to another. For a particular section of text, comprehension depends, in large part, on text information that preceded it. Proficient readers remember what was read earlier in a text and then connect it to what they are currently reading (Keene & Zimmermann, 1997). For example, readers need to remember characters, their traits, and their relationships; the order of events; causes and effects; foreshadowing; and key vocabulary terms within a text as they read. Authors usually expect the reader to make these text-to-text inferences within the specific text being read. They also may assume that the reader has read certain other texts, but authors have much less control over these text-to-*other*-texts connections.

Text-to-Self/World Inferences

When we make inferences, we connect the text information to our own experience and knowledge of the world. For example, I may think of the tree as a symbol of growth in a story, or the dry lake as a metaphor for death. As I read on, these inferences might be confirmed, perhaps in a class discussion, or we may conclude that they were nothing more than a tree and a dry lake. I may infer that, because I know ice floats, all other solid versions of a liquid will float. (I would be wrong.) Many authors expect readers to make text-to-self/world inferences—they want us to apply what we read and learn to past or present situations, problems, and contexts in the world.

Teachers must create environments in which students feel safe about making many and varied inferences. Students should be encouraged to discuss, interpret, define, argue, and write down their inferences about the text and how it relates to their lives and the world around them. Inference, because it extends past the known, is one of the main ingredients of creative thought and expanded learning.

The following questions can be powerful igniters of both text-to-text and text-to-self/world inferences. Ideally, we can figure out ways to make such inference-generating questions automatic:

Who is doing the action? Why?

How does a part fit into the overall text?

What are the effects of an event, both psychological and physical?

What feelings does a person experience?

What is the author's purpose?

What if I had been in that situation?

How does this apply to my life or the world around me?

What does this word mean?

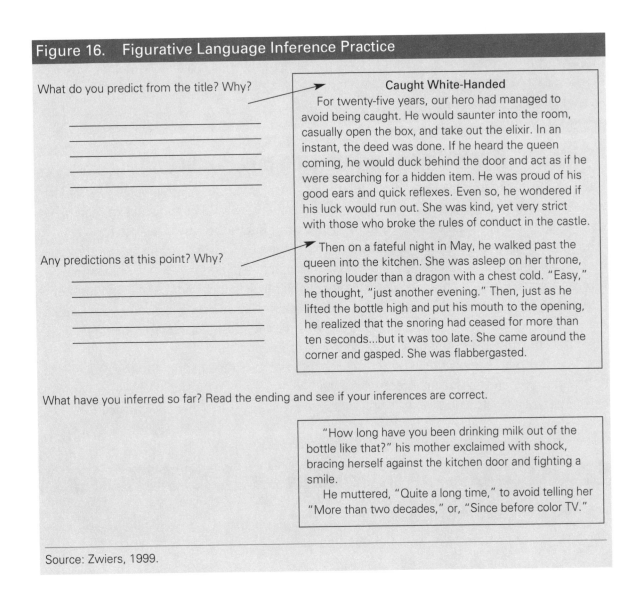

Figure 16. Figurative Language Inference Practice

What do you predict from the title? Why?

_____
_____
_____
_____
_____

Caught White-Handed

For twenty-five years, our hero had managed to avoid being caught. He would saunter into the room, casually open the box, and take out the elixir. In an instant, the deed was done. If he heard the queen coming, he would duck behind the door and act as if he were searching for a hidden item. He was proud of his good ears and quick reflexes. Even so, he wondered if his luck would run out. She was kind, yet very strict with those who broke the rules of conduct in the castle.

Any predictions at this point? Why?

_____
_____
_____
_____
_____

Then on a fateful night in May, he walked past the queen into the kitchen. She was asleep on her throne, snoring louder than a dragon with a chest cold. "Easy," he thought, "just another evening." Then, just as he lifted the bottle high and put his mouth to the opening, he realized that the snoring had ceased for more than ten seconds...but it was too late. She came around the corner and gasped. She was flabbergasted.

What have you inferred so far? Read the ending and see if your inferences are correct.

"How long have you been drinking milk out of the bottle like that?" his mother exclaimed with shock, bracing herself against the kitchen door and fighting a smile.

He muttered, "Quite a long time," to avoid telling her "More than two decades," or, "Since before color TV."

Source: Zwiers, 1999.

A key form of inference is interpreting figurative language. Readers must have a strong base of figurative experiences to be able to independently generate figurative ideas. Songs are the best places to start for many students. Have them bring in some examples to analyze. Analogies and fables can work as well. Figure 16 demonstrates figurative language inference practice with a short story that has readers guessing (inferring and predicting) right away, starting with the title.

Modeling

Teaching inferences involves a ton (figuratively speaking) of modeling. Repeated exposure and teacher scaffolding (e.g., asking the good questions that lead to inferences) are the best ways for students to cultivate inference habits. Of course, the danger of modeling can be too much teacher talk. Make sure students have frequent opportunities to do what you are modeling or they will tune out. Encourage risk taking, but always emphasize how important it is to build overall meaning of the text—and not to stray too far away from it. Students can get overly distracted from text meaning when they haphazardly construct inferences that are too disconnected from textual evidence.

Tools Chart for Inferring and Predicting

Table 13 shows the usefulness of this chapter's activities for various content areas. On the left side of the table, a ✓ in a column indicates that the activity is useful in that stage of reading. On the right side of the table, a ✓ in a column indicates that the activity is helpful for comprehension of common texts used in that content area. A ✓✓ on the right side of the table means that the activity is especially helpful for that type of text and that you should try it as soon as possible. Take the time, however, to look at all the activities and spend a few moments thinking about how you might use them in your teaching. I have been pleasantly surprised at the variety of creative ways in which teachers have adapted most of these activities and organizers to work in all content areas in all stages of reading.

Don't forget to apply the general teaching suggestions from chapter 2 to the activities in this chapter. When you find an interesting activity, refer to chapter 2 and ask how you can best integrate its instructional suggestions into the activity to meet your specific needs.

Table 13. When and Where to Use the Activities in Chapter 5						
Before Reading	During Reading	After Reading	Activity Name	Social Studies	Science	English/ EL
	✓	✓	Cause and Effect Timeline	✓✓	✓	✓
	✓	✓	Character Report Card	✓✓		✓✓
	✓		Cloze Connections	✓✓	✓✓	✓
	✓	✓	Dialogue Comic Strip	✓✓	✓✓	✓
	✓	✓	External-Internal Story Line	✓		✓✓
✓			Inference Advertisements	✓✓	✓	✓
✓	✓		Prediction Basketball	✓✓	✓	✓
✓	✓		Prediction Chart	✓		✓✓
	✓		Prediction Signals	✓	✓	✓✓
✓			Show and Not Tell	✓	✓✓	✓✓
✓	✓	✓	Sticky Symbols and Drawings	✓✓	✓	✓
	✓	✓	T+B=I Inference Machines	✓✓	✓	✓✓
	✓	✓	Text Transformation	✓	✓	✓✓

Activities for Inferring and Predicting

CAUSE AND EFFECT TIMELINE

The Cause and Effect Timeline can be used for narrative and expository texts. The graphic organizer asks students not only to determine the sequence of events in a story or historical account but also to establish or infer the causes of those events. Students can, if you so desire, be asked to draw lines to connect the events from the upper part of the graphic organizer to the causes in the lower part. You can use this activity for stories, novels, history texts, biographies, science observations, and more.

Procedure

1. Make a copy of the Cause and Effect Timeline reproducible on page 167. Cut out the two halves lengthwise, and fasten them together side by side to make one long timeline as follows:

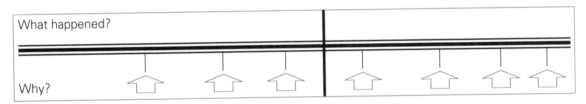

2. Above the thick line, write events with or without year dates. Each event should go above one of the lower arrows.

3. Put the causes of the events below the line, inside the arrows. Each cause should be directly under its corresponding event. Make sure you can support each cause with evidence. Causes can be inferred.

4. Draw additional lines, if applicable, to connect upper events to additional causes below; that is, some causes also will contribute to other events in addition to the ones written directly above them, or some events will, in turn, cause new events. Therefore, these new lines you draw will be diagonal. Students should be able to explain why they draw each additional line.

5. Connect more timeline halves, if necessary.

Variations

- Have students use the timeline to write a summary of a text that the timeline describes.
- Fill in an empty timeline to show students how to create a logical story or account using the timeline's event and cause categories. Explain how different events usually will have different paragraphs in the story.

• Have students take notes on the timeline about the sequence of events in a video or science experiment and then write a report on the experience.

CHARACTER REPORT CARD

This is an engaging activity in which students get to "grade" the characters in a book or history chapter on certain traits or qualities. The students must use evaluation thinking skills and must find evidence for their choices.

Procedure

1. Choose a story and decide which characters you would like to evaluate. Students can help you decide.

2. Brainstorm a list of up to four possible traits that the characters have to varying degrees. Traits can be positive or negative. (Have some traits in mind before generating a list with the students.)

3. List the character names on the left side of a sheet of paper and write the traits across the top, alternating with columns for grades, as shown:

Character	Courage Grade	Comments (Evidence)	Tenacity Grade	Comments (Evidence)
Jen	A	Because she faced up to Ron	B	She kept saving $
Octavio	B–	Lied about necklace	C	Quit school to work
Mirko	C	Let his brother…		

Following are some possible traits you may want to use:

Self-assured	Mischievous	Caring
Secretive	Creative	Naïve
Persevering	Patriotic	
Greedy	Patient	

4. Generate a grading system such as the classic A-B-C-D-F system; a system of points; designations of "Approaching Standard," "Meeting Standard," and "Exceeding Standard"; or some other system.

5. Show students how to start with the trait columns before entering the grades. Find evidence in the text for each character's traits and then discuss the grades with students. For example, you can model phrases such as, "I think she deserves an A in courage because she…."

6. Model for students how to respectfully disagree with another opinion and how to quote evidence. Instruct them to give more weight to evidence in the second half of the narrative than in the beginning, given that people change during stories.

7. Have students do this activity with partners or in groups.

CLOZE CONNECTIONS

This activity (adapted from Dewitz, Carr, & Patberg, 1987) is a simple way to show how we connect our background knowledge with text information to make an inference. We then continue to modify the inference based on new information in the text. This activity is especially helpful for building the habit of figuring out vocabulary in context, but it works well for inference, too.

Procedure

1. Find an appropriate text, preferably in electronic form so you can remove words with ease.

2. Find important words or phrases to take out. Look for a section that relates to each important phrase and replace these sections with lines that students can fill in. Tell students that it is not a test and that there are no wrong answers, strictly speaking. Tell them that the important thing to learn is to think about the sentence or paragraph and what makes the most sense in the blank. The inference process is what you want to see.

3. Create some sections that require students to write longer guesses (inferences) about what the author would have written in that spot.

4. Finally, have students underline the words and phrases (the text evidence) that helped them make their inferences.

5. Have students discuss their answers with other students and defend their inferences using the text and their own background knowledge.

DIALOGUE COMIC STRIP

This activity helps students to summarize and infer conversations that are important to the text. The Dialogue Comic Strip can be used with narrative or expository text. With expository text, the students must infer and empathize with the relationship between two objects, people, animals, or concepts and must generate a possible dialogue that shows that the students understand the key ideas in the text.

For example, in science class, a snake might say to a mouse, "I have adapted teeth that contain poison to kill you." The mouse replies, "I have adapted my ears to hear you slithering 10 feet away. Bye!" Or a geologist may say to a volcano, "Are you about to erupt?" It might reply, "No, I'm just venting a little steam." In social studies, a colonist may say, "King George, we really need to talk about this problem of taxation without representation. Our rights are...." In math, one side of an equation may say to the other, "If you get to be divided by 42, then my side gets to be divided by 42, too!"

Procedure

1. Model this process with several different texts if students have not done this activity often.

2. Give each student a copy of the Dialogue Comic Strip reproducible sheet from page 168. Tell students to modify or create three of the most important conversations from the text and fit them in the dialogue bubbles. Students should not copy any actual dialogue from the text. Encourage them to infer dialogues that might have happened, but point out that they should have evidence to support their inferred dialogues.

3. Have students put the speakers' names in the parentheses. They also can add quick drawings of the speakers, if desired.

4. Have the students write an explanation in each lower box for why each conversation was important. They should relate it to the main idea of the text.

5. Have students share their responses with a partner or group.

6. Share one or two student examples on the board or overhead projector.

Variation

Have students infer conversations that happened before or after the events of the text.

EXTERNAL-INTERNAL STORY LINE

This is a version of a story map (see chapter 3) with an inferential twist. Students need to infer a character's internal changes, thoughts, or feelings as the external events happen in a story. This shows an under-the-surface change in the story's characters and builds the habit of inferring character motives and actions from psychological factors.

Procedure

1. Model this procedure while reading aloud a simple text, or while reading aloud part of the text to be read by students.

2. Make a transparency from the External-Internal Story Line reproducible sheet on page 169 and place it on an overhead projector. Fill in the first event that happens in the story in box 1.

3. Think about and infer whether a character went through an internal change at that point.

4. Write the internal changes (e.g., personality, emotional growth, maturity, life lessons learned, etc.) in the ovals on the right, starting with oval 1.

5. Along with the actual changes in the ovals, write the evidence or reasons for the inner changes. Include how the external event might have affected the character's mental state.

6. When students do this activity on their own, have them share their answers with a partner or group. Then, have students share answers with the entire class, and work with them to create a whole-class diagram.

Variation

Inner-Outer Prediction Chart: This chart has emphasis placed on generating evidence for the predictions.

Character	Outer Predictions Events, Actions, Relationships	Why? (Evidence)	Inner Predictions Personality, Maturity, Learning, Emotions	Why? (Evidence)

INFERENCE ADVERTISEMENTS

This activity uses a series of magazine advertisements to show how their authors expect us to make inferences in order to influence us to buy their products. This activity grabs students' attention, because they see such advertisements on a daily basis and they do not like to be tricked into buying or doing anything. This activity is fun, motivating, and effective at garnering class participation. Remember to model the questions that generate the inferences, then to have students notice these questions. For example, ask, How does this saying influence potential buyers?

Procedure

1. Choose an advertisement to use with the class. Find a magazine with ads that use odd pictures and a clever line or two of text. Show only the clever saying from the advertisement on an overhead projector, without the picture. Ask students what they think it means.

2. Show the full advertisement with the picture and ask students its meaning.

3. Ask students what the reader has to know to understand the advertisement or to think it is clever.

4. Ask students why the advertisement's writers thought they could sell the product in this way.

5. Make a chart with space for a description of the picture, the saying, and the background knowledge that all feed into one space for the inference, as shown:

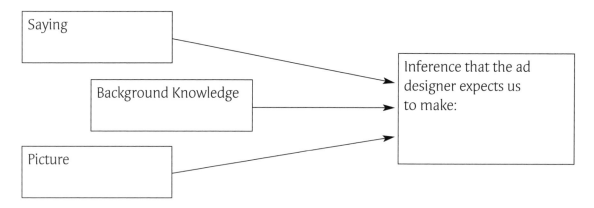

6. Ask students to bring in advertisements and have them be the teachers in the same activity.

Variations

• Show the picture with the text covered and ask students to guess what the advertisement is for and what the saying might be.

• Cover parts of the picture and unveil them, one part at a time, as students guess the advertisement's meaning.

• Bring in advertisements for the same type of product from different magazines and analyze how and why they are different.

PREDICTION BASKETBALL

This is a kinesthetic and cooperative activity that puts a little more fun into making predictions. It also can be used for other comprehension habits as a way of mixing up answers and creating random participation.

Procedure

1. Have students read a text and stop at a point you designate. Have each student write one major prediction on a half sheet of paper, along with his or her evidence for the prediction.

2. Put a makeshift basketball hoop (wastebasket, box, or coffee can) somewhere in the class. You can take it down and move it around to help students who are further away and to avoid having students get out of their seats.

3. Have students crumple up their predictions and try to throw them into the "basket."

4. Open and read the predictions that make it into the basket.

5. Have students randomly pick up the rest of the predictions that did not go into the basket, one prediction per student, and have each student read a prediction to a partner. Some students will not have one—they can just listen and ask for evidence or share a new prediction. Have the pairs discuss the quality of the predictions and the reasons each predictor had for his or her prediction.

PREDICTION CHART

This activity is helpful for training students to use good evidence for making predictions. It breaks down the process and shows students how prediction should naturally happen in the brain while reading. The Prediction Chart is most helpful for narratives, but I have seen science and social studies teachers use it successfully as well.

Procedure

1. Discuss with students why it is important to predict while reading. Create a list of reasons on the board. Discuss predictions about television shows, movies, and stories. Remind students that they are to be detectives who look for clues and put them together to solve a case (which will be understanding a story, in this instance).

2. Make a transparency from the reproducible Prediction Chart on page 170 (because you start with a movie, write *watch* or *look at* over the book icon to avoid confusion with the word *read*) and put it on an overhead projector. Start with the title of the movie and have students predict what the movie is about as you fill in the first box of the top row.

3. Ask students why they predicted what they did. Put the answers in the second box in the top row.

4. Now show the first five minutes of the movie or video. Stop it and ask students if any of the title predictions came true. If so, note them in the third column of the top row.

5. Have students help you fill in the second row by making new predictions in the first column and providing evidence in the second column.

6. Continue with another short portion of the video and then repeat the above steps to fill in the third row.

7. Optional: If you prefer to avoid photocopying, have students create their own three-column prediction charts on their own sheets of paper.

Variation

Picture Predictions: For this variation, cover a text or picture. In front of the class, uncover successive parts of the picture and have students generate hypotheses based on prior experience about what they think the picture is or what they think the text says *and why*.

Write the predictions on the left side of the Prediction Chart and students' reasons for the predictions in the second column. Have them notice how many of their reasons come from background knowledge. As the text is uncovered and predictions are shared, model the process of discarding (pruning) conflicting predictions by crossing them out on the Prediction Chart. Emphasize the process of creating new hypotheses based on new or revised background knowledge and schemata.

PREDICTION SIGNALS

Proficient readers have become accustomed over many years and pages to automatically recognize key signals in a text. These signals, some of which are in the left column in Table 14, are academic words and phrases that help the reader predict the content and type of text

Table 14. Prediction Signals	
If the Text Contains	**You Might Predict That You Will Find...**
A question	An answer
A subheading	Details that describe it
Therefore	A conclusion or outcome of previous text
For example Such as For instance In fact To illustrate this point	One or more examples that illustrate the main point of the paragraph or text
In other words That is Consists of Means	A definition or simpler explanation
However But Whereas On the other hand In contrast In comparison Yet	A difference or unexpected outcome
Just as Likewise Also Just like Similarly In the same way Moreover Furthermore	A continuation or comparison that shows similarities

coming up. They prepare the reader's brain to receive certain types of information that will help to form the main idea. The activity gives needed practice for readers in the recognition and use of text signals so that eventually their use becomes unconscious and automatic.

Procedure

1. Teach signal words to students during a minilesson or over the course of studying a long text that contains them.

2. Model how to make a quick note in the margin or on a sticky note when you encounter a signal word. Then, model how to make a prediction from what you read.

3. Have students practice making predictions and have them share their predictions with partners.

4. You may want to make a poster from Table 14.

5. Optional: For some of the signals, try creating hand gestures to use during read-alouds. (For example, for the word *however*, I move my arm to the left and then quickly reverse it to the right.)

SHOW AND NOT TELL

Show and Not Tell warms up the brain's "inference coals" and builds the habit of using clues to create meaning. It is a hands-on and kinesthetic way to hook students into the process of making logical inferences during reading by using evidence from the text and background knowledge.

Procedure

1. Bring unusual or unfamiliar objects into the classroom such as sporting gear, medical supplies, tools, machine parts, and so on.

2. Show each item, and have students think to themselves about what they infer that it does and why. Then, have students share their ideas in pairs and, finally, share as a whole class.

3. Use a two-column chart. Keep track of students' guesses on one side and their reasons for each guess on the other.

4. Add a clue, either verbal or visual, such as another item that goes with the one in question. For example, if the item is a golf ball washer, you might pull out a golf ball. Have students use the new clue to make another guess about the purpose of the item.

5. Tell the students what the object is and ask students to describe the process they used to narrow down their guesses (inferences).

STICKY SYMBOLS AND DRAWINGS

For this activity, students create symbols and drawings on sticky notes that become visual reminders of texts. Mental images help students to visualize text concepts and are more likely to remain in their long-term memories (based on work by Hyerle, 1996). Students must use inference to create symbols and to fill in parts of drawings not explicitly mentioned in the text. Even the initial process of creating symbols as a class or in small groups is very valuable.

Procedure

1. Explain concepts and ideas that might arise (e.g., character, metaphor, climax, compare and contrast, cause and effect) during comprehension of a difficult text. You may want to develop symbols for your class: For example, social studies classes may use symbols for greed, war, technology, art, religion, literature, disease, revolution, democracy, and lust for power.

2. Model how to create a symbol or drawing for a concept, and have students practice doing so in pairs. The symbols should not be too elaborate because they may be drawn many times.

3. Encourage students to identify ongoing concepts and themes in texts and to create corresponding symbols or drawings. Students can then draw symbols on sticky notes as they read a text.

4. You could even develop symbols for the comprehension habits in this book. When students catch themselves stopping to predict or summarize, they can quickly attach a sticky note with the corresponding symbol to the spot on the text. One suggestion is to predraw the symbols in order to avoid having students stop too long when reading a text.

5. Encourage students to develop their own symbols and drawings because ownership is nine tenths of an enduring skill. Each time students finish a whole story's worth of drawings, they can organize the sticky notes on sheets of paper and keep all the drawings in their notebooks.

T + B = I INFERENCE MACHINES

Inference machines are visual organizers that show what the brain is doing when it makes an inference. The brain looks at the text, thinks about how the text relates to something similar in the reader's background, then makes an assumption or guess that is connected to the main idea of the text in some way. The process is somewhat like an assembly line: The brain puts two things together—text information (T) and background knowledge (B)—to create a novel product of thinking—an inference (I). Hence, the title of the activity: T+B=I Inference Machines.

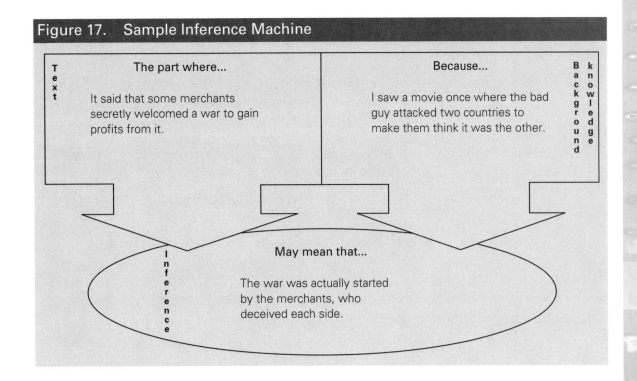

Figure 17. Sample Inference Machine

Text

The part where...

It said that some merchants secretly welcomed a war to gain profits from it.

Because...

I saw a movie once where the bad guy attacked two countries to make them think it was the other.

Background knowledge

Inference

May mean that...

The war was actually started by the merchants, who deceived each side.

Procedure

1. Begin by modeling this activity for students on an overhead projector. (See the reproducible form provided on page 171.) Pick an important part of the text and note it in the "text" box.

2. Although it seems logical (i.e., mathematical) to fill in the "background" box next, readers tend to generate the inference next. To create this inference, make a connection, conclusion, or educated guess about a result, prediction, or piece of the puzzle by thinking about the text. Think of causes and effects, author's purposes, clues provided by the author, and vocabulary with new or multiple meanings.

3. Think about the reason for your inference based on background knowledge, another part of the same text, something you have done or seen, or past or present issues in the world. Figure 17 shows a filled-in inference machine.

Variation

Venn Diagram: This activity is a simplified version of the T+B=I Inference Machines activity. It works because many students already are familiar with Venn diagrams. You simply "mix" text information with background knowledge to create the inference in the middle section of a Venn diagram, as shown here:

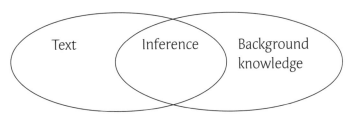

Text   Inference   Background knowledge

TEXT TRANSFORMATION

For this activity, students transform a text into a different genre. This requires a large amount of inference and comprehension of the important parts of the text. Examples include the following:

- Turning a textbook chapter into a newspaper article, poster, biography, interview, letter, narrative, poem, or news program (with accompanying video)
- Turning a narrative into a poem, letter, commercial, diary, play, song, comic book, or book jacket
- Turning a biography into a letter, interview, poem, short story, comic strip, or poster

You should eventually model how to transform a variety of texts. In the beginning of the year, however, you will probably concentrate on only a few types of transformations. Figure 18 offers two sample text transformations.

Procedure

1. Model the types of thinking skills that you want students to practice, such as cause and effect, fact and opinion, sequence, persuasion, and so on. Tell students that you want to see evidence of this thinking in their text transformations.

2. Emphasize that one must concentrate on the most important information in the text in order to carry over that information to a different text form. Tell students to think about what the author of the original text would want them to remember when creating a new version of his or her text.

3. If needed, you can use an intermediary scaffold, such as a graphic organizer for the main idea, to capture the elements needed for the new version of the text.

Figure 18.   Sample Text Transformations

Dear King George,

We are sick and tired of all your laws and rules. We do not have representation in your government and therefore we should not be taxed.

Some of the colonists have talked about revolution, but we simply want what is fair. Consider our request to have representatives with voting rights to hear our needs. If not, we don't know what will happen, but it might not be pretty.

Sincerely,
The colonists

Black Hole Chant

My name is Joe.
I live in a black hole.
The neighbors complain,
but I call it home.

We can't see straight,
we can't decorate.
Because gravity's so strong,
not even light escapes.

It's hard to see past the event horizon
and the sun got sucked in so it won't be risin.'

Generating and Answering Questions

* * *

A question is much more
motivating when it's your own.

Students are tired of answering questions. For years, they have sat in classes where a teacher or a text presents a long list of questions that they must answer promptly. Weeks of standardized tests, mostly composed of more questions, make matters worse. Students get praise or points for the right answers and sad looks or points off for the wrong answers. If boredom from these question sessions doesn't set in, frustration does. Rather than continue this stimulus-response game that covers standards on a cursory level at best, we need to let the students generate and answer their own questions to drive their learning. This gives students a more personal investment into what they will think about and what they will look for as they read.

Why is questioning on the part of the reader so important? Questions give us purpose for reading, and their answers help us actively shape the text's meaning (Ciardiello, 1998). Questions help us focus on the most important parts of text, and they help us to find the key information. Authors tend to write with several questions in mind that they intend to answer with their text. When we as readers ask similar questions, they will lead us to where the author wants us to go. The question-answer combination (in concert with inferences and predictions) is a set of "bearings" we take in order to find our position in a text, analogous to the use of stars for navigation by sailors. We hold a question in our minds, such as, How can I help students build the habit of questioning? (our question for this chapter), and this question becomes a post upon which we later attach the information in the text.

Our students already ask a myriad of questions about life. Why did she say that? What was the movie about? Who cares? How does this have anything to do with my life? What did you do last night? How can I make more friends? Where is my homework? How come I have to do this? Like the other comprehension habits, we need to shape and develop the questioning that students already do and transfer it into the arena of academic reading comprehension.

What are good questions? (That's a good question.) Good questions ask about connections between two parts of the same text, between the text and other texts or life experiences of the reader, and between the text and more general world events or situations. Good questions help a reader stay focused and moving toward the overall purpose of the text. Table 15 shows some good types of questions, with samples of each.

Table 15.   Asking Good Questions

We Need to Train Students to Ask About...	Sample Questions
The ways in which the text relates to real life	How does this compare to the 2003 war in Iraq? How could this affect the air in my community?
Character motives, ethics, symbolism, and metaphors	Why did she leave her family? Was that acceptable at that time? How can the river symbolize friendship?
Deeper concepts and more information than what the text offers (inferences)	I wonder why water floats in its solid state? What if it sank like most other precipitates? Why didn't they give up some land?
The text's main idea and theme	What is the author saying about animal adaptations? What was the gist of this story?
Varying perspectives	If I were the boy, what would I have done? I wonder what the enemy thought as he pulled the trigger?
Author's style, format, and purpose	I wonder why the author used first person? Why did the author use this strange dialogue? Why did she write this letter to the president?
Why certain parts were included or excluded by the author	Why did that character need to die at the end? Why is there an extra section on artificial diamonds in this chapter?
The meaning of key words and phrases	What does *numinous* mean? I wonder if *sidereal* means something to do with stars?
Cause and effect	Why did Napoleon start the war? How does a light bulb give off light? What were the long-term results of dropping the atom bombs in Japan?
Comparison and contrast	How is this novel similar to the last one? How is this president unlike the others?

Levels of Questions

The first thing that usually happens when we tell students to make up questions is that we hear a lot of poor questions. That is, students tend to avoid thinking about what they want to know, and they just blurt out the first thing that resembles a question. A good question helps the reader to understand the various layers of information that an author is trying to communicate to readers. Good questions come in three layers: On-the-surface questions, also known as "right there" questions, are the concrete and practical questions that help a reader keep track of explicit information. Under-the-surface questions, also called inferential questions, help a reader to understand implied or "read between the lines" information. They also require a reader to fill in needed concepts from background knowledge. Even deeper are the life application questions, sometimes called "text and me" questions, which help a reader connect the text to his or her own life or to the world. Good questions at all three levels do not occur spontaneously. Teachers need to model them on a daily basis in a variety of ways.

This book contains a reproducible poster of the different levels of questions that all readers should ask (see page 173). Feel free to copy, enlarge, and/or modify this poster and put it up for students to see and appreciate.

Good Questions for Before, During, and After Reading

Remember, reading comprehension is a three-stage process. Each stage includes questioning: We must ask good questions before we read to prepare us to find and store the information. During reading, we must ask questions to make sure we are sculpting the main idea and achieving the purpose we established for reading. After reading, we must ask questions to further organize what we have read and to fit it into the lesson we are learning. The following is a list of sample questions that facilitate comprehension in different stages of reading. Feel free to make your own list and to even create a poster for students to refer to daily.

Before

- Why am I reading this text?
- What do I already know about this topic?
- How can the text structure help me to read?
- What will this text be about?

During

- Is this text making sense?
- What just happened?
- What will happen next?
- Did I miss anything?
- What makes this text difficult to understand?
- How does _____ relate to _____?
- What does this _____ remind me of?
- What caused _____?
- What does _____ mean? Why do I think so?
- What would happen if _____?
- How does _____ affect _____?
- What information is important enough to remember as I read the rest of the text?
- What am I supposed to be learning by reading this text?
- Why is _____ important?

After

- So what?

- Did the reading end the way I predicted?

- What do I want to remember?

- How could I communicate what I read to someone else?

- Why did the author write this?

- In what ways is this text like anything else I have read?

- What was I supposed to learn by reading this text?

Tools Chart for Generating and Answering Questions

Table 16 shows the usefulness of this chapter's activities for various content areas. On the left side of the table, a ✓ in a column indicates that the activity is useful in that stage of reading. On the right side of the table, a ✓ in a column indicates that the activity is helpful for comprehension of common texts used in that content area. A ✓✓ on the right side of the table means that the activity is especially helpful for that type of text and that you should try it as soon as possible. Take the time, however, to look at all the activities and spend a few moments thinking about how you might use them in your teaching. I have been pleasantly surprised at the variety of creative ways in which teachers have adapted most of these activities and organizers to work in all content areas and in all stages of reading.

Don't forget to apply the general teaching suggestions from chapter 2 to the activities in this chapter. When you find an interesting activity, refer to chapter 2 and ask how you can best integrate its instructional suggestions into the activity to meet your specific needs.

Table 16.	When and Where to Use the Activities in Chapter 6					
Before Reading	During Reading	After Reading	Tool Name	Social Studies	Science	English/ EL
✓	✓	✓	Central Question Diagram	✓✓	✓	✓
		✓	Hot Seat	✓✓	✓	✓✓
✓	✓	✓	It Says, I Say, And So	✓✓	✓	✓
✓	✓		Question Starters	✓✓	✓	✓✓
		✓	Question the Author	✓✓	✓	✓✓
✓	✓		Question Think-Alouds	✓✓	✓✓	✓✓
✓	✓	✓	Question Tree and Sea	✓✓	✓✓	✓
✓	✓	✓	Socratic Sessions	✓✓	✓	✓✓
✓		✓	Vee Map	✓✓	✓	✓✓

Activities for Generating and Answering Questions

CENTRAL QUESTION DIAGRAM

This activity trains students to connect to evidence in their background knowledge in order to answer complex questions posed about a text. It teaches students to compare their opinions and reasons with those mentioned in the text. It also requires students to see both sides of an issue and to modify their background knowledge when necessary. This activity is based on work by Alvermann (1991) and Wiggins and McTighe (2000) on asking essential questions.

Procedure

1. Give each student a copy of the Central Question Diagram on page 172. Work with students to generate a central question from the text and have them write it in the center box. You might already have a central question in mind. Refer to your curriculum standards for the unit, if needed.

2. Before reading, have students individually generate their reasons for choosing "Yes" and/or their reasons for choosing "No" in response to the central question. (They can choose both, if they want.)

3. Optional: Have students discuss their reasons with a partner before reading the text.

4. Have students read the text, jotting down reasons for both positions on the appropriate sides of the diagram as they read.

5. Ask students to come to a conclusion and decide which answer is better, if either. Have them write their conclusions in the box at the bottom of the diagram.

6. Conduct a discussion on the conclusions and come to a consensus as a class. Emphasize the evidence used to support both sides of the issue.

HOT SEAT

The Hot Seat provides motivation to thoroughly understand a text, often by taking on different points of view. For example, when a student assumes the role of a character in a narrative or acts as a historical figure, the student can infer reasons for the character's actions by referring to evidence from the text or other sources.

Procedure

1. Model the process of assuming the role of the author, a historical figure, a scientific subject (e.g., raindrop, moon, molecule, octopus, tectonic plate, etc.), an expert on the text's subject, or a character from the text.

2. Give students sample questions or question starters on 3" x 5" cards to ask you. Sit in a specially designated seat at the front of the room (the hot seat). Say something such as, "I am Huck Finn. What would you like to know?" or "I am General Lee. Shoot your questions at me," or "I am a carbon molecule. Fire away," or "I am Steven Hawking. Any questions?" Let the students ask you questions, and answer them as the character you are playing.

3. Then, have students practice the activity themselves in pairs or in groups of four to six members. One student should assume the hot seat role and take the questions.

4. Other students ask questions about purpose, motivations, feelings, actions, or other content. They can use questions such as the following:

   - Why did you do this?
   - How did you feel about the other characters?
   - How did you change? Why?
   - What will you do now?
   - How did your invention change the world?
   - If you had..., how would the event or story have changed?
   - Why are you important for my life?

5. Play Whole-Class Hot Seat: Groups can nominate a student who did well in the small groups to go to the front of the classroom. Allow some time for students to prepare good questions. Optionally, you may want to chart questions into the three levels—on-the-surface, under-the-surface, and life application—and even evaluate the questions generated in terms of their helpfulness in understanding the text.

IT SAYS, I SAY, AND SO

This activity (adapted from Beers, 1998) helps students to look critically at the text and generate questions that call for inference and interpretation. The chart is useful for under-the-surface and life application questions.

It Says, I Say, And So provides a succinct method for building two habits at once: implicit questioning and inference. It shows students that it is OK—even helpful—to question a text and then guess the answers to those questions. Yet the activity also stresses the importance of basing one's questions and guessed answers on hard evidence found in the text. Also, the activity helps students to visualize connections (i.e., inferences) between the text and their own thinking processes. Finally, this is a simple activity that can be done many times across many different types of texts, both narrative and expository. If used enough, the process will become a key habit that will last throughout students' lives whenever they read.

Procedure

1. Give students some background on the topic to be studied and have them generate questions. Have students create a table on their own sheets of paper similar to the sample shown at the end of this activity; they should write their questions in the first column. (You also may put questions into this column in order to directly model certain types of questions.) Remember, asking good (implicit) questions requires *a lot* of modeling and scaffolding before students can do it on their own.

2. Optional: One helpful preparation activity is to brainstorm good questions and then choose the best ones. Then, go on to analyze *why* the best ones are good. See previous sections of this chapter for ideas on what makes a good question.

3. Have students look for text sections that could answer the question and copy them into the "It Says" column.

4. Have students use their inference skills to create their own interpretations of the text in the "I Say" column.

5. Have students use the first two columns as a foundation upon which they construct an answer in the "And So" column, as in this sample It Says, I Say, And So chart for a study of the ozone.

Question	It Says	I Say	And So
Why is the ozone layer depletion dangerous?	The layer prevents certain types of sunlight from reaching the planet's surface.	The more sun we get, the warmer it is, and ice may start to melt. Too much sun is also bad for skin.	If the ice melts, then the ocean level rises, and many places just above sea level may flood.

QUESTION STARTERS

Sometimes students need a little help to ask good questions. Starters such as the following give them some assistance in forming questions so that eventually they will not need help:

- Why did the man...?
- Who...?
- Why did they continue to...?
- If you had..., what would you have done?
- Should she have...? Why?
- Would you have...? Why?

- Why did the author include...?
- Why is the picture of...?
- What do you think happened after...?
- How might this chemical react with...?
- How would you solve this...?
- Why would you use a picture of...?

Procedure

1. Create the beginnings of questions (question stems) for the given text. Refer to the previous list for some ideas.

2. Have students use the question stems to create their own questions (they can work in pairs or individually). Emphasize that the students are to *act like teachers* and are to ask good questions that make us think (but that can be answered).

3. Have students first answer the questions verbally (if they are working in pairs) and then in writing. If they cannot answer a question, they should describe why they cannot answer it.

4. Have students read aloud their questions and answers to a partner and then to the class.

QUESTION THE AUTHOR

This activity (adapted from Beck et al., 1997) allows students to think about the techniques that authors use—or should use—to clearly communicate their ideas to readers. This type of critical reading empowers students to take a metacognitive look at texts and understand what makes them effective or not. When students realize that their lack of comprehension may in part be due to a poor quality of writing, they feel more empowered to analyze the text and pick it apart. A desired side effect, of course, is that they understand the text better when they must criticize and question it. This can, of course, ultimately translate not only into better comprehension but also into better writing and oral skills.

Procedure

1. Explain to students that some texts are not well written and that understanding what authors do and don't do can help comprehension. Point out that we can question the author's use of features and vocabulary, which gives us a better overall picture of text meaning.

2. Similar to a think-aloud, model the process of reading aloud and then asking a question directed to the author. For example, you may ask, Why would you include this paragraph in this text? Does it connect to a future part?

3. Model other questions to the imaginary author, such as the following:

- Why did you write this?
- What are you trying to tell me?
- Why are you telling me this?
- What's missing here?
- What do I have to know or figure out?
- How could you have stated this more clearly?
- What did you mean by this phrase?
- How does this connect with what you already wrote?
- Why did you use a _____ as the main character?
- Why did you use the analogy of a _____?
- What did you expect us to know already?

4. After showing students how to question the author about a variety of texts, have students practice the activity in pairs. Guide students and encourage them as they ask questions and use evidence from the text to support answers. One student plays the part of the author and the other asks the questions. Keep in mind that when students answer questions such as How can this be more clearly stated? they also will build essential summarizing habits.

5. Students can write down their questions (e.g., on sticky notes) if they think it will be helpful. Remind them that eventually they will be asking these questions automatically as they read.

QUESTION THINK-ALOUDS

Think-alouds can model for students the vital process of questioning that occurs during reading. You can verbalize questions that relate to the main idea, along with other types of questions that help guide you through the text.

Procedure

1. For a warm-up, use the Question Think-Aloud with atypical texts such as pictures, movies, songs, and math problems.

2. Preread the text you are going to model, and then fill in the ideas for good questions on a Think-Aloud Cheat Sheet such as the following sample (you can create one on a 3" × 5" index card).

Think-Aloud Cheat Sheet

Ask about the following:

Author's purpose	Vocabulary
Character motives and traits	Predictions
Literary devices	Connections to prior knowledge
Text structure	and the world
Pictures	

This will help show students the variety and quality of questions they should generate during reading. You can also have students create their own cheat sheets based on what you want to emphasize.

3. Read aloud the text with students. While reading aloud and pausing, make questions from titles, subtitles, and graphics within the text. Also do the following while reading aloud and modeling this activity:

- Think aloud the questions that we hardly ever notice that we formulate: Why is this here? Who was he? What's this word? What does the author mean by this?

- Think aloud when you find answers to your questions.

- Emphasize that the questions should relate to the text and should help us comprehend what the author is trying to say. (We could generate thousands of barely related questions that do not help comprehension at all.)

- Optional: During modeling, you can ask students to place the questions into on-the-surface, under-the-surface, or life application categories (see the Question Tree and Sea activity).

4. Have students practice thinking aloud in pairs. They also can start with a cheat sheet, if needed. Have partners write down a few of the best questions to share with the class later.

QUESTION TREE AND SEA

Good questioning is a vital habit for the comprehension of difficult material, and it can be especially powerful for English learners (Jimenez & Gamez, 1996). The Question Tree (see page 175) and Question Sea (see page 174) diagrams give students the scaffolding needed to develop the habit of asking explicit (on-the-surface) and, more importantly, implicit (under-the-surface and life application) questions. You can rename the question levels if you like. For example, some educators call them *right there*, *author and you*, and *on your own* questions (Helfeldt & Henk, 1990). Whatever names you give them, the Question Tree and Question Sea help you to show and model these various levels of questions. The Tree and Sea diagrams can be used with multiple types of images.

Procedure

1. Start with pictures, videos, pantomimes, and simple texts to generate questions, and use the Different Levels of Questions sheet from page 173 to brainstorm different questions.

2. Explain the different levels of questions and then have students help you place your questions in the correct levels of the Question Tree or Question Sea diagram. The goal is to have questions in all three categories that help you to better understand the text. For each question generated, have students think about whether the author would want his or her readers to ask that question or not.

3. Guide students through a written text and have them generate questions that relate to the text. Fill in questions where they belong on the diagram. Do this with both narrative and expository texts.

4. Remind students that under-the-surface and life application questions usually

- require extra thinking,
- have more than one answer,
- require more research,
- are not directly found in the text,
- involve opinions and educated guessing,
- refer to the author's message, and/or
- teach lessons about life, love, hope, meaning, truth, etc.

5. Have students share their best questions and discuss how such questions help with comprehension. Discuss what makes some questions relevant to the text and others not.

SOCRATIC SESSIONS

Let students know that Socrates—one of the greatest thinkers of all time—spent most of his time asking questions. In Socratic Sessions (adapted from Moeller & Moeller, 2002), students have the chance to discuss important questions inspired by the text. They also have a chance to "socratize" (i.e., keep asking deeper and deeper questions).

Procedure

1. Generate an initial implicit (under-the-surface) question that relates to the purpose of the text. The question often will contain some type of opinion, interpretation, or controversy.

2. Model how to ask further questions that bring up important points and counterpoints. That is, model how to dig deeper into the issues. For example, on the topic of drug legalization, deeper questions may be, Why do people want to legalize drugs? What does *addiction* really mean? Why do people use drugs?

3. Remind students that they may be accustomed to having teachers come up with these deeper questions most of the time, but now it is their turn. With enough practice, students' reading and thinking will improve drastically. Let students practice being Socrates—who, by the way, drove people crazy with his many radical questions.

4. Encourage students to engage in the following appropriate behaviors for discussion:

- Using the text to defend your position
- Listening well to others before responding to them
- Seeing multiple sides of an issue
- Using phrases such as "I agree with...and would like to add...," "I disagree with ...because...," or "Could you clarify the point about...?"

- Paraphrasing other students' responses (e.g., "So you are essentially saying that...," "So your point is....")

5. Have students summarize the session orally or in writing. If they are new to the summarizing process, you will need to model creating the summary, which includes the following:

- Thoughts about the initial question
- The influence of additional questions
- The comments of others
- What the text had to say or not say
- A final conclusion and how it may have changed over time

VEE MAP

A Vee Map (Roth & Verechaka, 1993) is a visual way to emphasize a key question in a text. The shape of the map shows that the question should be a below-the-surface or life application question that is central to the text (and to curriculum standards). This activity also has the advantage of incorporating prereading and summary components.

Procedure

1. Have students brainstorm about a topic (e.g., the Vietnam War).

2. Create a graphic that organizes the brainstormed information (Venn diagram, semantic web, etc.).

3. Create a Vee Map such as the one shown here.

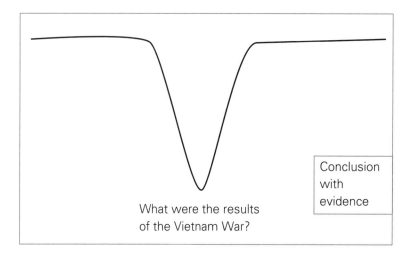

Each student can use his or her own paper to create individual maps, and/or you can create a class map on a large piece of poster paper. Put the notes from step 2 on the left side of the V.

4. Have students generate possible "big" questions about the topic. Choose one question you will emphasize and write it at the bottom of the V.

5. Have students read the text and take notes on the right side of the V on their own papers.

6. In the lower right corner, have students fill in the conclusion or answer and the supporting evidence from the text.

7. On the back of their papers, students can explain why this question is an important one. They can add any other questions that they deem important and explain why.

Understanding and Remembering
Word Meanings

* * *

The dictionary never seems

to get it right.

Many teachers consider a lack of vocabulary knowledge to be the primary reason for students' poor comprehension, especially in science and social studies classes. These teachers then proceed to look for ways to stuff students' brains with as many word meanings as possible. Unfortunately, a large number of vocabulary-teaching methods are limited to either the infamous "look-it-up, use-it-in-a-sentence, take-a-quiz-on-Friday" strategy or the "just-read-it" strategy. Rather than stuff students with word meanings, we need to teach students to teach themselves about words and their meanings. That is, we must train students to be constructivist detectives of meaning. They need to be able to quickly and automatically notice the clues inside and outside the new words they encounter. By the way, excluding the section on word parts, the theory and practice in this chapter is also applicable to groups of words such as phrases, sentences, and even paragraphs.

Teaching word meanings, especially before reading, has been found to be effective for word learning and text comprehension (Marzano et al., 2001). However, because the purpose of this book is to develop habits of comprehension, this chapter emphasizes ideas for developing the habit of figuring out words and using them to construct meaning. For those teachers who also want some guidelines for good instruction of vocabulary words, I do provide a "quality control" checklist to help you assess whether your arsenal of vocabulary teaching techniques aligns with the research on best practices.

Vocabulary instruction does not mean having students memorize a list of words and their definitions. This practice often is associated with extensive dictionary time and the creation of random sentences that contain the new words. Research shows that this method is not effective enough to warrant the time used for it (Nagy, 1988). Then again, just plain independent reading also is not sufficient for our below-grade-level readers. These students have not acquired the ability to figure out word meanings, hypothesize their meanings, retain them, and use them to understand complex texts, particularly science and social studies textbooks. We must not forget that students, on the average, acquire around 3,000 words per year in grades 4–12 (Nagy, 1988). That would be about 100–150 words per week—that's one long vocabulary quiz. Where do most of the 3,000 words come from? From the automatic habit of using context and word parts.

Therefore, the activities in this chapter are included to help you support and scaffold the development of these word meaning "subhabits": (a) using semantic and syntactic context clues; and (b) using the meanings of common roots, prefixes, suffixes, and similar words.

Using Context: Scoping Out the Word Neighborhood

Most of what we have learned has not been explicitly taught to us. We have observed, inferred, and built our background knowledge to form patterns of the way the world works. For this reason, all the cues that we recognize from past experience become clues that we use to create meaning in the present. These current clues trigger our background knowledge (i.e., schemata) to tell us the meaning that was associated with similar clues in the past. Then, we make an educated guess about the current meaning(s) of the clues.

We do this with words all the time: We use context clues to help us to create and sculpt meanings of unknown or multiple-meaning words (Allen, 1999). In a sense, we "scope out the neighborhood" around the word (or phrase) to guess the meaning that fits the best in those surroundings. For example, you probably automatically used context to extend the meaning of *sculpt* in the first sentence of this paragraph. You did not even begin to think that I was referring to the more common meaning, "to form a piece of art out of clay or marble." We start with the common or concrete and then extend and guess, depending on the context of the sentence or paragraph. Upon reading a recent article on drinking alcohol, a student once described to me how she used context clues help her figure out the meaning of the word *deleterious* when she saw it in front of the word *effects*. Her background knowledge told her that the effects of drinking alcohol (liver damage, nausea, etc.) were bad, and, therefore, she guessed that the word meant *harmful* or *negative*. Most of the words we know came from context—not just one or two experiences, but perhaps 7, 10, even 50 or more. Each exposure to a word provides further conscious and unconscious clues that help us to better sculpt or solidify its meaning.

Yet even before we expend energy on the figuring-out process, we need to judge whether the unknown words we encounter are important or not. Some less-important words may actually take up too much brain time and should be skipped. Be careful with expository texts, however, as many of their unknown words tend to be the most important for overall meaning and, therefore, should not be skipped. A simple way to check is to notice if the meaning of more than one paragraph hinges on the meaning of an unknown word. If so, we need to take the time to figure out the word.

Using Context Clues With Text Signals

We can point out the following context clues and have students watch for them. These are usually clues that the author purposely gives to help the reader.

- **Explanation or definition:** The author explains or defines the word in the same sentence in which it is introduced. Following are some signal words and punctuation for this type of clue and some sample sentences in which they are used.

Signal Words and Punctuation	Sample Sentences
is, are, has	A proton is a positively charged particle in the nucleus of an atom.
	Carnivores are animals and plants that eat meat.
	A person who is afraid of crowds has agoraphobia.
means	A democracy means that the government is formed by all the people.
defined as	The denouement is defined as the climax of a story.

- **Synonym or restatement:** The author uses more familiar terms to explain the new word. Following are some signal words and punctuation for this type of clue and some sample sentences in which they are used.

Signal Words and Punctuation	Sample Sentences
likewise	Jan looked at him with disdain. Likewise, he despised her.
especially	The war decimated the population. The South was especially short on labor in the years that followed.
or	The antediluvian, or ancient, carvings told us nothing.
in that	She was adroit at her job in that she could finish it in half the time of her coworkers.
similarly	Peregrine falcons migrate from pole to pole each year. Similarly, humpback whales make a long journey south each winter to breed.
in other words	His aphasia did not hinder him. In other words, his inability to speak didn't keep him from effectively communicating.
that is	His simple glance was a harbinger of danger. That is, his eyes were signs foretelling rough waters in their relationship.
a phrase set apart between commas	She used a metronome, a small machine that ticked out the timing of the music, as she practiced her violin.

- **Antonym or contrast:** The author offers the opposite meaning of the unknown word. Following are some signal words for antonym clues and some sample sentences in which they are used.

Signal Words	Sample Sentences
Some..., but others....	Some believed that the man was altruistic until the end, but others say that he gave only for selfish reasons.
On the other hand	She was audacious. On the other hand, he was timid and meek.
not	Francine was not blithe at all. She was sad and serious.
despite	Now they were confident, despite their usual diffidence.
although	He acts as if he agrees with the government, although I know about his iconoclastic beliefs.
yet	Its power seemed immutable, yet one day, it ended.
but	The gray kitten was lethargic in the morning, but at night he was quite lively and awake.
by contrast	She was quite efficacious in her job. By contrast, her brother wasn't able to do his work.
then again	Some liked his laconic speeches. Then again, others preferred longer and more detailed orations.
and then	We were getting along fine, and then we had our first altercation.

- **Cause and effect:** With a cause-and-effect clue, we automatically attempt to make the connections shown below. This process helps us guess word meanings.

Cause	Effect	Sample Sentences
Phrase or sentence with unknown word	Phrase or sentence with known words	The horse was so *fatigued* that he collapsed before he finished.
		Given the *paucity* of resources, the people were forced to move on.
Phrase or sentence with known words	Phrase or sentence with unknown word	The existence of a rattler in the Alaskan woods presented quite a *conundrum*.
		The drought lasted many years. Never had the land been so *desiccated*.

We predict the word's meaning as we think about how the causes relate to the effects, and then we read on to see if the prediction is confirmed. Some signal words from this clue type are as follows.

Signal Words	Sample Sentences
therefore	It occluded my vision; therefore, I crashed.
for this reason	She was a neophyte. For this reason, she had much to learn.
in this way	The shell was petrified. In this way, it was preserved in stone for millions of years.
consequently	They were a bellicose race. Consequently, their wars with neighboring nations depleted their resources.
given	Given the paucity of resources, she couldn't find enough information for her report.
resulting in	He had a proclivity for getting into trouble, resulting in frequent detentions.
such that	The insects were rapacious such that nothing in their path was left uneaten.
this is due to	He has a saturnine outlook on life. This is due to the death of his friend.

- **Examples of the word:** Some signal words for this type of clue are as follows.

Signal Words	Sample Sentences
such as	Many animals have mottled coats, such as the leopard, the ocelot, and the giraffe.
for example	He often was tenacious. For example, one time he climbed a mountain in a brutal storm, even after losing his food.
for instance	Some animals are omnivores. Bears, for instance, eat whatever meat or plants they can find.
once	He was zealous. Once, he sat on the courthouse steps for a week to get the city to change a law.
in one case	Many are xenophobes. In one case, a woman avoided people for two years.
one time	His loquacious speeches were famous. One time, he talked for three hours.

Using Context Without Signals

Semantic Context. The preceding section presented ways in which the author provides some extra contextual support in the text by using signal words or punctuation. But we also must be able to figure out a word that is not so obviously supported. In these cases, the reader must think beyond the sentence in which the word appears and use the bigger semantic picture to figure out the word's meaning. This process, according to many teachers, is a big challenge for their below-grade-level readers. It requires extra thinking (storing the word's possible meanings in the brain) because the clues are not as obvious or "local." The clues may be found several paragraphs or even many pages away. Consider the following example:

> He was quite *prolific* in his later years. During this time, he painted scenes from his hometown and neighboring villages. He painted streets, bridges, haystacks, cathedrals, and houses. He believed that almost every scene deserved to be put onto canvas. For this reason, he created so many paintings that his apartment could no longer hold them. He began to sell them for several dollars apiece. Now, long after his death, each painting is worth even less.

After reading the whole paragraph and looking for clues for the word *prolific*, such as "his many works of art," a reader might finally guess the meaning as "making many." (The reader may also associate the *pro-* in *prolific* with similar words: *produce, procure, proceed,* etc.) Then again, the reader may think *prolific* has another meaning, such as *poor* or *senile*. The reader would need to hold this "probable meaning" in the brain somewhere and recall it the next time the word *prolific* was seen in context, at which time he or she would compare it to the new context and then confirm or change it.

Pictorial Context. You might be surprised to know how many students do not even look at the pictures in the texts they read. Even fewer take the time to think about how the pictures support the text and its unknown words. This is unfortunate because sometimes the entire purpose of a picture is to explain a key word or concept. With think-aloud activities, you can show how important it is to consider the pictures and how they help us comprehend new words and concepts (Farr, 2001). Remind students that "a picture is worth a thousand words."

Syntactic Context. Syntactic context means using the location of the word in a sentence to figure out its grammar role, which then helps us figure out its meaning. If we know the unknown word is a noun, verb, adjective, or adverb, we can (a) get a better idea of what is missing or what we need to figure out (e.g., "I know this is an action"), and (b) decide if figuring out the word is important or not. Verbs and nouns tend to be more important than adjectives and adverbs in most texts.

Multiple Meanings Rule!

Most words have more meanings than we realize. I once heard someone estimate that 70% of the most commonly used words in English have more than one meaning. Yet we often do not realize this because we use context so quickly and automatically that the alternative meanings do not even pass through our minds. I realized this one day when an English learner said to me, "But I thought the word *cool* meant cold." I answered, "Hmmm, you're right, but in this context it means unexcited or unemotional." Even this definition differs somewhat from a third definition of being likeable and popular. Another example of multiple meanings is the word *revolution*:

- The people took up arms and started a revolution. (war and violence)
- The wheel made 54 revolutions before stopping. (physical turns)
- A revolution was happening inside of him. (inner change - psychological)
- His ideas revolutionized the film industry. (change in the way things are done)

I first thought of a revolution only as a military overthrow of a government. Gradually, as I saw the word in new contexts, I created more meanings based on my original definition (thereby building words upon words, year after year). I gradually built up a flexible meaning into something similar to "a radical and significant change" to make *revolution* fit each text's situation. This is what we do as we learn new words and new meanings for familiar words.

There are two steps for using context to figure out multiple meanings. For example, here are the two steps for the sentence "His *amorphous* lectures left her with many questions."

1. I first notice whether I already know at least one meaning of the target word (in this case, *amorphous*). My one known (concrete) meaning for the word is "without physical shape or form," such as what a cloud of mist might be.

2. I start from this known meaning and try to connect it with how it is used in the current text I am reading. In this case, my concrete meaning does not work. I must add an additional, more abstract meaning for the word so that it makes sense in this text. Therefore, I extend my original definition to mean "poorly formed" or "not clear."

This extension from a single meaning to multiple meanings, from the concrete to the abstract, and from the literal to the figurative presents one of the most challenging habits students must develop. It also is one of the most empowering for academic success. Therefore, we must help readers develop the habit of using their existing knowledge of a word and extending it to fit into the present context (Stahl, 1999). For example, consider the sentence "The first astronauts blazed the way to new frontiers in space." *Blaze* to a student may just mean "a fire." The reader needs to have the habit of thinking about the common qualities of *blaze* and relating them to what the text is trying to say. The reader might think, "Perhaps *blaze* has to do with using fire to clear away the land and make it easier to do something with it. So maybe it means that astronauts made the way easier for future travelers." In future texts, that reader may see the word *blaze* in similar contexts, such as "blazing a trail," and further confirm this guess.

To teach the habit of acquiring multiple meanings, you should model the process often for your students with think-alouds. That is, describe how you connect words to previous knowledge and how you then tweak your existing definitions to make a logical prediction for this new context. Verbalize how you visualize word meanings and connect certain features, or submeanings, to make the new meaning fit with the sentence. While reading aloud, pause at times to let students think about a word and its meaning. Then give students various levels of scaffolded practice in paired think-alouds that emphasize vocabulary. (Many practice activities are included in this chapter; see Appendix A for a starter list of multiple meaning words.)

Use the following types of tools for teaching students about multiple meanings:

- vocabulary graphic organizers, such as charts, that sort and define the variations of a word or term
- brainstorms that generate long lists of related words
- pictures, diagrams, and drawings that explain and show the meanings of difficult words

Word Surgery: Using Word Parts and Similar Words

Context (especially when used only one or two times) is not always enough to help us figure out a word. If we also employ the meanings of word parts and similar words, we can get even closer to the meaning the author intends. For example, if I have no clue of the meaning of *amorphous* from context, I might examine the prefix *a-* (which I know means "not") with the root *morph-*, which I know means "shape," to get a meaning such as "without shape or form; hard to grasp." Using knowledge of word parts, because it can be applied to many words, is an important subhabit of figuring out word meanings (Allen, 1999). We should teach students how to remember and use prefixes, suffixes, and root words in order to figure out unfamiliar words. (See Appendix B for common prefixes, suffixes, and roots.) This can become a habit that extends to other classes and texts for life. One way to model the use of word parts is by thinking aloud (see RATA activity in chapter 8) when you reach an unknown word. Stop and "cut up" the unknown word on the board, then compare the parts to known words. Students help to predict what the word means.

Similar Words and Cognates

Using similar words and cognates from other languages is another important vocabulary skill. Similar words often have similar word parts with similar meanings. For example, if a reader sees the word *antediluvian*, he or she may relate it to *antechamber* and *dilute* or *deluge*. This could lead to a rough guess of "before a flood," and in context would probably lead to the meaning of "ancient."

For English learners, depending on what their native language is, many "big" content words look similar to a word in their native language and often mean the same thing. These are called cognates. Students should be taught to watch for these similarities as they read. They also should hear the word pronounced in English because it may sound very different from how it is pronounced in the native tongue. Examples from Spanish include *revolución*, *popular*, *diligente*, *pronunciar*, and *actividad*.

Mores and Lesses of Vocabulary Instruction

Following are some general guidelines for teaching students how to build vocabulary. The lists are provided to remind you of the best practices and best uses of time for teaching vocabulary. Some mores and lesses might surprise you because they have been used for a long time in traditional instruction and assessment. Review each list and consider if and how much the mores and lesses fit your vocabulary instruction.

Do More

+ Use varied and interesting texts.

+ Teach vocabulary in the context of real reading.

+ Model vocabulary strategies all the way through grade 12.

+ Connect vocabulary to core concepts and related words.

+ Increase opportunities for students to use new words in and out of class.

+ Create opportunities for students to make inferences about words and talk about them.

+ Teach common prefixes, suffixes, and roots.

+ Provide minilessons on how to extend meanings of words from concrete to abstract.

+ Connect new words to students' background knowledge.

+ Provide narrative and expository reading options that relate to the curriculum and match the reading levels of the students.

+ Provide multimodal/multiple intelligences approaches for understanding and remembering words (drawings, symbols, movement, music, cooperation).

+ Provide time for a lot of reading.

Do Less

– Teach isolated vocabulary out of context.

– Use word lists that are unconnected to a text.

– Encourage rote memorization of definitions.

– Teach students to rely solely on context—or solely on decoding—to figure out words.

– Teach that all words must be figured out to understand a text.

– Encourage looking up definitions as the primary way of figuring out word meanings.

– Use vocabulary assessments that are not connected to real reading.

– Ask students to write original sentences using new words and concepts that they are just beginning to learn.

Tools Chart for Understanding and Remembering Word Meanings

Table 17 shows the usefulness of this chapter's activities for various content areas. On the left side of the table, a ✓ in a column indicates that the activity is useful in that stage of reading. On the right side of the table, a ✓ in a column indicates that the activity is helpful for comprehension of common texts used in that content area. A ✓✓ on the right side of the table means that the activity is especially helpful for that type of text and that you should try it as soon as possible. Take the time, however, to look at all the activities and spend a few moments thinking about how you might use them in your teaching. I have been pleasantly surprised at the variety of creative ways in which teachers have adapted most of these activities and organizers to work in all content areas and in all stages of reading.

Don't forget to apply the general teaching suggestions from chapter 2 to the activities in this chapter. When you find an interesting activity, refer to chapter 2 and ask how you can best integrate its instructional suggestions into the activity to meet your specific needs.

Table 17.			When and Where to Use the Activities in Chapter 7			
Before Reading	During Reading	After Reading	Activity	Social Studies	Science	English/ EL
✓	✓	✓	Connect the Words	✓✓	✓✓	✓
✓	✓	✓	Go Beyond the Verbal	✓✓	✓✓	✓
✓	✓		Guess and Adjust	✓✓	✓	✓
✓	✓	✓	Keywords Web	✓✓	✓✓	✓
	✓	✓	LitFigs	✓	✓	✓
	✓	✓	Multiple Meanings Table	✓✓	✓✓	✓
	✓		New Words in Context Chart	✓✓	✓✓	✓
	✓		RATA (Read-Aloud Think-Aloud) Word Clues	✓✓	✓✓	✓✓
	✓		Read a Lot	✓✓	✓✓	✓✓
	✓		SCUBA Diving Into Word Meaning	✓✓	✓	✓
	✓	✓	Self-Selected Vocab Quizzes	✓✓	✓	✓✓
✓	✓	✓	Target Words	✓✓	✓✓	✓
	✓	✓	Vocabulary Bank Notes	✓✓	✓✓	✓
	✓	✓	Word Bank	✓✓	✓✓	✓✓
		✓	Word Remembering	✓	✓	✓

Activities for Understanding and Remembering Word Meanings

Please note that the activities in this chapter were chosen for the following reasons: They do not spend large amounts of class time on just one word; they emphasize the use of context and word parts during reading of content texts; they require minimal dictionary use; and they challenge students to think about, process, and remember words in the construction of meaning.

CONNECT THE WORDS

This activity encourages students to see connections and relations between important vocabulary items. It becomes a visual way to make connections and remember the words—even after the test.

Procedure

1. Use the Connect the Words reproducible on page 176. Make a transparency of it to use for modeling this activity with the students. Identify the most important theme, word, or phrase in a lesson or section of text, and write it in the central diamond.

2. Find two or three other important words (or have the students find them, if you feel they are ready for this) and write them in the ovals at the outer corners of the sheet.

3. Think aloud (model) and describe the connections between the words in the ovals and the word in the center diamond. These connections should be written in the rectangles.

4. Have students work in pairs to generate one or two other important words to fill the remaining empty ovals. (Students can supply more words if you want to add ovals to the graphic.) Have students also fill in the remaining connection boxes. (See Figure 19 for a filled-in sample.) Pairs can ask one another, "How does this word relate to that word?"

5. Have pairs of students share their connections with one another.

6. Information from the boxes can later be used in writing compositions.

GO BEYOND THE VERBAL

Do everything possible to help students go beyond the written or verbalized definitions of difficult terms. Use examples, diagrams, visuals, pantomime, games, mnemonics, and so on. For many learners, the visual or kinesthetic image of the word will stick much better than the written or verbal explanations (Marzano et al., 2001).

Figure 19.   Sample Connect the Words Activity

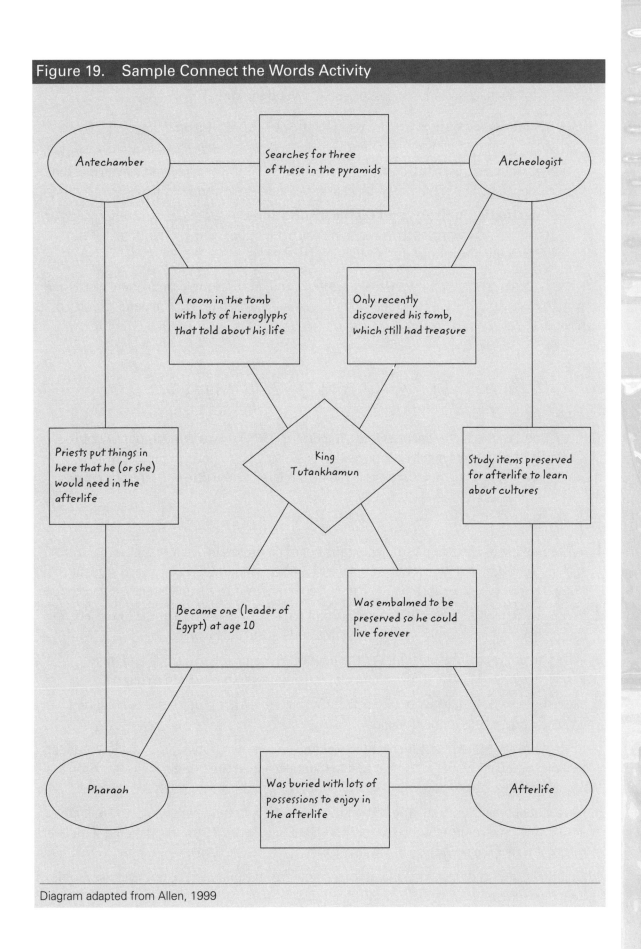

Diagram adapted from Allen, 1999

Procedure

1. Use the following association types for going beyond the verbal:

- **Visual associations:** Ways to associate the new word with an image (e.g., pictures, video, graphic organizers, real items).
- **Symbolic representations:** Representations of new words created by you *and* the students, such as semantic webs, charts, Venn diagrams, and so on.
- **Kinesthetic, auditory, and tactile associations:** Ways to do, experience, hear, or touch the new word, such as watching you act it out or acting it out themselves, performing music or chants, or handling real items.

2. Have students create their own visuals, symbols, and gestures for learning new words and word parts as another way to go beyond the verbal. They can practice in pairs, groups, or in front of the class.

GUESS AND ADJUST

This quick and easy activity (adapted from Poindexter, 1994) serves three important purposes: (1) building background knowledge for reading, (2) using word parts to predict word meaning, and (3) figuring out words using context related to the title and author's purpose.

Procedure

1. Write the title of a text to be studied on the board or, preferably, in a graphic organizer such as the Guest and Adjust form on page 177. Also, hand out a copy to each student to fill out while you fill out your copy. You can make your copy into a transparency, if you choose.

2. Write any other clue words that are important to the text in the oval at the lower left. You should have approximately 3 to 5 new words and 6 to 10 clue words.

3. Have students guess the meanings of the new words using the text's title and their knowledge of word parts. They should write their guesses in the middle column.

4. Have students do a Quickwrite (see activity in chapter 4) that predicts the text content; write the predictions in the triangle.

5. Read aloud the text while students follow along in their own books. Stop to allow students to look at the new words in context and to mentally adjust their original guesses. Stop at a point where you think students have had enough text to compare it to their sheets.

6. Have students finish reading the text on their own, and then fill in the adjusted meanings in the righthand column of the graphic organizer. See Figure 20 for a completed sample of the organizer. (The prediction is a little off.)

7. Optional: Have students write a final three-sentence summary of the text that uses some of the new words.

Figure 20.   Sample Guess and Adjust Activity

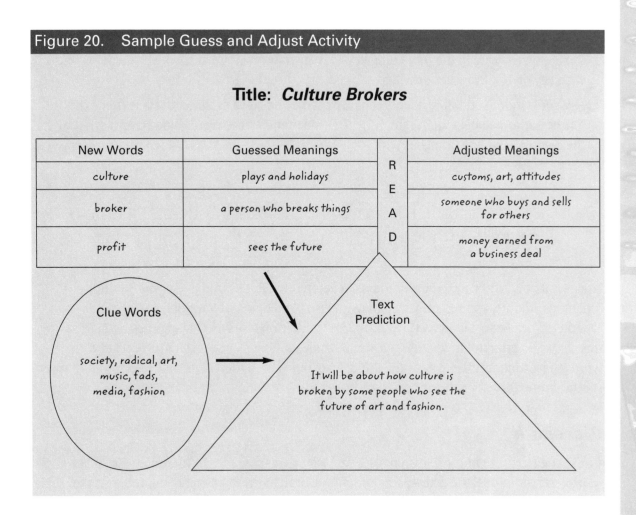

Title: *Culture Brokers*

New Words	Guessed Meanings	R E A D	Adjusted Meanings
culture	plays and holidays		customs, art, attitudes
broker	a person who breaks things		someone who buys and sells for others
profit	sees the future		money earned from a business deal

Clue Words

society, radical, art, music, fads, media, fashion

Text Prediction

It will be about how culture is broken by some people who see the future of art and fashion.

KEYWORDS WEB

We make many connections when we figure out and store word meanings. Similar to creating files on a computer, we create "files" in the brain, in which we store related words that somehow connect to the file name or category. This vocabulary web is a simple yet powerful way to develop the habit of creating connections between new words and the concepts that need to be learned.

Procedure

1. Use the Keywords Web reproducible on page 178. Write a central theme or concept in the center oval. Give a photocopy of the web to each student and make a transparency of it as well.

2. Place the web on an overhead projector and fill in two or three of the keys with important words to emphasize in the lesson or text the students are working on.

3. Have students copy the words onto their own papers and pick one or two more words from the lesson to write in the remaining keys. Have students write descriptive words around each key on the branches provided.

4. As a multimodal option, students can put a symbol next to each word. Have them choose symbols that will help them remember the meanings of the words, and have them draw their symbols on the branches with each word.

LITFIGS (LITERAL AND FIGURATIVE COLUMNS)

LitFigs is a powerful way to help students develop the habit of thinking about multiple meanings, idioms, and figurative language such as analogies, metaphors, and symbols (adapted from Bean, Singer, & Cowan, 1985). In addition to its use in language arts classes, this activity is effective in science and social studies classes. These classes have texts with words that students often know at a literal level but whose meanings they need to learn in the special contexts of science and social studies.

Procedure

1. Use the LitFigs reproducible on page 179. Make a transparency to use on an overhead projector to model the activity for students at first. In the right-hand column, put the unknown word or expression from the text. This word may be figurative, such as an idiom, symbol, or metaphor, or it may be an additional meaning of a known word (e.g., a mouse for a computer).

2. In the left column, write down what the word is actually describing in the text.

3. In the middle arrow, write an explanation of the word's meaning. Write down how the two meanings are similar, what the author was trying to emphasize, or why you think the author used this particular word (or why people, in general, use it). Figure 21 shows a sample form filled in.

4. Have students notice whether any language in the middle or left columns "came up figurative." That is, did the literal explanation also contain figurative terms? If so, place those terms in the right column and keep filling in the rows. For example, in Figure 21 the word *trapped* was used in the literal column. It was then put in the next figurative row and the word *escape* could even be put below it.

5. You may scaffold the activity by filling in certain boxes or columns beforehand and creating handouts from that, then letting the students fill in the rest.

6. Students can build up a large set of LitFigs throughout the year. Instead of the box-and-arrow graphic, you could have students use a simple grid with three columns that they can easily draw in their notebooks. Keep a large LitFigs chart on the wall, if desired.

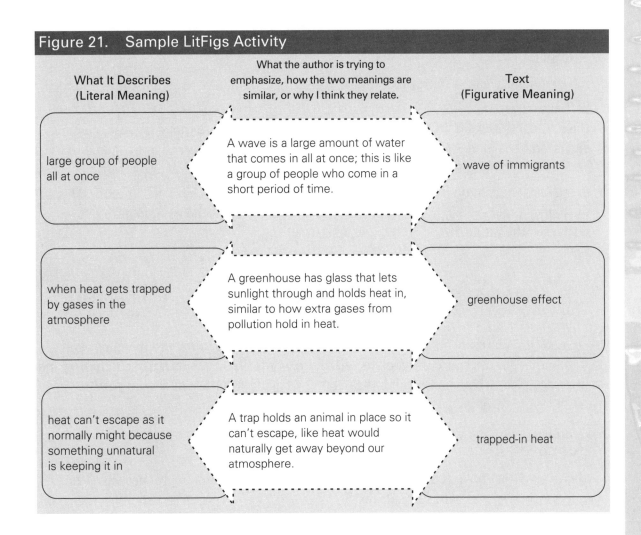

Figure 21.   Sample LitFigs Activity

What It Describes (Literal Meaning)	What the author is trying to emphasize, how the two meanings are similar, or why I think they relate.	Text (Figurative Meaning)
large group of people all at once	A wave is a large amount of water that comes in all at once; this is like a group of people who come in a short period of time.	wave of immigrants
when heat gets trapped by gases in the atmosphere	A greenhouse has glass that lets sunlight through and holds heat in, similar to how extra gases from pollution hold in heat.	greenhouse effect
heat can't escape as it normally might because something unnatural is keeping it in	A trap holds an animal in place so it can't escape, like heat would naturally get away beyond our atmosphere.	trapped-in heat

MULTIPLE MEANINGS TABLE

This is a quick activity that can benefit students who need to develop the habit of understanding multiple meanings and using word parts. Remind students that people often use one word for several different purposes. There usually is a reason that we use a particular word. For example, we say *mouse* for the computer accessory rather than *dog*, because the item looks like a mouse. This activity also can be done with the help of a dictionary, using it to provide extra meanings in the meaning boxes.

Procedure

1. Provide students with several important multiple-meaning words to discuss and look up, some of which may only have two meanings. Give each student a copy of the Multiple Meanings Table from page 180 (you can model the activity with a transparency of it), and have students write a multiple-meaning word in the first space in the left column.

125

2. Have students notice the parts of the word and write the parts and their meanings in the next column.

3. Have students create a short list of similar words that could have related meanings in the next column.

4. Have students look up the word in the dictionary and summarize (not copy) the meanings and definitions in the Multiple Meanings column. Optionally, you can have students discuss and mark whether the meanings are more abstract or concrete, literal or figurative.

5. In the far right column, have students write what the definitions have in common. (This is the higher-order thinking step that will help the students apply the word in different settings in the future.)

NEW WORDS IN CONTEXT CHART

The matrix in this activity helps students to systematically think about word meanings and then remember them. It also is a good record of the words that students are encountering and attempting to learn. The matrix builds the habit of using both context and word parts to figure out word meanings.

Procedure

1. Create a matrix similar to the one shown below (or have students create their own) and model how it is used with a sample text.

2. Put a sentence from the text with a new word or phrase in column 1 and circle the new word.

3. Put word parts and related words in column 2.

4. Use columns 1 and 2 to predict the word's meaning.

5. Read further in the text and see if the text helps form the word's meaning, and then discuss the word in class or use a dictionary to find the word's meaning.

6. Use or generate a sentence, rhyme, or picture that helps the students to remember the word's meaning.

1. Word or Phrase in Context	2. Word Parts, Related Words	3. Prediction of Meaning From Columns 1 and 2	4. Meaning From Discussion or Dictionary	5. Sentence, Rhyme, or Image That Helps Me Remember Its Meaning
She circumvented the fire by diving under it.	*Circum-*	Went around	Avoided	Circumference is round = go around

RATA (READ-ALOUD THINK-ALOUD) WORD CLUES

This activity, based on the think-aloud procedure (Farr, 2001), shows students how to figure out words while reading by using context and word parts. It is a way to verbalize the thought methods for figuring out new words, as outlined in the first part of this chapter. You can put the steps on a poster in your classroom for continued reference.

Procedure

1. Show students a poster such as the Word Meaning Checklist on page 184.

2. Choose a text with a few unknown words in it. They can be vocabulary words for the unit you are studying.

3. Read aloud the text and model how you think through the steps on the poster whenever you encounter a new word.

4. Use the checklist with the whole class participating.

5. Have students practice with the checklist in pairs or individually. You can make photocopies of the checklist to give to individual students, if desired.

READ A LOT

This activity is also called Sustained Silent Reading, Wide Reading, Drop Everything and Read, Free Voluntary Reading, Read in Peace, Independent Reading, and many other names.

Research abounds on the vast quantity of words that students learn from real reading, as compared to vocabulary tests and quizzes that "teach" vocabulary out of context (Nagy, 1988). Similar to the way in which we learn first and second languages, our brains grab onto unknown words as building blocks of understanding, generate possible word meanings, and retain the words for later testing and eventual solidification of their meaning. Therefore, we as teachers need to provide ample time for reading actual texts at the appropriate reading levels.

Procedure

1. Provide students with a wide variety of texts that contain new words and then give them time to read.

2. Make sure students are using "just right" texts—not too hard and not too easy. Generally, one or two unknown words per page will appropriately challenge students without overwhelming them. Five or more unknown words will often beget frustration.

Variation

Have students find three to five words during silent reading time and put them on sticky notes with a meaning guess below them (see example). They put the note next to the word in a text until they need to transfer it to a page in their notebook.

SCUBA DIVING INTO WORD MEANINGS

SCUBA (adapted from Salembier & Cheng, 1997) is a catchy acronym students can use to remember the important steps of figuring out an unfamiliar word: sounding it out, checking the clues, using the main idea, breaking the word into parts, and asking for help.

Procedure

1. Create a poster similar to SCUBA Word Meanings on page 181, or enlarge the reproducible version and display the poster in your classroom.

2. Model the SCUBA process for students by thinking aloud while you use it with a sample text.

3. Have students work in pairs to practice the SCUBA process. You can create SCUBA cards (four to a page) and have students write on the back, using SCUBA process for several words during reading.

4. After reading, hold a class discussion.

SELF-SELECTED VOCAB QUIZZES

If we must give quizzes, let's let students learn words that (a) they don't already know, and (b) are useful. This brief activity, which should take less than 10 minutes, is powerful because it gives students some choice in what they will learn. They take ownership of the words, which creates better retention.

Procedure

1. Let students choose five to seven words from their reading and have them write the words in their notebooks in two different spots: one spot for words and meanings, and the other spot for the words only. Students could even write the words on the left of a sheet of paper and the definitions on the right and fold the paper in half down the middle to hide the definitions. Some words may be "strongly suggested" or made obligatory by the teacher.

2. At quiz time, have students copy the words from their "words only" section and write them on a card or half-sheet of paper (which will be less intimidating than a full sheet of paper). They should then write the word meanings and/or a sentence with each word in it. They then grade themselves by using the definition sheets they created in their notebooks. You can circulate during this activity to observe and assess students' work.

3. Students can share a couple of words with a partner or the whole class for extra credit, if there is time.

TARGET WORDS

This activity is effective for several reasons: It helps students learn words in context, it preteaches vocabulary, and it helps build anticipation and questions as students use the words and sentences to predict the content of the text. This is an adapted version of the word knowledge rating activity described by Blachowicz and Fisher (1996).

Procedure

1. Find three to five key vocabulary words from the text. Copy the sentences in which they are found on the board or an overhead projector and underline or otherwise identify the selected vocabulary words. On their own paper, have students draw a target like the one shown here.

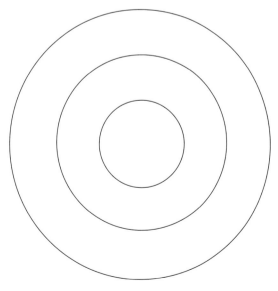

2. Have students read the sentences and write the vocabulary words on sticky notes, one word per note. Each sticky note should contain a word, its known or guessed meaning, and the student's guess as to its part of speech (noun, verb, adverb, adjective). Have students place these sticky notes on their targets as outlined in the following steps.

3. The innermost ring has the words that students know solidly with or without needing to use context to guess their meanings.

4. The next ring out has words whose meanings students are fairly sure of, or whose meanings students can figure out using context and word parts.

5. The outer ring contains words that are still confusing to students.

6. Have students work in pairs or triads to explain their guessed meanings and to compare meanings if their guesses differ.

7. Have students do a Think-Pair-Share or a Think-Write-Pair-Share (see chapter 4) about their prediction for what the text will be about, based on the words and the sentences. They should remember to give evidence for their predictions.

8. As students read the text, they can continue to add words to the target. They can discuss these words later with a partner or put them in a study word list in their notebooks.

VOCABULARY BANK NOTES

This activity is similar to many word map activities that abound in literature on teaching vocabulary (see Nagy, 1988). It also is very similar to using vocabulary study cards, but with a slightly more interesting twist that makes the words more valuable. You can, of course, guide students toward the more "valuable" words if they are choosing words that are too easy or not the target concept words you need to teach. The activity is geared more for middle school, but many high school teachers with whom I have worked have modified it with success.

Procedure

1. You and/or the students should choose words and terms that have "value" in your class and in other content areas.

2. Photocopy the Vocabulary Bank Note reproducibles on pages 182 and 183 (note there are front and back sides), and cut the copied pages to make one bank note per student. Have students fill in one or both sides of each bank note.

3. Have students create a list of the bank note words and put the list in their notebooks for later reference.

4. Have students show their bank notes to you or turn them in for you to assign values to the notes. Each note should be valued between $5 and $20. You should orally check to see if each student knows his or her word and why it is important. If not, no value is given to that particular bank note until the student knows it. Choose certain days of the week to have

students take five minutes to share and discuss their words with a partner. They share the notes they have been making that week during reading, homework, or other learning activities.

5. Optional: At the end of the quarter, semester, or marking period students can buy prize items for large sums of bank note money (e.g., a candy bar for $450). Remind them that they must still know all the words they "spend" in order to get their items.

WORD BANK

The best use of space on your wall may be an area you will call the Word Bank. Word banks are sections of the classroom wall that are devoted to the display and study of important words (Cunningham, 1995). New and important words in the bank can serve as a constant and quick reference for reinforcing content and academic concepts. The bank concept is a way to give different values to various words, which can be combined with the previous activity in this chapter, Vocabulary Bank Notes.

Procedure

1. Along with students, think about what categories to use for the words you will put in the bank. (I usually make two or three categories.) Use different colors for different categories. The headings might include ones such as these:

- Words From Chapter 5
- Words With Familiar Word Parts
- Culture Words
- Academic Language Words
- Idioms and Multiple-Meaning Words
- Long Words
- Algebra Words
- Words Borrowed From Other Languages
- Adjectives
- Favorite Long Words

2. Cut some pieces of paper (e.g., 8½" × 14" sheets cut the long way to become 4¼" × 14") on which to write the words, and then "prime the pump" by putting a couple of sample words up as you explain the categories. Each word should be written as large as possible, and its meaning should be written in small letters below it.

3. Have students read a text and choose words that they want to put on the wall, including choosing a category for each word. Have them justify why each chosen word is important to the current lesson or unit and why it goes into the particular category they say it does.

Variation

You can assign monetary values (as in the Vocabulary Bank Notes activity) to the relative importance of words. Students can argue for more value for certain words and less value for others. An example of the language they might use is, "This is an important word because...."

WORD REMEMBERING

Even if students are figuring out new words, they still need to remember what the words mean for future texts. Here is a quick way to help students get in the habit of remembering important words.

Procedure

1. Pronounce the word several times.

2. Relate it to other similar words that you know (e.g., *paramount* → *mountain*).

3. Create a visual image or connection in your mind for the word, using the text when possible. (Use mnemonic strategies.) I often remember the word *pedantic* by picturing an ant with glasses reading a large book.

4. Draw or cut out a picture that illustrates the word's meaning.

5. Make up a sentence or rhyme that uses the word and helps you to remember the meaning. For example, for the word *forge*, you could say, "The blacksmith has to forge five swords for King George."

6. Have students follow these steps on their own.

Monitoring One's Own Comprehension

* * *

You want me to retell what I read?
But I wasn't listening!

Comprehension monitoring, also called *metacognition*, is being aware of our level of understanding as we read and then using this awareness to guide us (Keene & Zimmermann, 1997). Comprehension monitoring is an unseen "higher level" of reading, similar to the unseen director of a play, who keeps the show running smoothly and fixes the problems as they arise. This director is behind the scenes, managing the actors (comprehension habits) to produce the play (text meaning).

The monitoring of one's own comprehension is difficult to teach. First, we must reflect on how we monitor our own comprehension when we read, and then we must figure out how to model that for our students. We must do whatever we can to make our thinking processes visible to students. As we do this, we create ways for students to practice comprehension monitoring enough so that it becomes a solid habit.

Basic elements of comprehension monitoring include the following:

- Establishing a purpose for reading, and keeping in mind whether the purpose is being met or not by checking to see whether each new piece of text fits the purpose for reading.

- Combining new information with previously stored information in your brain.

- Realizing when a current piece of text clashes with your evolving main idea or expectations.

- Controlling your attention, commitment, attitudes, and motivation during learning. Questions that help with this step include the following:

    Can I keep other things out of my mind long enough to concentrate on this text?

    Am I committed enough to read it all and go back over it, if necessary?

    Do I believe I have the ability to understand this?

    Am I motivated enough to expend the energy to understand this?

- Use "fix-up" strategies when comprehension breaks down. These are called *strategies* because they are more conscious and noticeable techniques (i.e., one can better remember using them) for overcoming comprehension problems than the automatic habits in other chapters. Fix-up strategies include the following:

- Rereading the text
- Reading further to see if things clear up
- Sounding out words
- Adjusting reading rate (slowing down or speeding up)
- Noticing extra clues such as text structure, pictures, introductions, back cover, questions, and so on
- Asking for help and using additional resources

Good readers do not just zoom in on the details at the expense of losing sight of the big picture that the author is trying to convey. Rather, good readers have the habit of zooming out to see the big picture—the main idea—in order to avoid getting lost. For example, as you read this book, you may focus on specific strategies that interest you, while at the same time staying aware of the overall purpose—that of building good reading habits in all students in all content areas.

In comprehension monitoring, a reader makes a split-second decision about whether he or she has comprehended the current sentence well enough to proceed to the next sentence. (You just did that if you are now reading this sentence.) We are constantly asking, Did the sentence fit well enough into my main idea for this text? If so, then we proceed. If not, we fix our comprehension. Many teachers, however, tell me that their students tend to vary—often drastically—in their criteria for attaining a satisfactory level of comprehension in order to continue forward in a reading. That is, students may not know when they are comprehending—or, even worse—when they are not. Some students, for example, may think that just saying all the words correctly is enough, and that by doing so the text will magically sink in by the time they finish it. Others may not recognize the importance of the unknown big words and therefore skip them, and still others may get through an entire text without establishing any purpose for reading it.

Students need to acquire the habit of establishing an overall purpose for reading (e.g., plot, description, persuasion, etc.) and then must learn to frequently zoom out to see if that purpose is being met, or if it needs to be modified in some way as indicated by the text's details. The following checklist helps students to notice when they are not comprehending.

Six signs that you are stuck in the mud of not comprehending:

- The pictures inside your mind stop forming or moving.
- Your questions and inferences are not getting answered.
- Your mind wanders from the text; you read it but are thinking about something else.
- The current page has nothing to do with what you thought the big picture or author's purpose was for the text.
- You cannot summarize the last few paragraphs or pages.
- Characters appear and you cannot remember who they are.

One subtle way to reduce these comprehension problems is to have students use bookmarks with reading and thinking reminders. For example, you can use or adapt the bookmarks found in Part III of this book: Comprehension Bookmark (page 185; see discussion in chapter 2), Reading Habits Bookmark (page 186), and THIEVES Bookmark (page 164; see related activity in chapter 4). Nudge students to use the bookmarks by announcing a "bookmark moment," in which students stop what they are doing to reflect on which bookmark items they are doing and not doing.

Motivation

Comprehension monitoring takes a considerable amount of mental energy. Much of this energy comes from motivation, both internal and external (Alvermann & Phelps, 2001). If a student is motivated to genuinely understand something in a text, he or she often will expend the energy to monitor comprehension in the reading process and work through problems. However, if he or she is not motivated, a reader will monitor comprehension just enough to get by. Just getting by provides a poor workout for the "mental muscles" of comprehension monitoring. Over time, obviously, lack of motivation contributes to "metacognitive atrophy" in reading.

The following are some motivation suggestions to use with students:

- Create interesting and fun learning tasks (not just "answer-10-questions" exercises).
- Provide texts that are interesting and relevant.
- Provide plenty of "frontloading," prereading, and background knowledge building.
- Provide enough time for the reading to be done.
- Provide opportunities for students to examine and share their thinking processes.
- Provide practice with practical and functional texts, including applications, articles, rules, directions, manuals, warranties, contracts, bills, letters, the "fine print," and so on. Very few classes ever teach how to comprehend and use these texts, yet much of real life requires knowing how to read them.
- Provide opportunities to practice with less and less teacher support over time. This allows students' comprehension monitoring to become second nature and eventually automatic.

Tools Chart for Monitoring Comprehension

Table 18 shows the usefulness of this chapter's activities for various content areas. On the left side of the table, a ✓ in a column indicates that the activity is useful in that stage of reading. On the right side of the table, a ✓ in a column indicates that the activity is helpful for comprehension of common texts used in that content area. A ✓✓ on the right side of the table means that the activity is especially helpful for that type of text and that you should try it as soon as possible. Take the time, however, to look at all the activities and spend a few moments

Before Reading	During Reading	After Reading	Activity	Social Studies	Science	English/EL
			Table 18. When and Where to Use the Activities in Chapter 8			
✓		✓	Discussion Starters	✓✓	✓	✓✓
	✓		Habit Stations	✓✓	✓✓	✓✓
✓	✓		Mental Multitasking Practice	✓✓	✓✓	✓✓
	✓		Multiple Intelligences Corners	✓✓	✓	✓✓
✓	✓	✓	Observation and Feedback Record	✓✓	✓✓	✓✓
✓	✓		RATA (Read-Aloud Think-Aloud)	✓✓	✓✓	✓✓
	✓		Read Aloud Everything	✓✓	✓✓	✓✓
	✓	✓	Reciprocal Teaching	✓✓	✓✓	✓✓
	✓		Think-Aloud 30-30-30 Scaffolding	✓✓	✓✓	✓✓
✓	✓		Think-Aloud Checklist	✓✓	✓	✓✓
	✓		Think-Aloud Hand Signals	✓✓	✓	✓✓
	✓	✓	Think-Aloud Note Grids	✓✓	✓✓	✓✓
	✓		Think-Notes	✓✓	✓	✓✓
✓	✓	✓	Why, Why, Why Chart	✓✓	✓✓	✓

thinking about how you might use them in your teaching. I have been pleasantly surprised at the variety of creative ways in which teachers have adapted most of these activities and organizers to work in all content areas and in all stages of reading.

Don't forget to apply the general teaching suggestions from chapter 2 to the activities in this chapter. When you find an interesting activity, refer to chapter 2 and ask how you can best integrate its instructional suggestions into the activity to meet your specific needs.

Activities for Monitoring Comprehension

DISCUSSION STARTERS

This activity should last the whole year. It helps students to broaden their types of thinking about reading through discussion with you and with other students. As students hear and use these discussion techniques, they acquire the habits of complex thinking on which these techniques depend. That is, if we provide academic language for students to process text information, they will be better able to comprehend the text. We are giving them linguistic tools to explore new ways of thinking.

Procedure

1. Make laminated signs or posters of some discussion starters to put on the wall. Some sample ideas are shown in Table 19.

Table 19.   Sample Discussion Starters

Predictions, Inferences, Questions

Prompts and Questions	Sample Response Starters
• Why do you think...? • What do you predict will happen? • What can you infer from...? Why? • Any questions about...? • Why did the author...?	• From the part about..., I infer that...because.... • I have a question about.... • I predict that...because.... • I think it means that.... • I wonder why....

Reactions, Opinions, Feelings

Prompts and Questions	Sample Response Starters
• What is your opinion about...? • How do you feel the author...? • What would you have done in...? • Does anyone disagree? Why? • If you were (character), how would you have...?	• In my opinion...because.... • I agree with (student's name) because.... • I disagree with (student's name) because.... • I was surprised when.... • When..., I felt.... • I think (person) should have.... • I was confused when.... • I was disappointed when.... • I would have...because....

Evidence, Connections

Prompts and Questions	Sample Response Starters
• What evidence from the text supports what you say? • Could you give an example of...?	• I think it means that...because.... • I would like to add to what (student name) said about.... • This relates to when I....

2. Explain each discussion starter and model how it can be used. For example, you can act out a concept and have students say, "I infer from your actions that you are frustrated." Or you might have students ask for evidence or examples when you say, "Babies who listen to Mozart end up smarter than those who listen to acid rock music."

3. Throughout the school year, continually refer students' attention to these discussion starters in order to expand and cultivate these ways of thinking about text. You also should constantly push students to supply text-based evidence for their classroom comments and opinions.

HABIT STATIONS

Once they have seen and practiced many of the habit-building activities in this book, students can practice them in a station format. Stations allow students to work on habits that need to be strengthened, and help make students aware of the different habits that happen in the same text. They allow for both individual and group constructivist work, with a choice of activities.

Procedure

1. For each of the six comprehension habits (organizing text information by sculpting the main idea and summarizing, connecting to background knowledge, making inferences and predictions, generating and answering questions, understanding and remembering word meanings, and monitoring one's own comprehension) prepare stations throughout the classroom with posters of habit-building practice activities, along with copies of graphic organizers and activity ideas (many of which can be found in this book). It is a good idea to color-code the activities for each habit by using colored paper or by having students use different colors of pens for the activities at each station.

2. Have students form groups and bring their text (group or individual) to a designated station.

3. Students work on one habit during a specific amount of time. Working on a habit can consist of taking notes on sticky notes, creating and filling in graphic organizers, responding to questions in a journal, drawing, and so on. Students can put their work into notebooks.

4. Have students bring their texts to another table after 5–15 minutes to use with the new station's habit.

5. Have students rotate two or three times and then have them share with their group some examples of habit use and the ways in which the habits help to comprehend the text.

MENTAL MULTITASKING PRACTICE

Remember Figure 1, Attention in the Reading Process (chapter 1, page 4)? Here is an engaging practice activity for developing more brain storage capacity in students as they read. During reading, we need to keep track of stores of facts, feelings, inferences, questions, predictions, and so on. All students can use more practice at storing and organizing information. This activity is a "quantity" exercise to address that need. This activity is just for quantity, though, so you will need to use other tools to help improve the quality of the thoughts.

Procedure

1. Give each student five 3" × 5" cards. Create an overhead with five sections, which you will use to model the notecards. Model steps 2 through 7 below, then put students in pairs.

2. Choose five of the following categories: inferences, predictions, facts, questions, word guesses, feelings, summaries, character traits, or causes and effects. Have students write each chosen category on one of their cards, with the name of the category in large letters on one side of the card.

3. Have students read a text and jot down notes on the appropriate cards, beneath the category headings.

4. Have students cross off items that are no longer helpful or have been contradicted or answered as they get further into the text.

5. When a student reaches four items on a card, he or she should quickly hand it to his or her partner.

6. The partner asks the student to recall the four items.

7. Partners should help each other if they cannot remember all the items. They can give one another clues instead of giving the outright answer.

8. If desired, you can allow "surprise checks" in which a partner spontaneously asks for a card or two and checks to see how much the other student remembers.

9. Later, you can gather the cards and assess how much and how well students are using the various comprehension habits.

MULTIPLE INTELLIGENCES CORNERS

Multiple Intelligences Corners allows students to understand a text through activities that emphasize different intelligences. The activity gives them a chance to use their stronger academic abilities (intelligences) while at the same time developing their weaker ones. You do not need to have students move around to various corners of the classroom, but it does add a little interest to the lesson. See Armstrong (2003) for some great ideas on using multiple intelligences to improve literacy.

Procedure

1. Observe and discuss with students which four intelligences would be good to use for the four corners. Ask students what they would like to work on and which intelligences help

them to understand when they read. (I have chosen visual, verbal, musical, and kinesthetic for this example; some other intelligences you may want to try are math and logic, interpersonal, intrapersonal, and naturalistic.) Create a station in the classroom for each of the four chosen intelligences.

2. Gather some practice activities that correspond to each intelligence and place them at the appropriate corner station. For example, there are many ideas you can use from this toolkit. For the Visual corner, you can use graphic organizers, drawings, art projects, and posters. The Music corner might include writing chants and songs in response to a text or video, listening to classical music while reading, and responding to songs or poems in a journal. The Kinesthetic corner might include the creation of hand motions, drama, manipulatives, and tableaus. The Verbal corner might have ideas for transposing genres, categorizing vocabulary cards, brainstorming ideas, prewriting, analyzing good writing samples, and creating newspapers, short stories, and magazines.

3. Have students start with one type of intelligence and then cycle through the intelligence corners, working in each corner for a set amount of time. Students can keep a notebook or a checklist for the varying types of work in each corner and can check these off each time to avoid repeating the same activity.

OBSERVATION AND FEEDBACK RECORD

Teacher observation is the best assessment of student reading habits. Feedback is a key component of student learning (Marzano et al., 2001). You can observe and interpret your students' comments as indicators of their comprehension habits. Table 20 shows some sample student comments.

Procedure

1. Make a table like Table 20 and use it to quickly jot down key phrases or sentences that students say during class discussions or readings. (You may only manage to write down a few comments a day, but this is fine.)

2. Later, go back and categorize the student comments you wrote and use this information to provide specific and helpful feedback to students about their thinking during reading. For example, you could say, "Great, Silvia, you connected to your background knowledge to help you understand this science concept!"

3. Optional: Place your filled-in table on an overhead projector and discuss the comments with a class.

Table 20. Student Comments and Comprehension Habits

Comprehension Habit	Student Comments
Summarizing	This section tells about the caste system in India and how it can prevent people from choosing what jobs they want to do.
Connecting to Background Knowledge	When he gave her the money, it reminded me of when I gave my brother money for his bicycle. I have a picture in my mind of a cluster of round protons and neutrons with tiny electrons buzzing around it.
Inferring and Predicting	I think the whales find warm and protected waters because their newborns are safer. I predict that the next section will explain how the magnets make the motor run.
Questioning	How did humans first discover how to make iron tools? Why did she kiss that frog?
Figuring Out Word Meanings	"His clandestine acts were eventually discovered." Clandestine must be something like hidden or secret.
Monitoring Comprehension	"The lion stacked the antelope?" That couldn't be right. I need to reread it.

RATA (READ-ALOUD THINK-ALOUD)

Think-alouds are times when you stop to describe aloud your thinking process while you are doing something (adapted from Davey, 1983; Farr, 2001). In our case, we are interested in making visible the fleeting habits of reading comprehension. RATA is short for Read-Aloud Think-Aloud, a special combination of reading aloud and modeling aloud one's thoughts for others to hear. RATA is good for times when you do the following:

- Realize you have come to confusing parts in a text, then clarify them with fix-up strategies
- Ask yourself questions
- Make predictions and inferences, and see if they are answered or confirmed
- Visualize what is happening in the reading and modify mental images, as text dictates.
- Connect to prior knowledge or experience and then prune away or discard connections that are not helpful
- Make analogies and modify them, as the text dictates
- Monitor your understanding of the author's purpose

Procedure

1. Use a wide variety of materials (stories, textbooks, essays, articles, graphs, pictures, etc.) to model. You also can bring in a text that is difficult for you (e.g., a college biology book) to give students a genuine sense of your thinking struggles and how you approach challenging texts.

2. Place the text you are reading on an overhead projector so students can follow along. Uncover the text as you read aloud, and then pause to make comments about what you are thinking in order to comprehend the text. (Do not do this too often, though, or the activity gets slow and tedious.)

3. Verbalize your thoughts about predictions, pictures, confusing parts, connections to background knowledge, and purpose for reading. Create minisummaries. Remember that think-alouds can be used for building other reading habits as well. In this case, though, you should emphasize how you monitor your comprehension, including modifying the main idea, using fix-up strategies (looking back, reading on), and connecting pieces of text. Figure 22 shows a sample think-aloud session, with the reading habits used for each step listed in parentheses after the step.

4. After reading a portion of the text in this manner (or whenever you feel it is appropriate), you can stop reading from time to time and ask students to think aloud to the class. Later, have students practice this activity on their own in pairs, reading aloud and stopping to think aloud to their partners.

Figure 22.   Sample Think-Aloud

Text: *The Adventures of Huckleberry Finn* by Mark Twain

1. *Evasion*? I'm not sure what this word means exactly, but I'm familiar with the term *tax evasion*, so I think this usage has to do with getting out of something or getting away with something. (word meaning)

2. With this part about a parade, I'm picturing big parades I've seen with marching bands that recognize military heroes for Veteran's Day, maybe. (activating prior knowledge and visualizing)

3. "for being prisoner for us..." Was Jim being a prisoner for Tom and Huck as a favor to them? Would Jim have gone on that adventure in the first place if he knew he was going to be set free via Miss Watson's will? Was all the trouble he went through worth more than $40? (asking questions)

4. This paragraph is confusing. I think that Jim is talking about being rich, but I'm not sure if he thinks he is rich now or thinks he's going to be richer in the future. I skipped over some words that may have been important. I'll reread this paragraph. (monitoring comprehension)

5. I think that we are going to learn how else Tom and Huck could start up their next adventure without money (since they don't have any at present), or a way that they could come upon some money to purchase "the outfit." (predicting)

6. Does Jim know something that Huck doesn't know and that I don't know? How does he know that Huck's father isn't coming back? (asking questions)

7. Now I definitely think that Jim must know something that he doesn't want Huck to find out, because he refuses to answer Huck's repeated questions. Jim isn't mean-spirited, so I think he's probably withholding information from Huck because he's protecting him from something. (inference)

5. Keep track of student think-aloud comments because such observations are excellent indicators of the students' strengths and weaknesses in reading. Use checklists, anecdotes, hand-held computers, or another convenient method for recording your notes.

6. Remind students that questions are good, confusion is OK if you fix it, and reading comprehension is proportional to the amount of hard thinking that we do.

Following are some think-aloud starter suggestions:

- I predict that the next section will be about…because….
- I would like to know more about….
- I wonder why….
- I have a picture in my mind of….
- I think that….
- This is like that time when I….
- This reminds me of….
- This is similar to how….
- I'm not sure what this word means. What word would make sense in this sentence? If I substitute the word _____, does it make sense enough to move on?
- I don't understand this section. I'll read ahead a few lines to see if it becomes clearer. If not, I guess I'll reread it.

Following are some good types of texts to use for think-alouds:

- Expository (articles, editorials, diagrams, charts, textbooks)
- Functional (directions, applications, warranties, maps, plans, prescriptions, recipes)
- Stories, songs, and poetry
- Pictures, art projects, problem-solving projects, paintings, advertisements
- Videos (stop video every few minutes to think aloud)
- Drawings, paintings, or objects made from modeling clay (e.g., one can verbalize one's thoughts while drawing, painting, or sculpting an animal, vehicle, or machine)

Variation

RATA Pair Notes: For this activity, one student in a pair reads aloud and thinks aloud, while the other listens and takes notes on a sticky note. The listener also categorizes each thought as one of the six reading habits presented in chapter 1. The reader then puts the notes at the spots in the text where he or she stopped to think aloud. Later the notes can be used to create written responses and collected (and categorized) on a page in the student's notebook.

READ ALOUD EVERYTHING

Too many teachers think that they should not read aloud because students aren't doing "the work." Actually, *not* reading aloud to students is much more harmful to many struggling readers who have not experienced good models of reading. Hearing the text read aloud allows students to see how the text should be read. Teachers in all content areas and classes should read aloud (Alvermann & Phelps, 2001).

Why read aloud? Because reading aloud does the following:

- Creates a community of learners
- Helps students develop interests for self-selection of reading material
- Models the joy of reading and learning from text
- Shows students how to use punctuation, intonation, and pauses to comprehend text
- Models to students the complexity of thinking involved in reading
- Builds...
    - Language fluency
    - Prior knowledge and practice connecting to prior knowledge
    - Students' understanding of story development and characterization
    - Listening skills and attention span abilities
    - Memory and summarizing abilities
    - Abilities to compare and contrast themes and characters
    - Habits of predicting, questioning, and visualizing
    - Abilities to interpret figurative language
- Provides...
    - Extensive practice in thinking about extended text
    - A common forum for discussing the text
    - Exposure to text and concepts that are above students' current independent reading levels

When should you read aloud? You should read aloud when you want to do the following:

- Emphasize the language in poetry, dialogues, or plays
- Introduce challenging texts and new concepts
- Grab students' attention at the beginning of a lesson
- Get students hooked into a long text
- Expose students to the text when the photocopier breaks or you do not have time to make photocopies

Procedure

1. Read aloud a large variety of materials—directions, novels, poems, articles, editorials, children's books, newspapers, textbook chapters, math story problems—to show students how they can read and think about these texts.

2. Read the first section, or up to half, of the assigned text to get students hooked into the reading. Have students read along, take notes, fill in graphic organizers, summarize, and/or make predictions as you read aloud to them. Stop at a crucial point to summarize, question, or predict, and then let students continue reading on their own.

In general, don't force students to read aloud, especially in front of the entire class. Create a safe environment where students can *occasionally* read aloud, but where students who choose not to read aloud will not feel left out.

RECIPROCAL TEACHING

When students discuss texts (narrative and expository) in groups, they develop academic thinking and language habits. Most cooperative groups have roles assigned to each student in the group, some of which are described in the procedures for this activity. One of the most popular versions of cooperative group work for text discussion is reciprocal teaching (Palincsar & Brown, 1984), which focuses on four comprehension habits: questioning, clarifying, summarizing, and predicting. This activity is particularly effective with challenging expository texts.

Procedure

1. Assign students to groups of four and have each group decide on the order of facilitation and on who will start as facilitator. Other members of the group can take on other roles such as notetaker, focuser, or word searcher.

2. Before reading, build students' interest in the text and engage the prior knowledge of the students by using anticipation guides (see chapter 4), semantic organizers (see chapter 3), brainstorming, THIEVES (see chapter 4), visual prompts, Quickwrites (see chapter 4), text scanning, minidramas, videos, and so on.

3. **Questioning:** Each group's facilitator decides on a stopping point in the text, and the students do silent reading as a group. When all members finish (early finishers can jot down notes), each group's facilitator asks for an on-the-surface and an under-the-surface question (see chapter 6) from the group or asks a question to other group members. They all discuss possible answers to the question. The group discusses how important the question might be to the text's overall meaning. (They can even put the questions on a continuum of importance, as shown here.)

What color was the car?		Who was Dana?		Why did she run away?
Least important	Less important		More important	Most important

4. Clarifying: Each group's facilitator asks for or gives clarification of concepts or vocabulary.

5. Summarizing: Each group's facilitator summarizes the reading, and the other students add to (or subtract from) the summary.

6. Predicting: Each group's facilitator predicts what happens next in the text, based on prior evidence: "I predict that...," and "My evidence is...." Other students can agree or disagree and give their evidence for doing so.

7. Continue the process with other members of the groups facilitating, or have each student lead a strategy: One student can be the Questioner, another student the Clarifier, another the Summarizer, and another the Predictor.

8. Give the students the following norms for group interaction (if desired, you can put these on a poster to hang in the classroom):

- Everybody helps.
- Give reasons for your suggestions.
- No one is finished until everyone is finished.
- You have the right to ask for help.
- You have the duty to offer help.
- You have the duty to play your role.

For extra support and accountability, you can have students use a graphic organizer such on the one on page 187. Feel free to modify the one provided.

THINK-ALOUD 30-30-30 SCAFFOLDING

In this activity, which could also be called 30-30-30 RATA (see the RATA activity in this chapter), the text is divided into thirds and reading and thinking are scaffolded. Each 30 roughly stands for a percentage of the total amount of text read by the teacher or the students. (For example, 30% of 12 paragraphs is 4 paragraphs.) Each percentage is changeable depending on the text and the students.

Procedure

1. Model prereading strategies by thinking aloud, and elicit student think-alouds to establish the author's possible purpose and predict the text's contents. You also can build or connect to student's background knowledge at this time.

2. For the first 30% of the text, read and think aloud while students listen and (optionally) take notes. You can emphasize certain habits (e.g., summarizing, questioning, etc.) for students to practice with the teacher (second 30%) or independently (third 30%).

3. For the middle 30% of the text (or up to 50% for difficult texts), read aloud and stop occasionally to allow students to think aloud, either with partners or the whole class. Students can take notes during this section if you like.

4. For the last 30% of the text, have students read silently and take notes on sticky notes, paper, or graphic organizers to practice the think-aloud habits you want to emphasize.

5. During postreading, think aloud again to model the process of bringing text parts together and determining the author's purpose.

Variations

- Have students use the Reading Habits Bookmark (page 186) or Comprehension Bookmark (page 185) to spark think-aloud ideas.

- Use this approach for activities other than reading, such as making clay objects, drawing, writing a poem, organizing a presentation, creating a webpage, etc. Think-alouds with these activities can be effective because they make the "model" thinker's thoughts visible to the learners in a variety of contexts. Try the activities in the following order, which is from concrete to abstract: Think aloud while making a clay figure, then think aloud while drawing, then think aloud with narrative, then with expository text.

THINK-ALOUD CHECKLIST

The Think-Aloud Checklist is a way to keep track of the comprehension habits and their roles in constructing meaning. You can use this activity with many of the other tools in this toolkit. You also can and should use it with other forms of information processing such as videos, songs, dialogues, art, and math problems.

Procedure

1. Give each student a copy of the Think-Aloud Checklist (see page 188) and explain each item on the list, using examples. Have students brainstorm examples of what a person would say for the different habits.

2. Read aloud and stop at times to think aloud. Students take notes on your thoughts. Let students discuss their marks with a partner, if desired. Try to voice thoughts in as many categories on the checklist as possible. For possible texts, encourage students to bring in samples of texts that you might be unfamiliar with or have trouble easily understanding, such as textbooks in subjects other than the one you teach, or lyrics from songs that are popular with students. You can use warranties, research articles, or legal documents—anything you might struggle to understand.

3. Give students examples of helpful thoughts, which get a score of 2 on the checklist. These can include thoughts that relate to the main idea and author's purpose, and thoughts that show comprehension the way the author probably intended. Then, also give examples of less helpful thoughts (score of 1), which are random or tangential thoughts that may actually hinder comprehension (e.g., "The greenhouse effect reminds me of my uncle's green house that we painted last year. I fell, and that hurt me.").

4. Put a blank checklist on the overhead projector and fill it in together as a class (using just a few examples) as students share how they interpret each of your think-aloud comments. You also could have a student fill the checklist in while you read and think aloud. The process of assessing you will help students notice the use or lack of habits in their own reading. In addition, assessing you familiarizes them with the habits and gives them the rare experience of being the assessor.

5. Once students are comfortable with the process, have them use the checklist in pairs: One student reads and stops to think aloud, while the other uses the checklist. Pairs offer more practice and students are more likely to share their thoughts in smaller settings. As above, the partner uses the Think-Aloud Checklist to assess the reader's ability to construct meaning and monitor comprehension.

6. To assess students, have each student read. As a student reads, he or she pauses at certain points to verbalize his or her thinking process to you. Pauses can be student- or teacher-initiated. Simply record the types and quality of comments made by each student.

Variation

Have students do a self-assessment using the following prompts:

- My most common type of comment was _____ because _____.
- The type of comment I think I should make more often is _____ because _____.
- Thinking aloud helped me _____ with this text.

Complete the following prompts yourself about the students:

- Student strengths noted are _____.
- Areas for improvement are _____.
- The most common type of comment by this student is _____.
- A type of comment to include more often in the next think-aloud is _____.

THINK-ALOUD HAND SIGNALS

This activity is a kinesthetic way to involve students during read-alouds and think-alouds. Research abounds showing the success of using extraverbal ways to reinforce concepts (Druyan, 1997; Marzano et al., 2001). And movement is more fun than simple desk work for most struggling students, especially when they have to learn challenging and abstract concepts.

Figure 23. Descriptions of Hand Signals for Comprehension Habits
Background Knowledge: One hand next to your ear, with one hand waving behind you
Summarizing: Both hands up, thumbs and index fingers framing a big, imaginary picture and then reducing it
Questioning: Both hands palms up, next to shoulders
Inferring: One hand palm down, moving from high to low, as if being submerged in water
Prediction: Hand held horizontally above the eyes, as if looking far off into the distance
Word Meaning Using Parts: Chopping motion with one hand
Word Meaning Using Context: Each hand held up in the shape of a C; hands are then moved further apart
Monitoring Meaning: Index finger on temple

Procedure

1. First, do a teacher-directed version of the activity: Read aloud to the students and think aloud as you read. Have the students listen to your think-aloud, mentally categorize each thought, and then respond with the corresponding hand signal from the list in Figure 23. This can show you which students do and do not understand the various reading habits, so that you can provide extra support to students who need it. It also is a quiet activity.

2. When students are ready for more responsibility, do a student-directed version of the activity. This can be later in the same text or with a new text. Read aloud to the students and stop at a certain point, telling the students to do the hand signal that corresponds to their current thought. You can call on a student or two. For example, you could say, "Lupe, I noticed from your hand motion that you made an inference. What inference did you make?" Then, you could ask the class, "Did anyone else make that inference?"

3. You also can stop at some points during the read-aloud and give a hand signal that prompts students to use the indicated habit. They can write down their results or thoughts and/or share their thoughts with the class.

4. When you feel that students are ready, have them do an independent version of this activity: Students can work in pairs, following the procedure outlined in step 1 above. One student can be the teacher while the other is the student and then the partners can switch roles.

Variation

You also can make up hand signals for other thinking skills such as compare and contrast, evaluate, persuade, fact versus opinion, cause and effect, and so on.

THINK-ALOUD NOTE GRIDS

Think-Aloud Note Grids are checklists for students to use while you are modeling a think-aloud or when they are thinking aloud in pairs. Students can use two types of grids, one for recording another's thoughts and one for recording their own thoughts. Feel free to change the right-hand columns of the grid as desired to include any type of habit or thinking skill that you wish to emphasize. By analyzing students' think-aloud notes, you can assess the quantity and quality of their thoughts during reading.

Procedure

1. Teach students the comprehension habits you want to emphasize and how to categorize them when they hear another person describe his or her thoughts during reading. Practice with the Think-Aloud Note Grid (see reproducible form on page 189) by making up think-aloud statements and having students discuss which column to check for each one. You can do this step on an overhead projector.

2. Give each student a copy of the Think-Aloud Note Grid. Start by modeling the think-aloud process with a high-interest activity such as interpreting a picture, watching a video, reading a cartoon, or reading an advertisement.

3. Present the video, picture, text, or other medium, and think aloud as you go through it. Have students take very quick and short notes on your think-aloud in the "Thoughts" column of the grid as you think aloud.

4. Have students categorize each of your think-aloud thoughts by placing one (or more) x marks in the right-hand columns.

5. Have students discuss their notes and your thoughts in pairs or groups to reach a consensus or to notice patterns. For example, you may want to have them tell you which habits you used frequently and which ones it appears you need to work on.

6. Have students take notes on their own thoughts as they read a text, and have them notice which habits they used frequently or infrequently. This is a great chance for students to take metacognitive stock of their reading behaviors.

THINK-NOTES

This is a variation of thinking aloud in which the reader writes down thoughts on sticky notes next to the text (see Figure 24). This is effective for building the habit of comprehension monitoring because it is simple enough to do on a daily basis.

Procedure

1. For modeling, use an overhead projector with colored transparency squares that imitate sticky notes. Read aloud to the students, writing your thoughts on these notes to

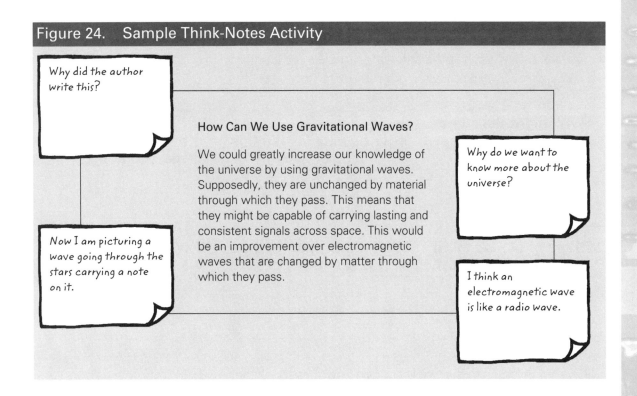

Figure 24. Sample Think-Notes Activity

Why did the author write this?

Now I am picturing a wave going through the stars carrying a note on it.

How Can We Use Gravitational Waves?

We could greatly increase our knowledge of the universe by using gravitational waves. Supposedly, they are unchanged by material through which they pass. This means that they might be capable of carrying lasting and consistent signals across space. This would be an improvement over electromagnetic waves that are changed by matter through which they pass.

Why do we want to know more about the universe?

I think an electromagnetic wave is like a radio wave.

emphasize the overall gist of the text and any problematic points that you encounter. You can put different types of thoughts on different colors of notes. For example, summaries may go on yellow, inferences on pink, questions on blue, and vocabulary on green.

2. You also can have students cut different shapes of notes to use for different comprehension habits. A diamond shape could be the evolving main idea, a circle could be a question, and so on. Put an initial for the habit at the bottom of each note (e.g., B for background knowledge, M for main idea, S for summarizing, I for inferring, P for predicting, Q for questioning, W for word meanings, C for monitoring comprehension, etc.).

3. For practice, have students go through the process with various types of text. You can require a minimum amount of certain colors or shapes of notes, if necessary. Help students who are having trouble by offering more examples.

4. When finished, students can collect the notes in a journal and organize them by type or by importance to the meaning of the text. Then, students can critique their notes and see if they can improve in certain areas.

WHY, WHY, WHY CHART

The Why, Why, Why Chart is a simple activity for building the vital habit of setting up a purpose for reading different types of text. It challenges students to think about various purposes for reading and to think about the topic of each text.

Procedure

1. Create a chart, such as the following sample, on a laminated poster or written on note cards, an overhead projector, or in students' notes. Feel free to modify the questions.

WHY might the author write this type of text (genre)?	WHY do people read this type of text?	WHY might the author have written this particular text?
WHY might I read this if I didn't (don't) have to?	WHY did the author give the text this title?	WHY might the teacher want us to read this?

2. Give a minilesson to the whole class on how these questions can help comprehension. Discuss how writing is communication and knowing why the author wrote it helps us see what he or she was trying to communicate. That is, it helps us focus on the main message of the text. Ask students, Why is this "why" question important? for each of the six in the chart.

3. Have students fill in the chart as they read a particular text.

4. Hold a class discussion after reading to see if any of the answers changed and to synthesize what was learned.

PART III

Reproducibles

KEYWORD CONSTRUCTION

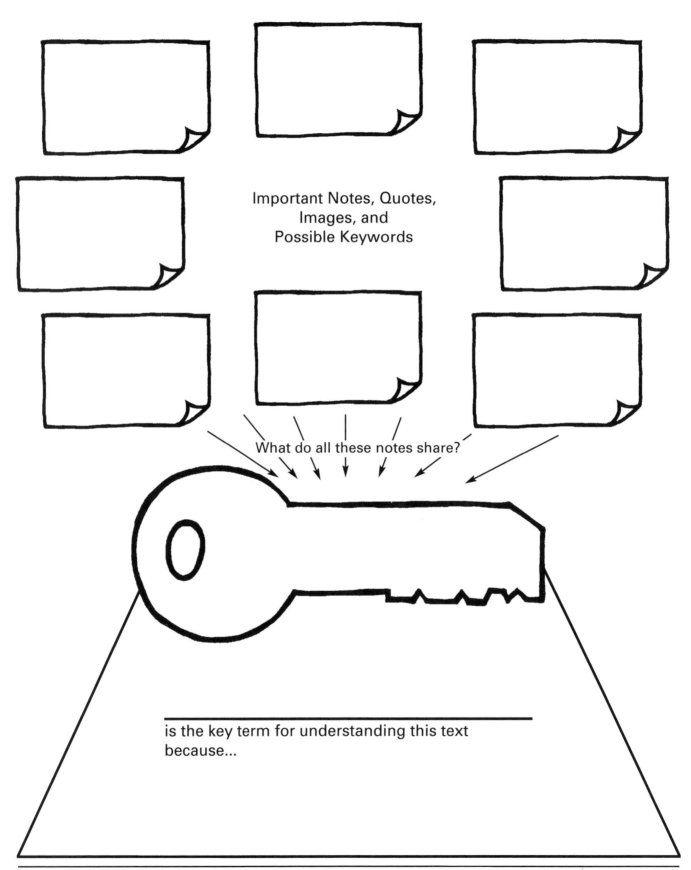

Important Notes, Quotes,
Images, and
Possible Keywords

What do all these notes share?

_____
is the key term for understanding this text
because...

MAIN IDEA MEMORY STORAGE

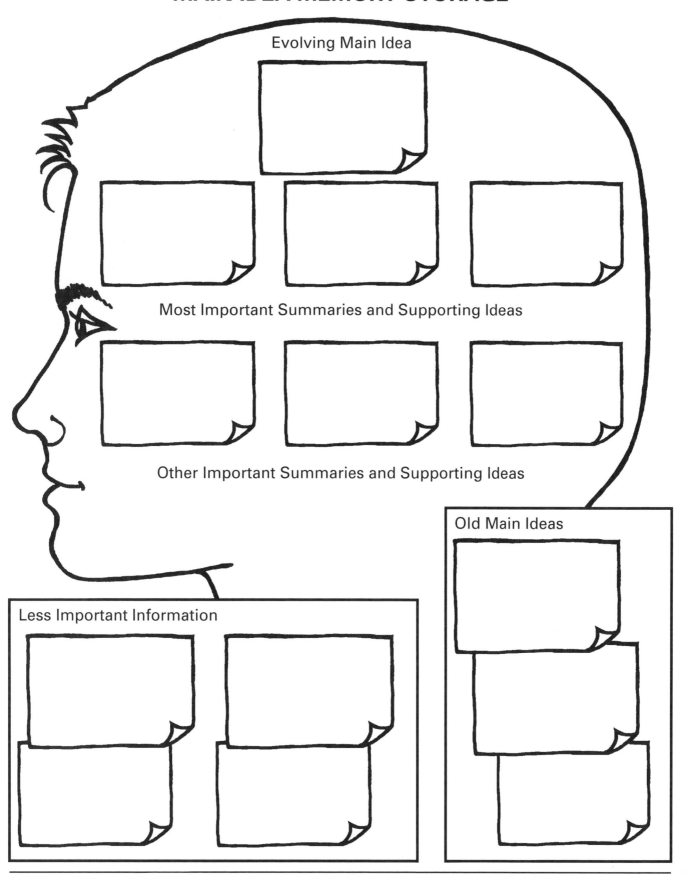

Evolving Main Idea

Most Important Summaries and Supporting Ideas

Other Important Summaries and Supporting Ideas

Old Main Ideas

Less Important Information

STEPS FOR PURPOSE

☐ Look at text clues: title, summaries, subtitles, introductions, pictures, and so on.

☐ Listen to the **teacher's** explanations for why you are reading the text. (Hot Tip! Directly ask the teacher's purpose for assigning the text.)

☐ Think about current lessons and objectives, and about how this text might fit into what you are learning.

☐ Think about why the **author** took the time to write this text. What does the author want readers to know or do as a result of reading it?

☐ Use the above steps to help form **your own** purpose for the text. What might you get out of reading this text? What could be interesting about this? Ask yourself, "Why am I reading this?" and have at least one answer that keeps you going.

☐ The purpose may change while reading. Be ready and flexible.

Teacher's Purpose   Author's Purpose

My Purpose

STORY MAP

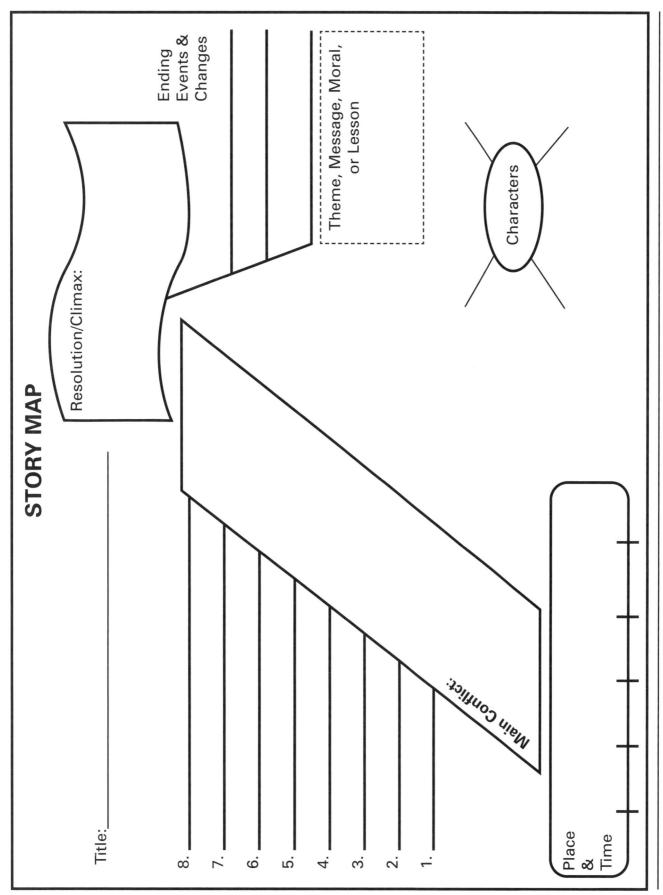

Title: _____

Ending Events & Changes

Resolution/Climax:

8.

7.

6.

5.

4.

3.

2.

1.

Main Conflict:

Theme, Message, Moral, or Lesson

Characters

Place & Time

WEBPAGE TEMPLATE

Title:	
	Main Idea | Connections to My Life | Questions
Causes	
Effects	
People	
Places	
Purpose	

 (See related activity on page 52.)

ANTICIPATION GUIDE

Topic/Text _____

Before reading, look at each statement and decide whether you agree or not. Put the letter that corresponds to your opinion on the line on the left side. Write your reason under "Why?" After you read the text, do the same on the right side of the page.

A = Agree strongly   a = Agree somewhat   d = Disagree somewhat   D = Disagree strongly

Before Reading   After Reading

____ 1. [   ]   ____
       Why?

____ 2. [   ]   ____
       Why?

____ 3. [   ]   ____
       Why?

____ 4. [   ]   ____
       Why?

Building Reading Comprehension Habits in Grades 6–12: A Toolkit of Classroom Activities by Jeff Zwiers. Copyright © 2004 by the International Reading Association. May be copied for classroom use. (See related activity on page 60.)

BACKGROUND KNOWLEDGE BACKPACK

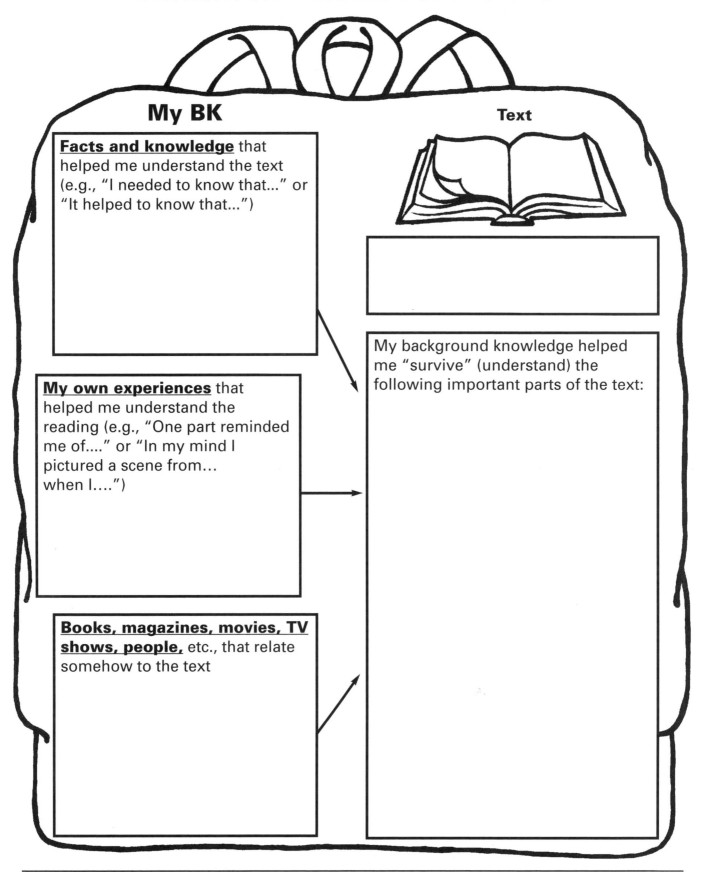

My BK

Facts and knowledge that helped me understand the text (e.g., "I needed to know that..." or "It helped to know that...")

My own experiences that helped me understand the reading (e.g., "One part reminded me of...." or "In my mind I pictured a scene from... when I....")

Books, magazines, movies, TV shows, people, etc., that relate somehow to the text

Text

My background knowledge helped me "survive" (understand) the following important parts of the text:

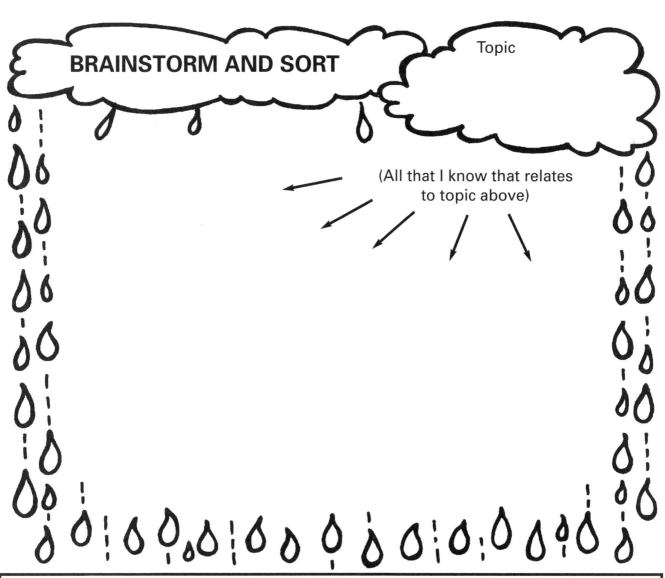

BRAINSTORM AND SORT

Topic

(All that I know that relates
to topic above)

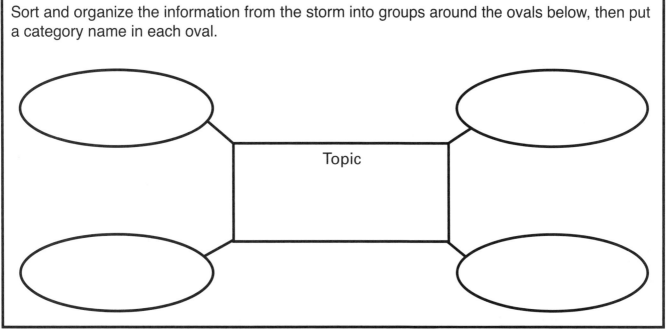

Sort and organize the information from the storm into groups around the ovals below, then put a category name in each oval.

Topic

CATAPULT INTO LITERATURE PRACTICE

Covers (front and back): What do the covers (words and pictures) show us about what we might visualize in the story? What does the back cover tell us about the story (the words, pictures, or both)?

Author: What is the author's background? Has he or she written any other stories that might be like this? What were they about? Are the same characters in this story as in the others?

Title: What does the title lead us to predict about the story? What questions do you have about the title?

Audience: For whom was this story written? Old; young; male; female; city-dwelling; country-dwelling; past, present, or future readers?

Page 1: Read page 1 and think about what the story might be about.

Underlying message or purpose: With what you have thought about so far, what message or purpose might the author have for the readers? What might be the deeper meaning? How might it connect to your life?

Look at any visuals, maps, and sketches in the text. As we look through the story, what do the pictures, sketches, diagrams, or maps tell us?

Time, Place, Characters: From clues so far, what can we say about when the story takes place, where it takes place, and the characters? What can we guess might happen to the characters?

CATAPULT INTO LITERATURE PRACTICE

Covers (front and back): What do the covers (words and pictures) show us about what we might visualize in the story? What does the back cover tell us about the story (the words, pictures, or both)?

Author: What is the author's background? Has he or she written any other stories that might be like this? What were they about? Are the same characters in this story as in the others?

Title: What does the title lead us to predict about the story? What questions do you have about the title?

Audience: For whom was this story written? Old; young; male; female; city-dwelling; country-dwelling; past, present, or future readers?

Page 1: Read page 1 and think about what the story might be about.

Underlying message or purpose: With what you have thought about so far, what message or purpose might the author have for the readers? What might be the deeper meaning? How might it connect to your life?

Look at any visuals, maps, and sketches in the text. As we look through the story, what do the pictures, sketches, diagrams, or maps tell us?

Time, Place, Characters: From clues so far, what can we say about when the story takes place, where it takes place, and the characters? What can we guess might happen to the characters?

PATH TO PURPOSE

THIEVES BOOKMARK

T **Title**—Read the title of the chapter and predict what the chapter is about.

H **Headings**—Look at all headings and the table of contents. Turn them into questions that the text will probably answer.

I **Introduction**—Read the introduction and any questions or summaries at the beginning. Predict the main idea.

E **Everything I Know About It**— Think of everything I have seen, read, or done that may relate to this text.

V **Visuals**—Look at pictures, graphs, diagrams, or maps, and read their captions. Notice lists with letters or numbers that point out important information. Read all the notes in the margins and notice **bold** and *italicized* words. Make notes (or a web) of what I plan to learn.

E **End-of-Chapter Material**—Read end-of-chapter material, such as summaries or questions that I will try to answer by reading.

S **So What?**—Why did the author write this? Why am I reading this? Knowing the purpose helps me comprehend. (S can also stand for text structure.)

THIEVES BOOKMARK

T **Title**—Read the title of the chapter and predict what the chapter is about.

H **Headings**—Look at all headings and the table of contents. Turn them into questions that the text will probably answer.

I **Introduction**—Read the introduction and any questions or summaries at the beginning. Predict the main idea.

E **Everything I Know About It**— Think of everything I have seen, read, or done that may relate to this text.

V **Visuals**—Look at pictures, graphs, diagrams, or maps, and read their captions. Notice lists with letters or numbers that point out important information. Read all the notes in the margins and notice **bold** and *italicized* words. Make notes (or a web) of what I plan to learn.

E **End-of-Chapter Material**—Read end-of-chapter material, such as summaries or questions that I will try to answer by reading.

S **So What?**—Why did the author write this? Why am I reading this? Knowing the purpose helps me comprehend. (S can also stand for text structure.)

THIEVES PRACTICE

T From the title, predict what the text is about.

H Look at all headings (and the table of contents) and then turn two of them into important questions that you think the text will answer (Why...? How...?).

I Use the introduction and first paragraph to predict the main idea (or to create a big question you think the text will answer).

E Write down everything you know about the topic. Use the back of this paper, if necessary. Circle any of your notes you would like to know more about, or write a question about them.

V List three important visuals found in the text and predict how they will help you understand the text.

E Guess the answers for the end-of-chapter questions, read any summaries, and write down every boldface or italicized word.

S So what? Why do you think the author wrote this text? What does its structure tell you?

THIEVES PRACTICE

T From the title, predict what the text is about.

H Look at all headings (and the table of contents) and then turn two of them into important questions that you think the text will answer (Why...? How...?).

I Use the introduction and first paragraph to predict the main idea (or to create a big question you think the text will answer).

E Write down everything you know about the topic. Use the back of this paper, if necessary. Circle any of your notes you would like to know more about, or write a question about them.

V List three important visuals found in the text and predict how they will help you understand the text.

E Guess the answers for the end-of-chapter questions, read any summaries, and write down every boldface or italicized word.

S So what? Why do you think the author wrote this text? What does its structure tell you?

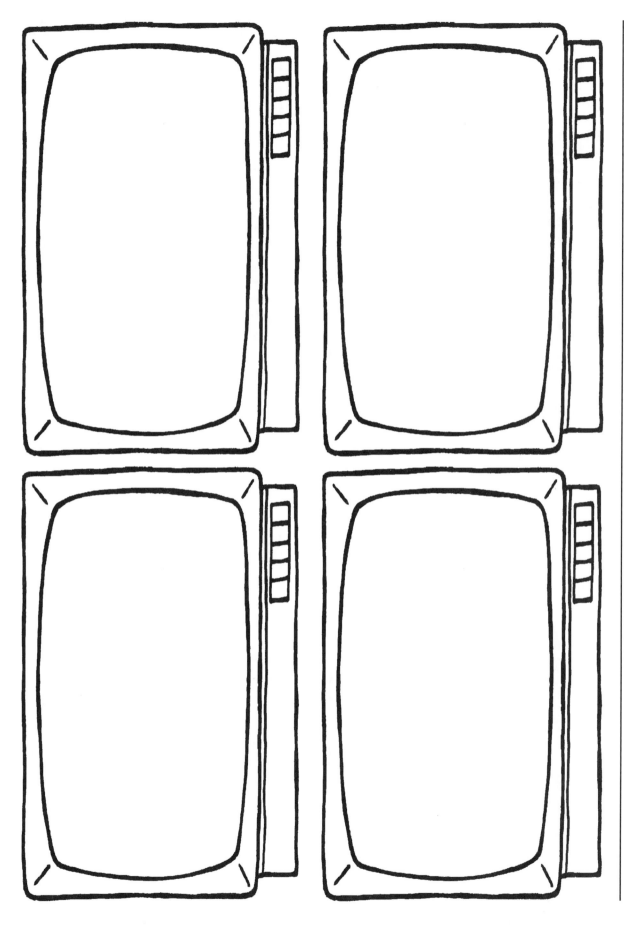

VISUALIZATION STATIONS

CAUSE AND EFFECT TIMELINE

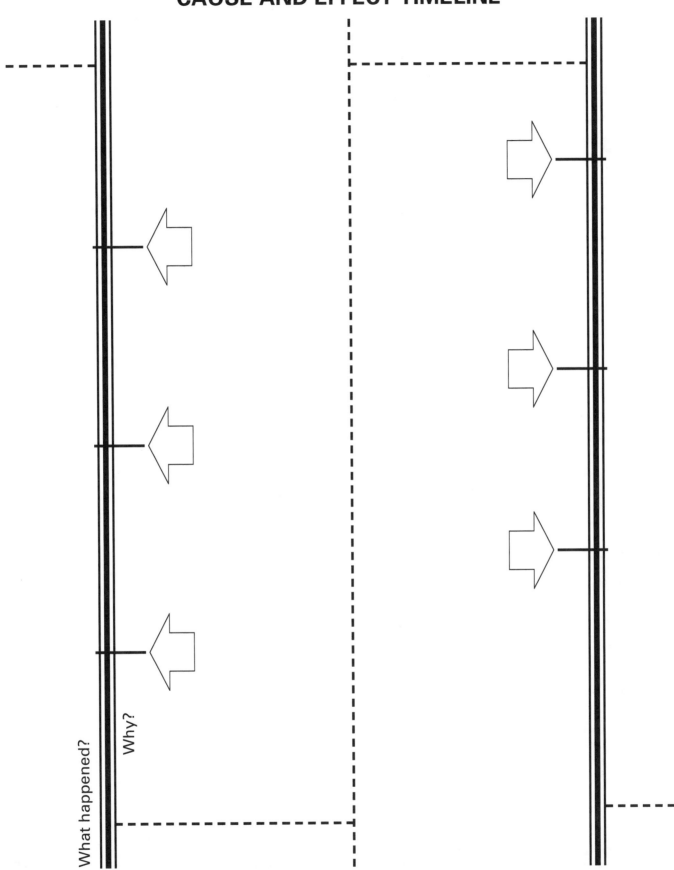

What happened?

Why?

DIALOGUE COMIC STRIP

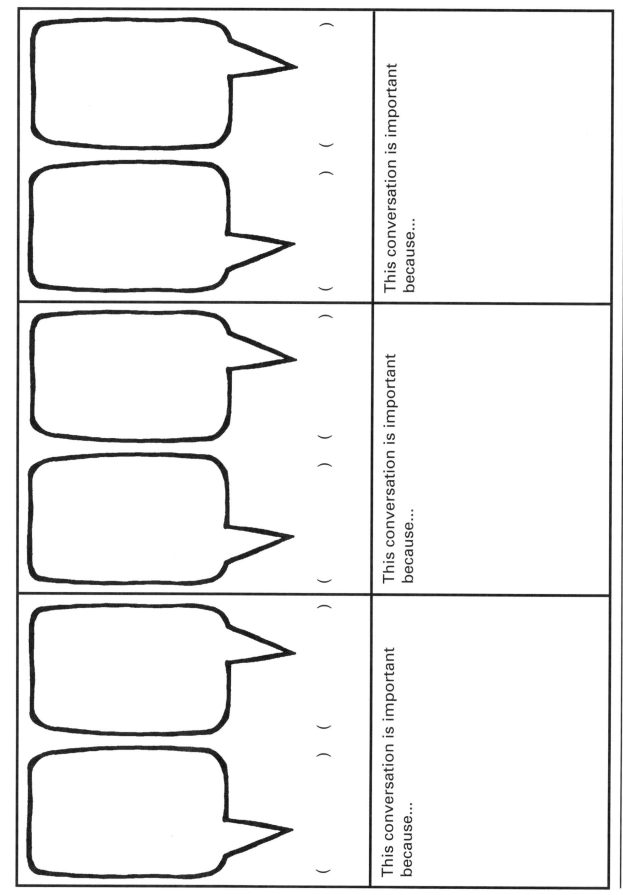

This conversation is important because…

This conversation is important because…

This conversation is important because…

EXTERNAL-INTERNAL STORY LINE

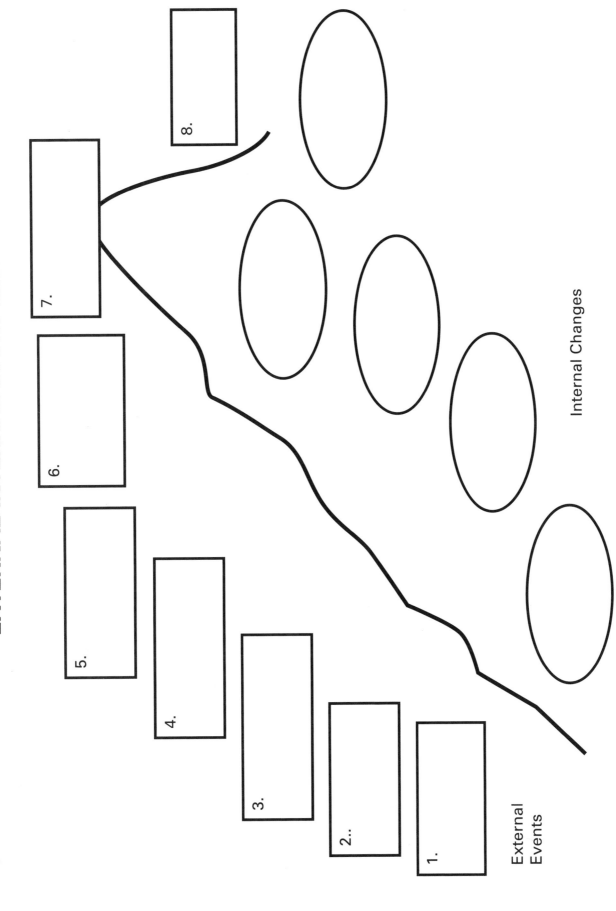

External Events

Internal Changes

PREDICTION CHART

Student Name _____

Text Title _____

What do you think the next part is about? (Be specific) Pg.		Why? (Use evidence from text, pictures, and/or your prior knowledge)		Was your prediction confirmed or not? How do you know? Pg.

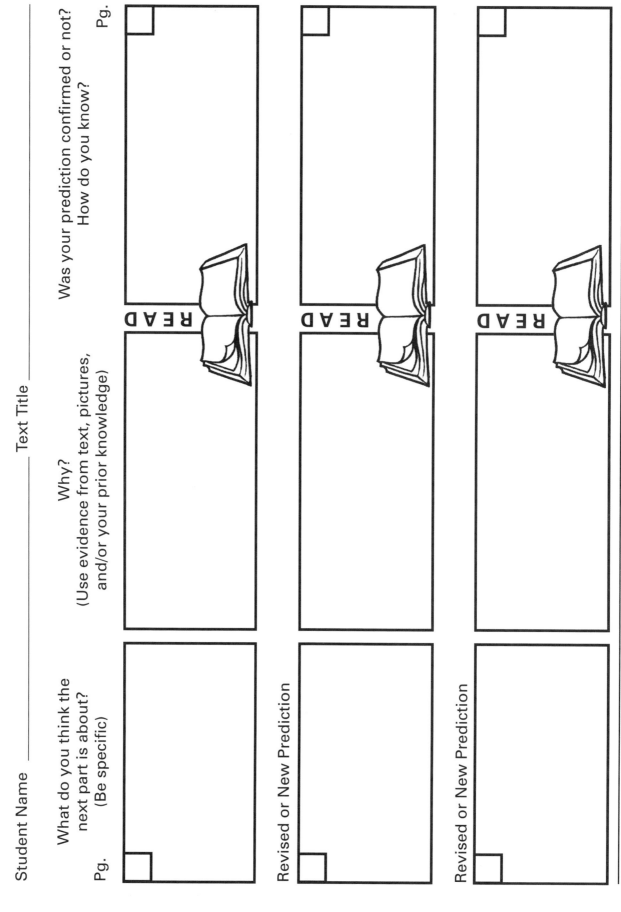

Revised or New Prediction

Revised or New Prediction

T+B=I INFERENCE MACHINES

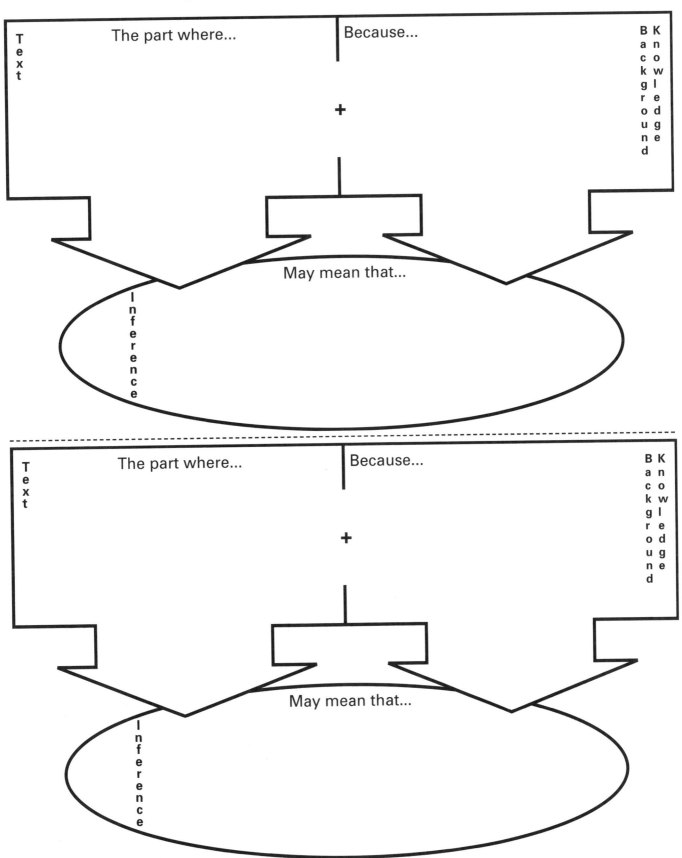

CENTRAL QUESTION DIAGRAM

Question with Should..., Could...,
Would..., or Do you think that....

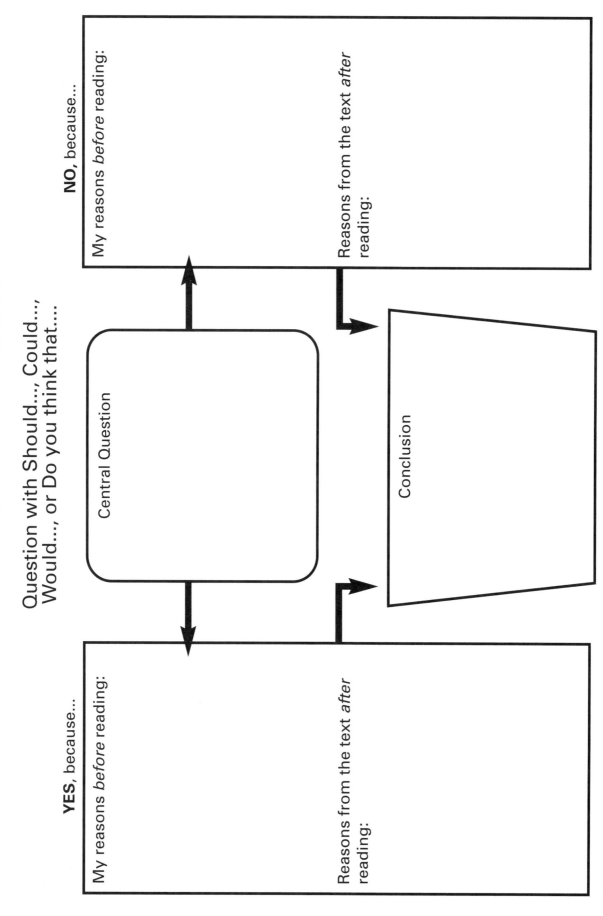

YES, because...

My reasons *before* reading:

Reasons from the text *after* reading:

Central Question

Conclusion

NO, because...

My reasons *before* reading:

Reasons from the text *after* reading:

Source: Adapted from Alvermann, D.E. (1991). The discussion web: A graphic aid for learning across the curriculum. *The Reading Teacher, 45,* 92–99.

DIFFERENT LEVELS OF QUESTIONS

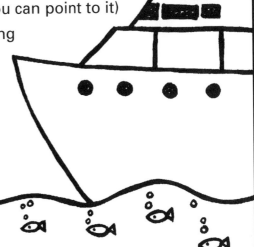

On-the-Surface Questions

• Usually have one correct answer found in the text (you can point to it)

• Involve summarizing, paraphrasing, and literal retelling

• Inquire about facts, details, and events

• Often begin with *Who*, *What*, *Where*, or *When*
  (some on-the-surface questions may begin with
  Why, *How*, *Should*, *Could*, or *Would*)

Under-the-Surface Questions

• Can have more than one correct answer

• Are not explicitly stated in the text

• Often begin with the words *Why*, *How*, *Should*, *Could*, or *Would* (some under-the-surface questions may begin with *Who*, *What*, *Where*, or *When*—often followed by "do you think..." and then often followed by another *Why?* question)

• Usually require one or more of the following:

  • Filling in gaps, making inferences, "reading between the lines"

  • Predicting, speculating, asking what the text means

  • Hypothesizing and evaluating

  • Challenging the text

  • Experimenting, solving problems, thinking divergently

  • Reflecting, expressing major understanding

Life Application Questions

• Connect the text to self or knowledge of the world

• Ask about author's purpose, message, moral, or symbolism

• Explore cultural or psychological ideas

• Extend beyond the text into the reader's own experience

• Include opinions

• May include "How does this part relate to my past, present, or future?"
  "What is my opinion about what the text says?"
  or "How does this text help me learn what I need to learn?"

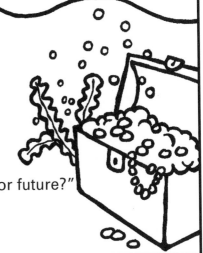

QUESTION SEA

On-the-Surface Questions

Who...?   Where...?   When...?   What...?

Under-the-Surface Questions

Why...?

Would...?

How...?

What if...?

Life Application Questions

If I were..., how...?

How does this text relate to real life?

QUESTION TREE

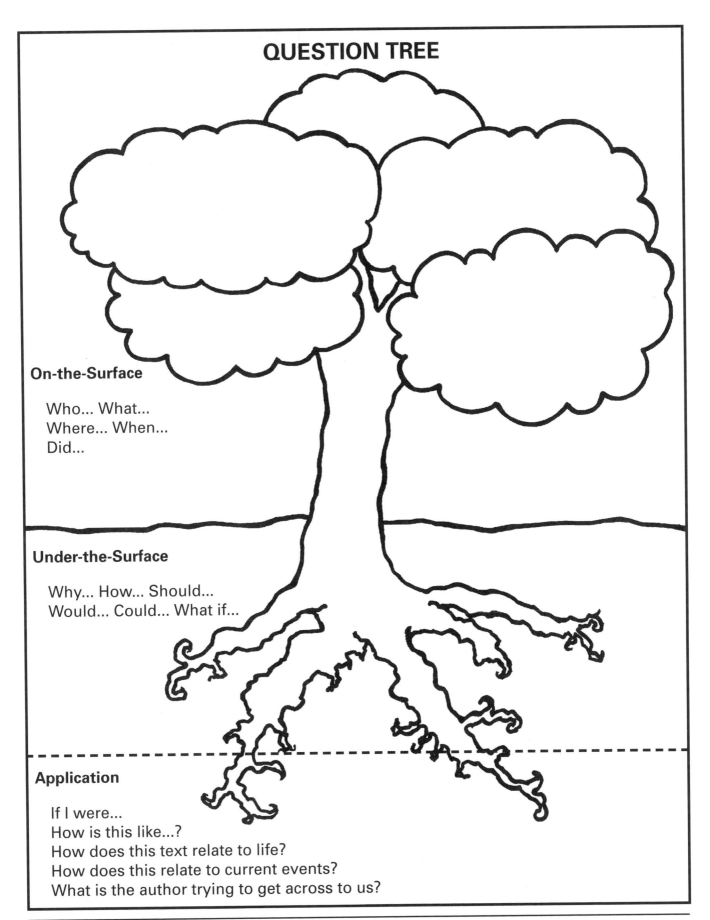

On-the-Surface

Who... What...
Where... When...
Did...

Under-the-Surface

Why... How... Should...
Would... Could... What if...

Application

If I were...
How is this like...?
How does this text relate to life?
How does this relate to current events?
What is the author trying to get across to us?

CONNECT THE WORDS

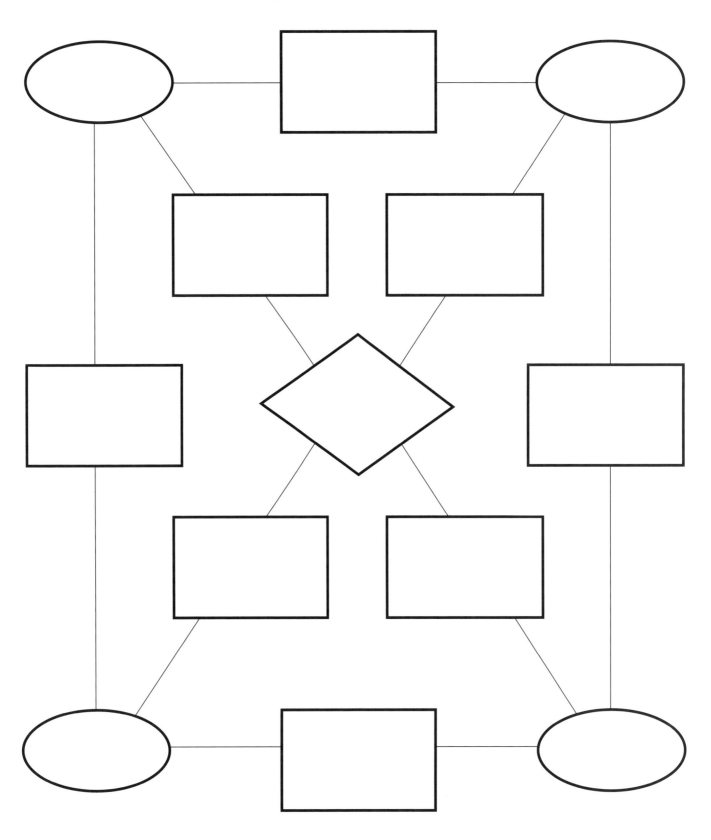

Source: Adapted from Allen, J. (1999). *Words, words, words: Teaching vocabulary in grades 4–12*. York, ME: Stenhouse.

GUESS AND ADJUST

Title:

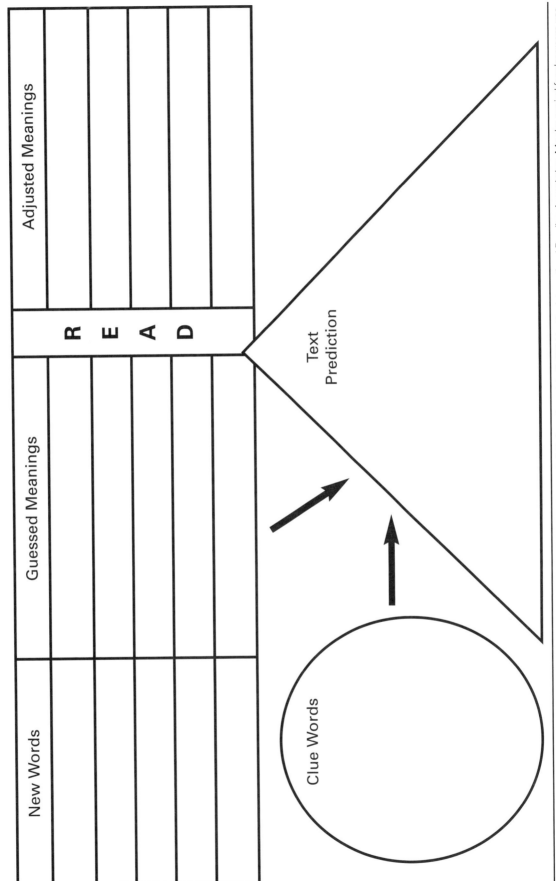

New Words

Guessed Meanings

R
E
A
D

Adjusted Meanings

Text Prediction

Clue Words

Building Reading Comprehension Habits in Grades 6–12: A Toolkit of Classroom Activities by Jeff Zwiers. Copyright © 2004 by the International Reading Association. May be copied for classroom use. (See related activity on page 122.)

KEYWORDS WEB

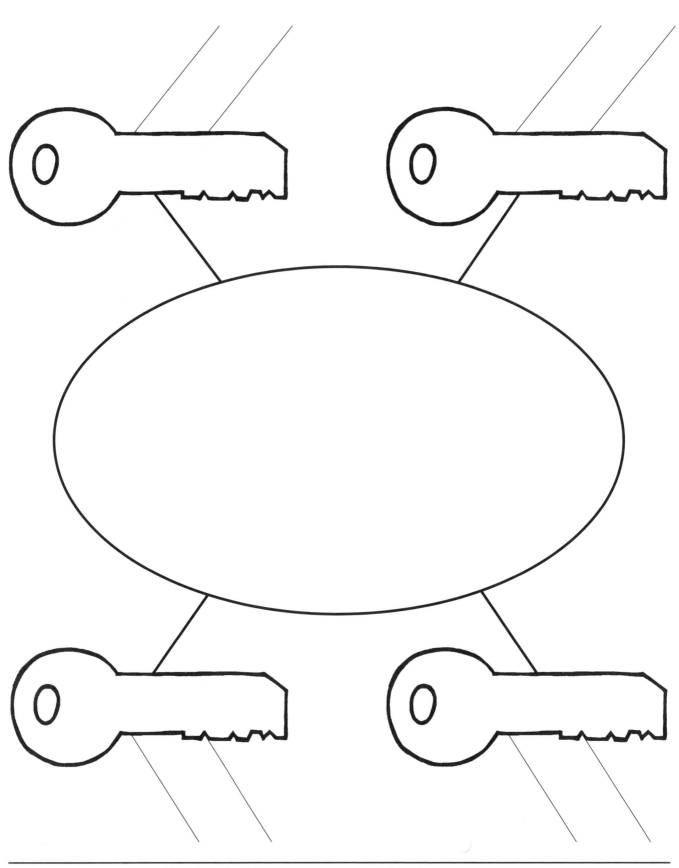

LITFIGS

What It Describes
(Literal Meaning)

What the author is trying to
emphasize, how the two meanings are
similar, or why I think they relate.

In the Text
(Figurative Meaning)

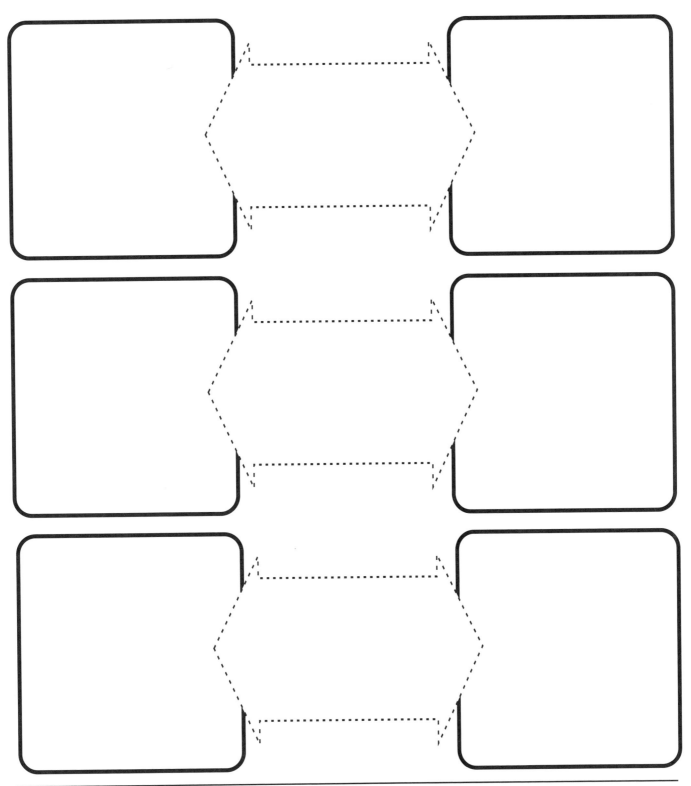

MULTIPLE MEANINGS TABLE

Word	Word Parts and Meanings	Similar Words	Summaries of Multiple Meanings	What They Have in Common
			1. 2. 3.	
			1. 2. 3.	
			1. 2. 3.	
			1. 2. 3.	
			1. 2. 3.	

SCUBA WORD MEANINGS

S **Sound** it out. Say the whole word to yourself a couple of times.

C **Check** the clues in the sentence and paragraph and think about what word would fit best in place of the unknown word.

U **Use** the text's main idea and the pictures to make a good guess for the word's meaning.

B **Break** the word into parts that have meanings that you recognize, and/or think of similar words.

A **Ask** for help from a peer or teacher, or use a glossary or dictionary.

Source: Adapted from Salembier, G.B., & Cheng, L.C. (1997). SCUBA-dive into reading. *Teaching Exceptional Children, 29*(6), 68–71.

Examples of the Word

VOCABULARY BANK NOTE

Word (or Phrase)

Name

$

President Vocab U. Lary

Why This Word Is Important:

Meaning in Sci., S.S., Lit., Math

Other Meaning(s)?

Sentence Using the Word:

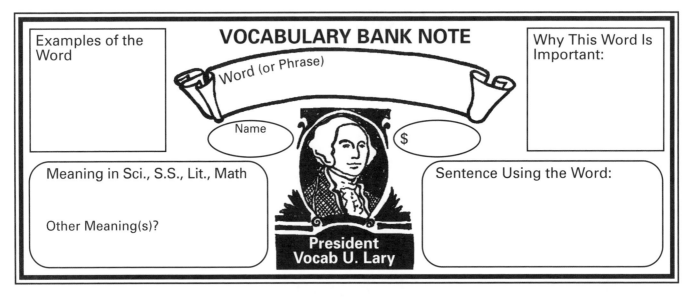

Examples of the Word

VOCABULARY BANK NOTE

Word (or Phrase)

Name

$

President Vocab U. Lary

Why This Word Is Important:

Meaning in Sci., S.S., Lit., Math

Other Meaning(s)?

Sentence Using the Word:

Examples of the Word

VOCABULARY BANK NOTE

Word (or Phrase)

Name

$

President Vocab U. Lary

Why This Word Is Important:

Meaning in Sci., S.S., Lit., Math

Other Meaning(s)?

Sentence Using the Word:

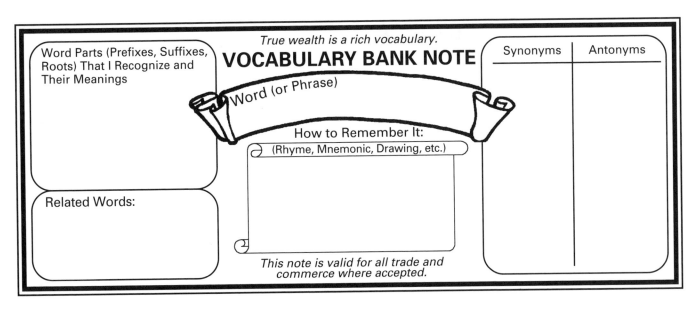

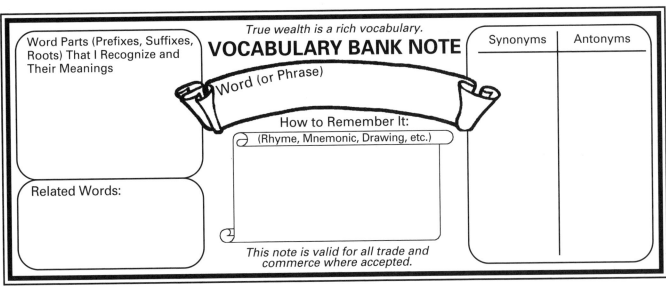

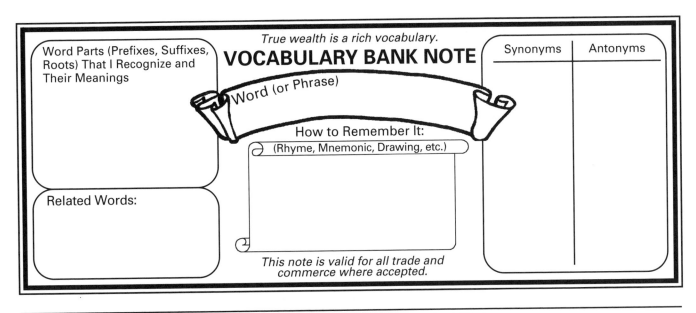

WORD MEANING CHECKLIST

IMPORTANCE

☐ Is the word important enough to figure out? Do I need to know it to understand the text?

CONTEXT

☐ How do the sentence, paragraph, and nearby pictures give me clues to the word's meaning?

☐ Which known word or phrase could I use to replace the unknown word?

☐ Does my replacement make sense grammatically?

☐ Does my replacement fit into the overall text meaning?

WORD PARTS

☐ Which parts of this word have meanings that I recognize?

☐ What are some words I know that are similar or have similar parts?

PREDICTED MEANING

☐ When I combine the previous two steps, what is the best meaning that I can store in my mind for now?

☐ How can I best remember the meaning?

COMPREHENSION BOOKMARK

BEFORE reading, I...

☐ Know the **purpose** of reading

☐ Use **prereading** techniques (THIEVES or CATAPULT)

☐ Think about what I **already know** about this topic

☐ Make **predictions** about what I think the text will tell me

WHILE reading, I...

☐ Stop to **visualize, summarize parts, ask questions**, and organize thoughts

☐ **Reread** parts I don't understand

☐ **Predict** and then confirm or change my predictions

☐ **Figure out unknown words** by using the words around them and word parts

☐ **Organize** information with notes or drawings in the space below:

AFTER reading, I...

☐ **Write** a quick summary of the reading in my learning log to remember it

☐ Go back and look at the **notes** I made to organize them

☐ **Think** about how the reading relates to classroom learning and life

☐ **Reflect** on how well I read

COMPREHENSION BOOKMARK

BEFORE reading, I...

☐ Know the **purpose** of reading

☐ Use **prereading** techniques (THIEVES or CATAPULT)

☐ Think about what I **already know** about this topic

☐ Make **predictions** about what I think the text will tell me

WHILE reading, I...

☐ Stop to **visualize, summarize parts, ask questions**, and organize thoughts

☐ **Reread** parts I don't understand

☐ **Predict** and then confirm or change my predictions

☐ **Figure out unknown words** by using the words around them and word parts

☐ **Organize** information with notes or drawings in the space below:

AFTER reading, I...

☐ **Write** a quick summary of the reading in my learning log to remember it

☐ Go back and look at the **notes** I made to organize them

☐ **Think** about how the reading relates to classroom learning and life

☐ **Reflect** on how well I read

READING HABITS BOOKMARK

B **Background Knowledge** It will probably help that I already know.... This part connects to what I know about....

M **Main Idea and Author's Purpose** So far, this text is about.... The author wrote this in order to....

S **Summarizing** This section or paragraph was about....

Q **Questioning** I wonder why.... How....

I **Inferring** I bet that... because.... I think that.... Based on this part, I assume that....

P **Predicting** I predict that... because....

W **Word Meaning** This word means...because it has the word part.... The word means...because of its context....

M **Metacognition** I don't get it; I will read it again.... I will read on to see if this part gets clearer to me....

READING HABITS BOOKMARK

B **Background Knowledge** It will probably help that I already know.... This part connects to what I know about....

M **Main Idea and Author's Purpose** So far, this text is about.... The author wrote this in order to....

S **Summarizing** This section or paragraph was about....

Q **Questioning** I wonder why.... How....

I **Inferring** I bet that... because.... I think that.... Based on this part, I assume that....

P **Predicting** I predict that... because....

W **Word Meaning** This word means...because it has the word part.... The word means...because of its context....

M **Metacognition** I don't get it; I will read it again.... I will read on to see if this part gets clearer to me....

RECIPROCAL TEACHING GRAPHIC ORGANIZER

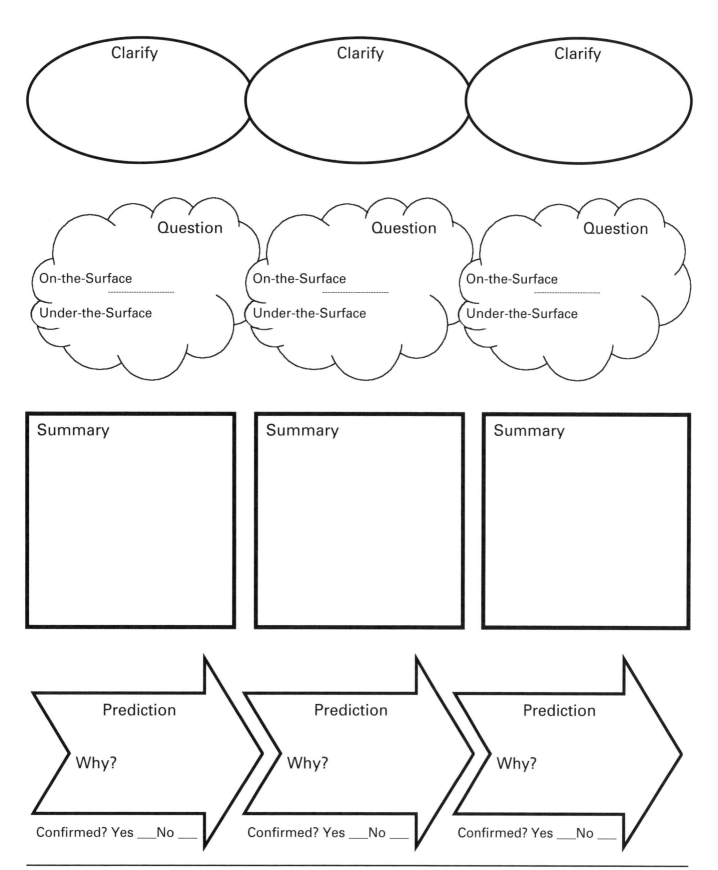

Clarify

Clarify

Clarify

Question

On-the-Surface

Under-the-Surface

Question

On-the-Surface

Under-the-Surface

Question

On-the-Surface

Under-the-Surface

Summary

Summary

Summary

Prediction

Why?

Confirmed? Yes ___No ___

Prediction

Why?

Confirmed? Yes ___No ___

Prediction

Why?

Confirmed? Yes ___No ___

THINK-ALOUD CHECKLIST

I think...

I remember when...

This boils down to...

I predict that... because

Comprehension Habits	2 = *Helpful* 1 = *Attempt*					
BKN: Connects to background knowledge (self/world)						
Connects to previous part of the text or to other texts						
Notices a conflict with background knowledge						
Background Knowledge Notes:						
SUM: Summarizes to reduce and remember information						
Connects summaries to **main idea and/or author's purpose**						
Summarizing Notes:						
INF: Makes logical **inferences** based on BK and text **evidence**						
Makes logical **predictions** based on BK and text **evidence**						
Confirms or **disconfirms** inferences and predictions						
Inference and Prediction Notes						
QUE: Generates good **questions** that provide direction or purpose						
Hypothesizes, seeks, and notices **answers** while reading						
Question Notes:						
WOR: Uses **context clues** to figure out words						
Uses knowledge of **word parts** to figure out words						
Word Meaning Notes:						
MON: Makes statements or questions indicating **confusion**						
Uses **fix-up strategies** (look back, read ahead)						
Uses **text structure**						
Challenges text; critiques style, format, clarity						
Comprehension Monitoring Notes:						

THINK-ALOUD NOTE GRID

#	Notes on _____'s thoughts	Use Background Knowledge	Fix up and Monitor Comprehension	Predict or Infer	Question	Summarize	Figure Out Vocabulary (Context/Word Parts)	Main Idea/Author's Purpose

APPENDIX

A Few Multiple-Meaning Words

This appendix contains examples of words with more than one meaning. Use them to show students how words can have both concrete and abstract meanings, and how a reader must use context to figure out which meaning is which. For example, consider the multiple meanings of *bank* in this sentence: "The man was on the bank until it fell into the river."

arms
- ☐ appendages with hands
- ☐ weapons for war

bank
- ☐ a depository for money
- ☐ land on the edge of a river

bit
- ☐ piece of metal that goes in a horse's mouth
- ☐ past tense of *bite*
- ☐ a small amount (e.g., just a little *bit*)

book
- ☐ to reserve a spot or flight
- ☐ a bound text with pages

can
- ☐ to be able (e.g., I *can* go)
- ☐ a metal container

case
- ☐ a situation or legal action (e.g., The *case* was unsolved)
- ☐ a receptacle for storage (e.g., guitar *case*)

date
- ☐ a social engagement
- ☐ a specific day on the calendar (e.g., Today's *date* is...)

fair
- ☐ legal and equitable
- ☐ a place with rides and cotton candy
- ☐ pleasant (e.g., The weather is *fair*)

fire

☐ to get rid of an employee
☐ flames and heat
☐ to shoot a weapon

game

☐ willing or interested (e.g., I'm *game* to try eating bugs)
☐ a sports contest (e.g., a baseball *game*)

get

☐ obtain (e.g., *Get* me a hamburger)
☐ become (e.g., I *get* angry when...)
☐ come (e.g., *Get* over here!)
☐ understand (e.g., I *get* it)
☐ receive (e.g., You'll *get* a cold out there)
☐ be allowed to (e.g., I *get* to go to the zoo today!)

grave

☐ a tomb or other burial place
☐ serious (e.g., The situation was *grave*)

jam

☐ a spread made from fruit
☐ to pack tightly (e.g., *Jam* another coat in the case)
☐ a clog (e.g., traffic *jam*)

kind

☐ gentle and benevolent
☐ type (e.g., What *kind* of animal is that?)

last

☐ to endure (e.g., It will *last* forever)
☐ final

light

☐ pale (e.g., a *light* color)
☐ visible energy used to illuminate an area (e.g., Turn on the *light*)
☐ to enliven (e.g., *light* up a room)
☐ not heavy

long

☐ extending for a great distance or time (e.g., a *long* rope)
☐ to want intensely (e.g., I *long* to see you)

mean

☐ nasty, unpleasant, or aggressive (e.g., The bully was *mean*)
☐ to intend (e.g., I *mean* what I say)
☐ a mathematical "middle" (e.g., The *mean* score was 43)

net
- ☐ remaining after all deductions (e.g., The *net* profit was $5.00)
- ☐ loosely woven fabric (e.g., The fish escaped from the *net*)

note
- ☐ written records (e.g., Take *notes* for me)
- ☐ a musical tone
- ☐ to be aware of (e.g., *Note* the differences)

over
- ☐ above, on top of
- ☐ done, finished

palm
- ☐ the inner part of the hand
- ☐ a type of tree
- ☐ a hand-held computer

pass
- ☐ to go from one place to another
- ☐ to die (e.g., *pass* away)
- ☐ a ticket or permission slip (e.g., a hall *pass*)
- ☐ to throw a ball to another player in a game
- ☐ to hand something to someone (e.g., *Pass* me the peas, please)

play
- ☐ to sound an instrument or participate in a game
- ☐ a drama presented on a stage

present
- ☐ a gift
- ☐ here (e.g., She is not *present* today)
- ☐ to show or introduce (e.g., May I *present* to you...)

press
- ☐ to push down
- ☐ news media

race
- ☐ a group of people
- ☐ a speed contest for runners, cars, bicycles, and so on

rest
- ☐ to relax
- ☐ remainder (e.g., I'll eat the *rest*)

sole
- ☐ the bottom of a shoe
- ☐ a flat fish
- ☐ only (e.g., The *sole* reason is that I love you)

spell
- ☐ to write or say letters in the correct order (e.g., *Spell* your name)
- ☐ a period of time (e.g., Stay a *spell*)
- ☐ a magical incantation

spring
- ☐ the season after winter
- ☐ a bouncy wire
- ☐ a source of water
- ☐ an act of jumping, or fast growth

staff
- ☐ a stick or pole
- ☐ a group of workers

state
- ☐ condition (e.g., in a sad *state*)
- ☐ one of the divisions of a country (e.g., the *state* of Delaware)
- ☐ to say (e.g., Please *state* your name)

tire
- ☐ to become fatigued
- ☐ a rubber cushion around the wheel on a car

wake
- ☐ the churned waves behind a boat
- ☐ to come out of sleep
- ☐ a viewing before a funeral

wave
- ☐ a surge of an ocean or a sound
- ☐ to move the hand in greeting

well
- ☐ healthy (e.g., I feel *well*)
- ☐ a pit from which to draw water

will
- ☐ to intend (e.g., I *will* go)
- ☐ desire or preference (e.g., It is his *will* for you to go)
- ☐ a legal document for the disposition of property (e.g., He put it in his *will*)

yard
- ☐ three feet
- ☐ the land in front of or behind a house

Prefixes, Suffixes, and Roots

Chapter 7 highlights the importance of learning how to figure out words by using their parts. The following is a convenient list that you can teach in creative ways to students so they can quickly figure out many words without having to consult a dictionary. One good way to teach them in general, of course, is for you to highlight word-part words that arise in context during the school year.

Word Part	Meaning	Sample Words
PREFIXES		
a-, an-, ab-	not, without	abnormal, amoral, apathy, atypical
ambi-	both	ambidextrous, ambiguous
ante-	before	antecedent, antechamber, anteroom
anti-	against	anticlimax, antidote
bene-, bon-	good, well	benediction, benefactor, benefit, bonanza
bi-	both, double	bicycle, bifocals, bilateral, biweekly
circum-, circ-	around	circumference, circumnavigate, circumspect
co-, col-, con-, com-	together, with	codependent, coexist, collect, collide, committee, congregation, conspire, convention, correlation, correspond
contra-, contro-, counter-	against	contradict, contraindication, controversy, counterpart
de-	from, down, away, off, undo	deceive, decline, deduct, defame, depart, depress, derail, derive
dia-	through, between	diagonal, dialogue, diameter, diatribe
dis-, dys-	apart, not, reverse, badly	disincentive, disinterested, dismiss, dissatisfied, distinct, distort, dysentery, dystrophy
ex-	out, from, former	exception, exclude, exhale, expose, extract
extra-	beyond	extracurricular, extraneous, extraordinary, extraterrestrial
fore-	before, in front	forecast, foregone, foreleg, foreshadow
homo-	man, one	homogenous, homophone

Word Part	Meaning	Sample Words
hyper-	over, above	hyperactive, hyperextension, hypersensitive, hyperthermia
hypo-	under	hypodermic, hypothermia, hypothesis
in-, im-, il-, ir-	1-in, into, within	illustrate, implicit, imply, import, income, inhabit, innate, involve, irrigate
	2-not	illegitimate, improbable, inactive, inane, incompatible, inept, irregular
inter-	between	interchange, interrupt, intervene
intra-, intro-	within, into	intramural, intravenous, introduce, introspection
macro-	large, excessive	macrocosm, macroeconomics
mal-	poor, badly	maladjusted, malady, malicious, malnourished
meta-	beyond, outside, change	metabolism, metacognition, metamorphosis, metaphor
mis-	wrongly, incorrect	misfire, misfit, misguide, misinterpret, misquote, mistreat, mistrust, misunderstand, misuse
mono-	one	monochrome, monopoly, monotone
neo-	new	neoclassic, neophyte
non-	not	nonexistent, nonsense, nonviolent
paleo-	ancient	paleography, paleontology
para-	beside, almost	parachute, paramedic, paraphrase, parasite
peri-	around	pericardium, perimeter, peripheral, periscope
poly-	many	polygamy, polyglot, polygon
post-	after	posterity, posthumous, postpone, postwar
pre-	before in time, place, or order	precede, predict, prefer, prefix, preheat, preliminary, premature, premise, pre–Revolution
pro-	forward, for	procure, produce, prohibit, promote
quad-	four	quadrangle, quadrant, quadruplets
re-	back, again	reclaim, regain, reproduce, rescind, revise
retro-	backward	retroactive, retrospect
sub-	under	subdermal, subjugate, submerge, substandard, subterranean

Word Part	Meaning	Sample Words
syl-, sym-, syn-, sys-	with, together	syllogism, symbiosis, symbol, symphony, synchronization, system
trans-	across, through, beyond	transatlantic, transfusion, transit, transmigration, transmit
ultra-	beyond, excessive	ultraconservative, ultramodern, ultraviolet
un-	not, reverse	undo, unfair, unkind, unpretentious
uni-	one	uniform, unify, unilateral, united

SUFFIXES

Word Part	Meaning	Sample Words
-age	act of, collection of (v, n)	espionage, forage, passage, portage, salvage
-ance, -ancy	action, state, process (n)	allowance, persistence, resistance
-ar, -er, -or	one who, that which (n)	amplifier, collector, preacher, teacher, walker
-asis, -osis	process, condition (n)	hypnosis, osmosis, psychosis, stasis
-ate	make, cause (v)	congregate, cooperate, correlate, desegregate, meditate
-cide	kill (n)	genocide, homicide, pesticide, suicide
-dom	quality, office (n)	boredom, freedom, kingdom, wisdom
-ee	one who receives action (n)	employee, interviewee, nominee, trainee
-en	make (v), made of (adj)	darken, frozen, golden, wooden
-ese	language of, native person of (n), of a particular group (adj)	Balinese, Brooklynese, Chinese, Japanese, Maltese
-fy	make (v)	amplify, calcify, certify, clarify, classify, simplify
-ice	condition, quality (n)	artifice, justice, malice
-ion, -sion, -tion	state of, act of, results of (n)	infection, inspection, opinion, reflection, rejection, suspension
-ism	system, condition (n)	activism, idealism, hedonism, plagiarism, racism
-ist	a person who, that which (n)	activist, artist, cyclist, racist
-ity, ty	quality, state of (n)	activity, creativity, frailty, sensitivity

Word Part	Meaning	Sample Words
-ive	having, making, causing (adj)	aggressive, conclusive, creative, exclusive
-ize	make, carry out (v)	criticize, hypothesize, realize, summarize, theorize,
-less	without (adj)	careless, brainless, fruitless, heartless, useless
-ly	manner of (adv)	boldly, callously, carefully, haphazardly, mindlessly, surreptitiously
-ment	process, result of, act of (n)	amendment, endowment, experiment, government, sediment
-ness	state of, condition of (n)	darkness, duress, emptiness, helplessness, robustness
-ology, alogy	study of, theory (n)	astrology, biology, genealogy, ideology, neurology
-ous	having (adj)	malicious, pernicious, perspicacious, spacious, superfluous, unconscious
-tude	condition of (n)	altitude, amplitude, attitude, fortitude, vicissitude
-y	inclined to have (adj)	greedy, itchy, needy, seedy, shady

ROOTS

am, amor	love, like	amiable, amorous, enamored
anthro	humankind	anthropologist, anthropomorphic, philanthropy
arch	first, top, head	archaic, archangel, archetypical, monarch, matriarch, patriarchal
auc, aug	increase	auction, augment
aud	listen, hear	audience, audio, auditory, inaudible
aut, auto	self	autocracy, automation, autonomous, autopilot
belli	war, violent	bellicose, belligerent, rebellious
bio	life	autobiography, biome, bionic, biopsy, biosphere
carn	flesh	carnivore, incarnation
cede, ced, ceed	surrender, yield, move	cede, concede, intercede, precede, proceed, recede, succeed
chron	time	chronicle, chronological, synchronize
civ	citizen	civic, civil, civilian, civilization, civilize, civvies
claus, clud, clus	close, shut	claustrophobia, conclude, exclude, preclude, recluse

Word Part	Meaning	Sample Words
cogn, gnos	know	cognition, cognizant, diagnose, Gnostics, prognosis
card, cord, cour	heart, center	accord, cardiopulmonary, cordial, courage, discord
corp	body	corporation, corporeal, corps
cosm	world, universe	cosmic, cosmos, microcosm
cour, cur, curs	run	concur, concurrent, courier, cursive, incur, occur
cred	believe	accredited, credentials, credit, creed, incredulous
crease, cresc, cru	grow, rise	accrue, crescendo, decrease
dem	people	democracy, demographics, epidemic
derm	skin	dermal, dermatologist, epidermis, taxidermy
dic, dict	speak, say	benediction, dedicate, dictate, dictator, edict, indicate, verdict
duc, duct	lead, guide	conduct, deduce, produce, viaduct
dur, dura	lasting, hard	durable, duration, endure
end, endo	within	endogenous, endoskeletal
erg	work	erg, ergometer, ergophobia
fac, fic, fect	make, do	faculty, fiction, infection, manufacture
fer	carry, bear	ferry, fertile, infer, refer
fid, feder	trust	confident, federal, fidelity, infidel
fin	end	confine, define, finale, finite, infinity
flu, fluc, fluv	flow	fluctuate, flue, fluent, flush, fluvial
forc, fort	strong	forceful, forte, fortify, fortitude
fract, frag	break	fractal, fraction, fragile, fragment, refract
gen	produce, birth, race	congenital, gender, genealogy, generate, genetic, genus, indigenous
geo	earth	geographic, geometry, geothermal
germ	essential, cause	germ, germane, germinate
grad, gress	go, step	aggressive, congress, degrade, digress, gradation, gradual, graduate
gram, graph	write	biography, geography, orthography, photography, sonogram, telegram
grat	pleasing	congratulation, grateful, gratitude, gratuity, ingrate

Word Part	Meaning	Sample Words
greg	crowd, gather, group	aggregate, congregate, gregarious, segregate
hab, habit	live, have	cohabitate, habitat, habitual, inhabit, rehabilitate
hetero	different	heterogeneous, heterosexual
hydr	water	dehydration, hydrogen, hydraulic, rehydrate
jud	lawyer, judge	judge, judiciary, prejudice
liber, liver	loosen, free	deliberate, deliver, liberal, liberation
loc, loco	place, near	allocate, collocate, local, locality, locomotive, relocate
locut, loqu	speak	circumlocution, loquacious, soliloquy
log, logy	word, study	analogy, apology, dialogue, illogical, prologue, theology
magn	great	magnanimous, magnification, magnificent, magnitude
man	hand	emancipation, manage, manicure, manifest, manipulate, manual
medi	half	median, mediate, medieval, mediocrity, medium
mem	remember	commemorate, memoir, memorial
migra	wander	immigrant, migration, migratory
mori, mors, mort	death, mortal	immortal, moribund, mortify, mortuary
morph	shape, form	amorphous, metamorphosis
nov	new	innovative, nova, novel, novice, renovate
omni	all	omnipotent, omnipresent, omniscient
ortho	straight, correct	orthodontist, orthodox, orthogonal, orthopedic
path	feeling, suffer	antipathy, empathy, pathetic, sympathy, telepath
pend, pens	weigh, hang	compendium, impending, pending, pendulum, pensive, suspend
phon	sound	cacophonous, euphonious, phonograph, symphony
photo	light	photoelectric, photogenic, photosynthesis, photon

Word Part	Meaning	Sample Words
pon, pos	put, place	deposit, disposition, exponent, oppose, postpone, postulate, posture, proponent, propose
port	carry	import, portable, report, support, transport
prim, proto	first	primal, primary, protagonist, prototype, protozoan
recti, reg	straighten	direct, incorrect, rectangular, regiment, regulate
rupt	break	corruptible, erupt, interrupt, rupture
scrib, script	write	describe, manuscript, prescription, scribble, scribe
secu, sequ	follow	consecutive, consequence, non sequitur, subsequent, sequential
sens, sent	feel	dissension, sensation, sensory, sentimental
solu, solv	loosen	absolve, resolute, resolve, solvent
spec, spic	look	aspect, conspicuous, despicable, expect, inspect, introspective, perspective, perspicacious, respect, retrospect, specimen, spectacle
spire	breath	aspire inspire, perspire, respire, spirit
strict	make tight	constrict, restrict, strict, stricture
tele	far	teleconference, telepathy, telephone, telescope
tempo	time	contemporary, extemporaneous, temporal
terra	earth	extraterrestrial, terrain, territory
tox	poison	antitoxin, intoxicated, toxic
trib	bestow, pay	attribute, contribute, retribution, tributary
vac	empty	evacuate, vacant, vacation, vacuole, vacuous, vacuum
val	worth, strength	evaluation, valiant, valid, valor
vers, vert	turn	advertise, avert, divert, invert, revert
vict, vinc	conquer	convince, evict, invincible, victor, victory
vid, vis	see	invisible, supervision, video, vista
voc	call	advocate, invoke, provoke, vocabulary
vor, vour	eat	carnivore, devour, herbivore, omnivorous, voracious
zo	animal	protozoan, zodiac, zoology, zooplankton

REFERENCES

Allen, J. (1999). *Words, words, words: Teaching vocabulary in grades 4–12*. York, ME: Stenhouse.

Alvermann, D.E. (1991). The discussion web: A graphic aid for learning across the curriculum. *The Reading Teacher, 45*, 92–99.

Alvermann, D.E., & Phelps, S.F. (2001). *Content reading and literacy: Succeeding in today's diverse classrooms* (3rd ed.). Boston: Allyn & Bacon.

Armbruster, B.B., Anderson, T.H., & Meyer, J.L. (1992). Improving content-area reading using instructional graphics. *Reading Research Quarterly, 26*, 393–416.

Armstrong, T. (2003). *The multiple intelligences of reading and writing*. Alexandria, VA: Association for Supervision and Curriculum Development.

Aronson, E. (1978). *The jigsaw classroom*. Thousand Oaks, CA: Sage.

Baumann, J.F. (1986). *Teaching main idea comprehension*. Newark, DE: International Reading Association.

Bean, T., Singer, H., & Cowan, S. (1985). Analogical study guides: Improving comprehension in science. *Journal of Reading, 29*, 246–250.

Beck, I.L., McKeown, M.G., Hamilton, R.L., & Kucan, L. (1997). *Questioning the author: An approach for enhancing student engagement with text*. Newark, DE: International Reading Association.

Beers, K. (1998). *Reading strategies handbook for high school*. Austin, TX: Holt, Rinehart and Winston.

Blachowicz, C., & Fisher, P. (1996). *Teaching vocabulary in all classrooms* (2nd ed.). Englewood Cliffs, NJ: Prentice Hall.

Bleich, D. (1975). *Reading and feelings: An introduction to subjective criticism*. Urbana, IL: National Council of Teachers of English.

Brown, J.E., & Stephens, E.C. (1999). *A handbook of content literacy strategies: 75 practical reading and writing ideas*. Norwood, MA: Christopher-Gordon.

Buehl, D. (2001). *Classroom strategies for interactive learning* (2nd ed.). Newark, DE: International Reading Association.

Carr, E.M., & Ogle, D. (1987). K-W-L Plus: A strategy for comprehension and summarization. *Journal of Reading, 30*, 626–631.

Ciardiello, A.V. (1998). Did you ask a good question today? Alternative cognitive and metacognitive strategies. *Journal of Adolescent & Adult Literacy, 42*, 210–219.

Cunningham, P.M. (1995). *Phonics they use: Words for reading and writing*. New York: Addison-Wesley/Longman.

Davey, B. (1983). Think aloud: Modeling the cognitive processes of reading comprehension. *Journal of Reading, 27*, 44–47.

Delpit, L. (1995). *Other people's children: Cultural conflict in the classroom*. New York: The New Press.

Dewitz, P., Carr, E.M., & Patberg, J.P. (1987). Effects of inference training on comprehension and comprehension monitoring. *Reading Research Quarterly, 22*, 99–122.

Dole, J.A., Duffy, G.G., Roehler, L.R., & Pearson, P.D. (1991). Moving from the old to the new: Research on reading comprehension instruction. *Review of Educational Research, 61*(2), 239–264.

Druyan, S. (1997). Effect of the kinesthetic conflict on promoting scientific reasoning. *Journal of Research in Science Teaching, 34*(10), 1083–1099.

Duffelmeyer, F.A., Baum, D.D., & Merkley, D.J. (1987). Maximizing reader-text confrontation with an extended anticipation guide. *Journal of Reading, 31*, 146–150.

Farr, R. (2001). Think-along/think-alouds and comprehending lead to better comprehension. *The California Reader, 34*(2), 29–33.

Fletcher, C.R., & Bloom, C.P. (1988). Causal reasoning in the comprehension of simple narrative texts. *Journal of Memory and Language, 27*(3), 235–244.

Freire, P., & Macedo, D. (1987). *Literacy: Reading the word and the world*. Westport, CT: Bergin & Garvey.

Friend, R. (2001). Teaching summarization as a content area reading strategy. *Journal of Adolescent & Adult Literacy, 44*, 320–329.

Gambrell, L.B., & Bales, R.J. (1986). Mental imagery and the comprehension-monitoring performance of fourth- and fifth-grade poor readers. *Reading Research Quarterly, 21*, 454–464.

Gardner, H. (1999). *Frames of mind: The theory of multiple intelligences*. New York: Basic Books.

Gillet, J.W., & Temple, C. (1999). *Understanding reading problems: Assessment and instruction* (5th ed.). Boston: Allyn & Bacon.

Guthrie, J.T., & Wigfield, A. (2000). Engagement and motivation in reading. In M.L. Kamil, P.B. Mosenthal, P.D. Pearson, & R. Barr (Eds.), *Handbook of reading research* (Vol. 3, pp. 406–424). Mahwah, NJ: Erlbaum.

Helfeldt, J.P., & Henk, W.A. (1990). Reciprocal question-answer relationships: An instructional technique for at-risk readers. *Journal of Reading, 33,* 509–514.

Hibbing, A.N., & Rankin-Erickson, J.L. (2003). A picture is worth a thousand words: Using visual images to improve comprehension for middle school struggling readers. *The Reading Teacher, 56,* 758–770.

Hyerle, D. (1996). *Visual tools for constructing knowledge.* Alexandria, VA: Association for Supervision and Curriculum Development.

Irwin, J.W. (1991). *Teaching reading comprehension processes* (2nd ed.). Upper Saddle River, NJ: Pearson.

Jaworski, A., & Coupland, N. (Eds.). (1999). *The discourse reader.* London: Routledge.

Jimenez, R.T., & Gamez, A. (1996). Literature-based cognitive strategy instruction for middle school Latina/o students. *Journal of Adolescent and Adult Literacy, 40,* 84–91.

Johns, J.L., & Berglund, R.L. (2001). *Strategies for content area learning: Vocabulary comprehension response.* Dubuque, IA: Kendall/Hunt.

Johnson, D., & Pearson, P.D. (1984). *Teaching reading vocabulary* (2nd ed.). Austin, TX: Holt, Rinehart and Winston.

Kagan, S. (1997). *Cooperative learning.* San Clemente, CA: Kagan Cooperative.

Keene, E.O., & Zimmermann, S. (1997). *Mosaic of thought: Teaching comprehension in a reader's workshop.* Portsmouth, NH: Heinemann.

Lyons, C.A., & Pinnell, G.S. (2001). *Systems for change in literacy education: A guide to professional development.* Portsmouth, NH: Heinemann.

Manz, S.L. (2002). A strategy for previewing textbooks: Teaching readers to become THIEVES. *The Reading Teacher, 55,* 434–435.

Marzano, R.J., Pickering, D.J., & Pollock, J.E. (2001). *Classroom instruction that works: Research-based strategies for increasing student achievement.* Alexandria, VA: Association for Supervision and Curriculum Development.

McLaughlin, M., & Vogt, M. (2000). *Creativity and innovation in content area teaching.* Norwood, MA: Christopher-Gordon.

Merkley, D.M., & Jeffries, D. (2001). Guidelines for implementing a graphic organizer. *The Reading Teacher, 54,* 350–357.

Moeller, V.J., & Moeller, M.V. (2002). *Socratic seminars and literature circles for middle and high school English.* Larchmont, NY: Eye on Education.

Nagy, W.E. (1988). *Teaching vocabulary to improve reading comprehension.* Newark, DE: International Reading Association.

Ogle, D. (1986). K-W-L: A teaching model that develops active reading of expository text. *The Reading Teacher, 39,* 564–570.

Palincsar, A.S., & Brown, A.L. (1984). Reciprocal teaching of comprehension-fostering and comprehension-monitoring activities. *Cognition and Instruction, 2,* 117–175.

Peregoy, S.F., & Boyle, O.F. (2000). *Reading, writing, and learning in ESL: A resource book for K–12 teachers* (3rd ed.). Reading, MA: Addison-Wesley.

Poindexter, C. (1994). Guessed meanings. *Journal of Reading, 37,* 420–421.

Pressley, M., Burkell, J., Cariglia-Bull, T., Lysynchuk, L., McGoldrick, J.A., Schneider, B., et al. (1990). *Cognitive strategy instruction.* Cambridge, MA: Brookline.

Readence, J.E., Bean, T.W., & Baldwin, R.S. (2001). *Content area literacy: An integrated approach* (7th ed.). Dubuque, IA: Kendall/Hunt.

Robb, L. (2003). *Teaching reading in social studies, science, and math.* New York: Scholastic.

Roth, W., & Verechaka, G. (1993). Plotting a course with vee maps. *Science and Children, 30*(4), 24–27.

Ryder, R.J., & Graves, M.F. (2002). *Reading and learning in content areas* (3rd ed.). Chichester, UK: John Wiley.

Salembier, G.B., & Cheng, L.C. (1997). SCUBA-dive into reading. *Teaching Exceptional Children, 29*(6), 68–71.

Sampson, M.B. (2002). Confirming a K-W-L: Considering the source. *The Reading Teacher, 55,* 528–532.

Stahl, S.A. (1999). *Vocabulary development: From reading research to practice* (Vol. 2). Cambridge, MA: Brookline.

Stone, C.L. (1983). A meta-analysis of advanced organizer studies. *Journal of Experimental Education, 51*(4), 194–199.

Taba, H. (1967). *Teacher's handbook for elementary social studies.* Reading, MA: Addison-Wesley.

Taylor, B.M., Graves, M.F., & van den Broek, P.W. (2000). *Reading for meaning: Fostering comprehension in the middle grades.* New York: Teachers College Press; Newark, DE: International Reading Association.

Tierney, R.J., & Readance, J.E. (1999). *Reading strategies and practices: A compendium* (5th ed.). Boston: Allyn & Bacon.

Urquhart, A.H., & Weir, C.J. (1998). *Reading in a second language: Process, product, and practice.* New York: Longman.

U.S. Bureau of Census. (1993). *Current population reports, P25-1104: Population projections of the United States, by age, sex, race, and Hispanic origin: 1993 to 2050.* Washington, DC: U.S. Government Printing Office.

Van Allen, R., & Allen, C. (1976). *Language experience activities.* Boston: Houghton Mifflin.

Villaume, S.K., & Brabham, E.G. (2002). Comprehension instruction: Beyond strategies. *The Reading Teacher, 55,* 672–675.

Vygotsky, L.S. (1978). *Mind in society: The development of higher psychological processes* (M. Cole, V. John-Steiner, S. Scribner, & E. Souberman, Eds. & Trans.). Cambridge, MA: Harvard University Press. (Original work published 1934)

Wiggins, G. (1998). *Educative assessment: Designing assessments to inform and improve student performance.* San Francisco: Jossey-Bass.

Wiggins, G., & McTighe, J. (2000). *Understanding by design.* Englewood Cliffs, NJ: Prentice Hall.

Wilhelm, J.D. (2001). *Improving comprehension with think-aloud strategies: Modeling what good readers do.* New York: Scholastic.

Zwiers, J.A. (1999). *Caught white-handed.* Unpublished short story.

Additional Suggested Resources

Adams, M.J. (1990). *Beginning to read: Thinking and learning about print.* Cambridge, MA: The MIT Press.

Allington, R.L. (1998). *Teaching struggling readers: Articles from* The Reading Teacher. Newark, DE: International Reading Association.

Bear, D.R., Invernizzi, M., Templeton, S., & Johnston, F. (1999). *Words their way: Word study for phonics, vocabulary, and spelling instruction* (2nd ed.). Englewood Cliffs, NJ: Prentice Hall.

Bos, C.S., & Vaughn, S. (2001). *Strategies for teaching students with learning and behavioral problems* (5th ed.). Boston: Allyn & Bacon.

Brozo, W.G., & Simpson, M.L. (1998). *Readers, teachers, and learners: Expanding literacy across the content areas* (3rd ed.). Englewood Cliffs, NJ: Prentice Hall.

Burke, J. (2000). *Reading reminders: Tools, tips, and techniques.* Portsmouth, NH: Boynton/Cook.

Clay, M.M. (1993). *Reading recovery: A guidebook for teachers in training.* Portsmouth, NH: Heinemann.

Collins, A., & Smith, E.E. (1980). *Teaching the process of reading comprehension* (Tech. Rep. No. 182). Urbana: University of Illinois, Center for the Study of Reading.

Cooper, J.D. (1996). *Literacy: Helping children construct meaning* (3rd ed.). Boston: Houghton Mifflin.

Daniels, H. (1994). *Literature circles: Voice and choice in the student-centered classroom.* York, ME: Stenhouse.

Gunning, T.G. (2002). *Building literacy in the content areas.* Boston: Allyn & Bacon.

Haggard, M.R. (1985). An interactive strategies approach to content reading. *Journal of Reading, 29,* 204–210.

Harvey, S., & Goudvis, A. (2000). *Strategies that work: Teaching comprehension to enhance understanding.* York, ME: Stenhouse.

Lenski, S.D., Wham, M.A., & Johns, J.L. (1999). *Reading and learning strategies for middle and high school students.* Dubuque, IA: Kendall/Hunt.

Marr, M.B. (2000). The value of perspective taking for improving comprehension. *The California Reader, 34*(1), 7–12.

Marzano, R.J. (1988). *Dimensions of thinking: A framework for curriculum and instruction.* Alexandria, VA: Association for Supervision and Curriculum Development.

Marzano, R.J., Pickering, D., & McTighe, J. (1993). *Assessing student outcomes: Performance assessment using the dimensions of learning model.* Alexandria, VA: Association for Supervision and Curriculum Development.

McCarney, S.B. (1993). *Pre-referral intervention manual.* Columbia, MO: Hawthorne Educational Services.

McCormick, S. (1995). *Instructing students who have literacy problems* (2nd ed.). Englewood Cliffs, NJ: Merrill.

Miller, W.H. (1993). *Complete reading disabilities handbook: Ready-to-use techniques for teaching reading disabled students.* San Francisco: Jossey-Bass.

Pritchard, R. (2000). *Strategic teaching and learning: Standards-based instruction to promote content literacy in grades four through twelve.* Sacramento: California Department of Education.

Radencich, M.C., Beers, P.G., & Schumm, J.S. (1993). *A handbook for the K–12 reading resource specialist.* Boston: Allyn & Bacon.

Ruddell, M.R. (1996). *Teaching content reading and writing.* Boston: Allyn & Bacon.

Shanker, J.L., & Ekwall, E.E. (1997). *Locating and correcting reading difficulties* (7th ed.). Englewood Cliffs, NJ: Prentice Hall.

Taggart, G.L., Phifer, S.J., Nixon, J.A., & Wood, M. (1999). *Rubrics: A handbook for construction and use.* Lanham, MD: Scarecrow Press.

Walker, B.J. (1999). *Diagnostic teaching of reading: Techniques for instruction and assessment* (4th ed.). Englewood Cliffs, NJ: Prentice Hall.

Wilhelm, J.D., Baker, T.N., & Dube, J. (2001). *Strategic reading: Guiding students to lifelong literacy 6–12.* Portsmouth, NH: Heinemann.

Wilhelm, J.D., & Smith, M.W. (1996). *"You gotta BE the book": Teaching engaged and reflective reading with adolescents.* New York: Teachers College Press.

INDEX

Note: Page numbers followed by *f* and *r* indicate figures and reproducibles, respectively.